NOW REVISED AND UPDATED FOR THIS EDITION

It's not far from the Windmill Theatre, through the streets of the West End, to the Middlesex Hospital. For Peter Sellers it was a lifetime's journey that took him – in so many guises – from his debut on the comedy test track to his sad and untimely end.

On the way he became so many characters, a multitude of voices and faces from the myriad lunacy of the Goons to the je ne sais quoi of Inspector Clouseau.

Never far from the headlines either as the whirlwind suitor of Britt Ekland or one of filmland's very hottest properties, this sensitive and private man won a special place in the hearts of the millions he entertained.

Witty, charming, possessed of a rare genius, Sellers will live for an eternity as one of the very finest comic actors of more generations than one.

'An absorbing new profile-in-depth.'
THE SUNDAY PEOPLE

'Engrossing reading.'
MANCHESTER EVENING NEWS

'Excellently readable.'
THE SUNDAY TELEGRAPH

PETER SELLERS

THE MASK BEHIND THE MASK

PETER EVANS

SEVERN HOUSE

For Mark and Lisa

This revised and updated edition published 1981 by
SEVERN HOUSE PUBLISHERS LTD
144–146 New Bond Street, London W1Y 9FD
First published in Great Britain in 1969 by
Leslie Frewin Publishers Limited
© 1968, 1969 and 1980 by Peter Evans

ISBN 0–7278–0688–2

Printed in Great Britain by The Anchor Press Ltd
and bound by Wm Brendon & Son Ltd,
both of Tiptree, Essex

Contents

Death as a Prologue

A FEW MINUTES after 2.30 a.m., Pacific Coast Time, his heart stopped beating. It was Tuesday, 7th April, 1964, and he was thirty-eight years old. The heart attack he had feared for most of his adult life had finally come. It came fifteen hours after the registrar at the Cedars of Lebanon Hospital in Los Angeles had, with clinical neatness, recorded his admittance for rest and observation following a 'moderate coronary attack' at his rented Beverly Hills home the evening before: Sellers, Peter. Caucasian. Male. English. Consulting physician Dr Rex Kennamer. Next of kin Mrs Britt Sellers, wife.

The Cedars is a most exclusive hospital smoothly catering to the ailing affluent of Hollywood. Famous profiles and million-dollar legs are not unusual there, and the staff has long learned to accept even the legendary as patients and not celebrities.

There was no fuss, no excitement about the eminent yet oddly nondescript patient who arrived at the hospital that morning with a young wife who was still little more than a bride.

The English actor, bespectacled, tieless, showed no significant signs of his impending danger. There was no hint that in a few hours he would be dead.

He was pale and perhaps nervous, that was all. He talked quietly with his wife, teasing her about some curious mis-pronunciation of a word her Swedish tongue had failed to negotiate.

A reception clerk remembers: 'He just looked very tired, very drawn, like a guy who has lost a lot of beef too fast. But he was ambulatory and I figured he was another nervous exhaustion case from Big H.'

He was taken to a sixty-five-dollar-a-day suite on the

7

second floor. He was given sedatives, and Britt held his hand until he slept. As all consciousness left him he said: 'You know you've married a star now, Britt. You've got to have top billing to get into a five-star joint like this.'

She smiled at the private joke. She had often told him, truthfully, that she had never heard of Peter Sellers until the day they met in London.

Now she carefully moved her hand from his and bent down and kissed his sleeping lips. She remembers the faint chill on them, and she felt 'sort of apprehensive but unbelieving'.

After all, they had been married only forty-six days – not all of those spent together – and, at twenty-one, determinedly optimistic, youthfully resilient, she was easily able to push that most fearful thought from her as she left the hospital.

Outside, alone in the warm California sunshine, she suddenly felt a long way from home. Her platinum hair, which was meant to give her a sophistication she felt she needed to please her older, more worldly husband, only emphasised the child in her small face, now naked and pale.

The last day and night had been tough. She returned to their home in Hillcrest Road, high above Sunset Boulevard, above the date palm trees and the pink and orange and white stucco houses with their threatening fairy-book look of impermanence.

Hollywood was not her favourite town.

But 924 Hillcrest was the most beautiful house she had ever seen, let alone lived in, this unknown actress from the chilled suburbs of Stockholm.

Crowded with exotic plants and decorated with fine Florentine furniture on cool Italian marble floors, it was everything she believed a Hollywood home should be. And more than that, it was everything a young girl's honeymoon home should be.

But now it was empty, without the stereo sound of jazz, of Getz and Hines and Coltrane, that he liked to play loud and almost continually, and she felt oddly nervous.

His children Michael and Sarah, from his first marriage, now visiting during their Easter holiday from school in England, had been taken for a drive. The servants, after a bizarre labour dispute (the marble floors, they insisted, were both hazardous and hard on their feet), had walked out a few hours earlier. An empty house with marble floors is emptier than a vacant mausoleum. It was in this petrified atmosphere that Britt Ekland Sellers found herself examining for the first time their extraordinary relationship.

She had known her husband only eleven days before they married, and they were still slowly discovering and exploring each other, both as lovers and as people.

Some seventeen years younger than Sellers, a man who was still in almost every way a stranger in her life – and, although she did not know it then, almost certainly always would be – she knew still the anguish of sudden shyness in his presence, and this both puzzled and disturbed her.

She made an effort to think in English. She was infatuated, she knew that. She was wildly flattered. She was *imponerad* . . . impressed, yes. And *fascinerad* . . . fascinated.

She stopped. It was becoming an exercise in passive defence, like whistling in the dark. For Britt was perfectly aware that she had married a man she did not love in any language.

She sat on the bed and wept.

Later that morning, composing herself, she put a call through to her mother, Maj Britt Ecklund (Britt had taken Sellers' advice to change the spelling of her surname), in Stockholm.

She said that Peter had gone into hospital for a few days. It wasn't at all serious, she insisted, and she was simply calling for a chat, politely ignoring the fact that it was costing three dollars a minute. Unsure of her English, she desperately wanted to talk to somebody in her own language. She talked for more than thirty minutes, compulsively and occasionally with an almost childlike eagerness, about, her mother thought, the most trivial things.

9

She talked about the weekend that had started so well and was to bring her, at that moment, so unknowingly close to tragedy.

Saturday morning, 4th April, after coffee and fresh orange juice, they rose at ten o'clock. Outside they could hear Sarah, just seven years old, and Michael, then ten, playing by the pool, their laughter and childish sounds very clear and homely in the rich and splendid silence of Beverly Hills.

They decided to go to Disneyland.

By eleven o'clock, after taking a call from Bryan Forbes, the director and a close friend, in London, they were ready to leave.

The car nosed down the sharp ski-sloping driveway and Sarah fell forward in her seat. 'Into the valley of death . . .' Sellers laughed, catching his daughter around her waist and hugging her to him until the car levelled out on the road, '. . . and out again.'

It was a fine day without smog. When it was time to finally leave Disneyland the children pleaded to stay. Sellers gave in and booked rooms at a local hotel. 'Do I spoil them?' he asked Britt seriously. 'Yes,' she told him with affection. 'You spoil us all terribly.'

Sunday morning, 5th April, shortly after lunch, they drove back to Beverly Hills without haste, avoiding the freeways, the radio loud and the children and their father singing the commercials and inventing mad new lyrics.

That night the children went to bed early. Sellers and Britt had dinner alone, played some Brubeck, watched television, and talked for a while.

Britt thought he looked tired.

Certainly he was a very worried man. Run-down for some weeks, with a stye on his eye that had already interrupted shooting on the film he was making for director Billy Wilder, he was now confronted with a massive 1·5 million dollar breach of contract suit, 20th Century-Fox was bringing over his wife's walkout from a movie in London called *Guns of Batasi*.

10

Incensed, the studio had accused him of inducing her absence. Britt, he answered, was suffering from emotional and physical exhaustion.

'He tried to hide it but I knew the whole business was depressing him very much,' said Britt later.

It is not hard to trace the source of Sellers' anxious state of mind.

Guns of Batasi was to have been Britt's first movie under the contract she had signed with Darryl F. Zanuck. Zanuck was an old-style Hollywood mogul, perhaps the last of his kind. 'A gross exhibitionist and sensualist', according to his biographer Mel Gussow in *Don't Say Yes Until I Finish Talking,* Zanuck had a curious habit of interviewing young actresses in hotel suites while wearing little more than a Mark Cross silk kimono and a cigar. The actress Viviane Ventura told me how she had once been interviewed by the old mogul at the George V hotel in Paris. After a few preliminaries, his robe fell open and he made an unmistakable pass at her. She gripped his proferred penis very hard. 'If you don't behave like a gentleman, I'm going to pull you all the way to the nearest police station and report you for indecent exposure', she told him with remarkable presence of mind.

Perhaps he admired her spirit; perhaps he was deeply impressed by her performance in *A High Wind in Jamaica.* Miss Ventura was flown to New York, ensconced at the Drake Hotel, and given a seven-year contract with Zanuck's 20th Century-Fox.

Zanuck's weakness for foreign actresses was notorious. He had had famous liaisons with many of the ladies he put under contract: Bella Darvi, Juliette Greco, Irina Demick and Genevieve Gilles were among his *protégées*.

In 1963, after some television and stage work in Sweden, Britt went to Rome to pursue her acting ambitions. 'Spaghetti Westerns' had just taken Europe by storm and the city was bustling with movie producers, the studios were humming with activity.

Noticed in a Via Veneto sidewalk café by Hollywood

talent scouts, according to a legend perpetuated in studio bio's, Britt was taken to the Excelsior Hotel to meet Zanuck.

Zanuck liked what he saw.

Britt was sent to New York, ensconced at the Drake Hotel, and in due course given the ubiquitous seven-year contract with 20th Century-Fox.

Sellers knew all this. On the surface, he seemed the essence of suavity and worldliness. He was well received in Hollywood's best homes. He mixed in the highest society. He knew how to order and appreciate the finest wines. He could handle cannabis and cocaine. His shirts and suits and shoes were custom-made by the finest craftsmen in London and Paris.

But behind this assured image, he was wracked with adolescent self-doubts. In Hollywood, separated from his young bride, he became anxious. Anxiety turned to jealousy. Jealousy became a rage.

The idea that his wife was a Zanuck discovery nagged him. He was also trying to come to terms with the fact that Britt had not been exactly the immaculate maiden he had imagined her to be when they first met. Perhaps misguidedly, but with remarkable frankness, she had made a clean breast of her less-than-nunnish past.

There was a hell of a lot of tension and distrust about. Despite her vehement denial, Sellers was convinced that Britt had slept with Zanuck, was sleeping with Zanuck, and would have to go on sleeping with Zanuck.

Sellers' suspicion was a secret known only to a few close aides and one they guarded well. They did their best to play down the irrational outbursts and the effect it was having on his work; it was becoming difficult to hide the deteriorating relationships at the studio.

Sellers could not bring himself openly to rage against Zanuck, even to Britt. 'His pride wouldn't let him admit that he was worried about being cuckolded by a near-septuagenarian. (Zanuck was sixty-three.) What he did was typical Pete. He invented a more suitable suspect to attack.'

The scapegoat – 'Sellers' surrogate suspect', one of Britt's girlfriends called him – was his wife's leading man in *Guns of Batasi,* an actor named John Leyton. In cables and phone calls and letters, Sellers poured out his love, his misgivings, his fears, and his jealous fantasies to his bride. Over and over again he questioned her about Leyton. Did he ever visit her dressing room? Had he made a pass? Did she fancy him? Did she look forward to their love scene together? The atmosphere grew hot with Sellers' demands for confessions, details, written-in-blood pledges. 'There was a lot of self-flagellation in Pete.'

'Peter used Leyton to release all his pent-up anger, this terrible jealousy. But it was Darryl Zanuck who haunted his imagination', I was told. 'And we didn't know it then, of course, but this whole business . . . it was the beginning of a much deeper malaise.'

Britt was knocked off-balance. For the first time she saw the sudden incongruous shift in his emotional behavior; she was particularly alarmed by his unfounded outbursts against an actor she barely knew. When they had parted in England a few weeks before, Sellers was full of confidence, full of loving trust, full of hope. Now this. It did not make sense.

When Sellers asked her to fly to California for the Easter weekend, she knew she could not refuse. In the middle of shooting her own movie at Pinewood studios, the trip was against the terms of her contract, against the terms of her insurance, against all the rules of the game. She left Heathrow on Thursday evening; she would return in time for shooting the following Tuesday.

Much to everybody's dismay, Sellers persuaded her to quit the picture and stay with him in California. 'As if he didn't have enough problems, this was asking for trouble', said an aide.

But for Sellers it was 'one in the eye for that shit Zanuck'.

Zanuck hit back with the massive breach-of-contract suit.

'It was getting pretty hairy', agent Dennis Selinger said.

'Pete always had a great talent for complicating his life.'

That Sunday evening, after the day at Disneyland with the children, Britt and Sellers went to bed early. Her time in California, despite all the legal pressures, had been a loving success. They had renewed the joys of their early days together in London. Sellers seemed to be his old self again. Britt was convinced that his strange behaviour during their brief separation had been a temporary aberration.

To help him unwind, Sellers opened a bottle of his favourite champagne. They sat in bed and sipped the wine, talking, listening to music. They made love. They used amyl nitrate poppers – a volatile drug which acts with great speed to relieve spasms and dilate blood-vessels in heart patients – to heighten and sustain the moment of orgasm. Sellers, who had been using amyl poppers for about a year, got his supply from a doctor who had been advising him on slimming.

After they had made love, Sellers went to the bathroom. He was halfway across the room when he stopped – the way a man stops who has just thought of something very important he has forgotten to do. It was a dead stop and very still.

It felt like a sudden, sharp attack of indigestion, only far worse than any indigestion he had every known. Hesitantly, his hand moved to his chest.

'Peter?' said Britt.

'My whole chest seems to be on fire.'

He still didn't move.

A few days earlier he had read an article in *Reader's Digest* about heart attacks. He now wondered if it was perhaps his imagination running wild. He walked slowly, like a man on a tight-rope, across the bedroom and sat on the edge of the bed.

The fire in his chest got worse. Still he waited, afraid to articulate his fear.

The concern in Britt's voice had now reached her face.

'Peter?' she said again.

'You'd better call Kennamer, Britt,' he said at last. 'My

14

chest feels like a bloody oven.'

Dr Rex Kennamer, a tall, lean man with an earnest, distinguished face that hasn't seen too many hard winters, arrived at the house sometime shortly before midnight.

The pain in Sellers' chest had eased a little but he had been visibly shaken.

Kennamer, one of America's most respected heart specialists as well as a fashionable physician, almost certainly knew before taking a cardiogram that the actor had suffered at least a mild coronary that night.

They did not tell him about their use of amyl nitrate poppers.

He gave him an injection to ease the pain and sleeping tablets to get him through the night. Britt did not sleep.

The following morning, Monday, 6th April, too early to be carrying good news, Kennamer returned to the house on Hillcrest Road.

'You've had a mild heart attack,' he told Sellers. He had been treating Britt in the 20th Century-Fox case and knew all about the pressures on the actor. 'I think,' he now said with a pleasant unalarming firmness, 'we'd better get you into Cedars for a few days so we can keep an eye on you. See that you don't attempt any four-minute miles. I also want to carry out a few more tests.'

Sellers remembers no particular emotion at the news, only perhaps a small sense of relief that the heart attack he had feared so long – and more acutely since his father's fatal coronary seventeen months before – had finally come and that it was not so bad after all.

Britt packed an overnight case for Sellers and they drove with Kennamer to the hospital, where this singular international star became another Caucasian male victim of a moderate coronary attack in the city of Los Angeles that day.

At the studios, director Billy Wilder heard the news and was not in a very good humour. Already the film *Kiss Me Stupid*, with Kim Novak and Dean Martin, was proving to be an unhappy one. Sellers and Wilder, of different generations, different temperaments, and different styles,

15

were not hitting it off, and their professional rapport was fragile. Worse, the astute veteran Wilder knew he was working with a weak and witless script that was persistently defying the maddest invention of both Sellers and himself.

'This,' Wilder told his assistants when he got the message, 'is all we needed. Jesus H Christ! Is he really sick or just shamming? Because if he's trying to duck out now . . .' He suspended shooting for the day and withdrew to his office to reorganise the production schedule around the British actor's absence.

By midday he knew it was a hopeless exercise, involving vast expense. He decided to temporarily close down the picture. The publicity department was told to announce that Sellers had collapsed. 'Until we know how serious it is,' said Wilder in a carefully worded statement to the wire services, 'we must wait. If it is that serious, then, of course, we must find a replacement.'

Privately he moaned: 'Who the hell can replace the bastard?'

Wilder, an average-sized man with close-cropped hair and a guttural Austrian accent that makes most of his words sound menacing, even the occasional kinder ones, was then sixty years old. He had twenty Academy Award nominations, half a dozen Oscars, and several fortunes to his credit, and was already regarded as one of Hollywood's most famous living landmarks, or accident black spots in the opinion of some. His sense of humour, Hollywood-honed, is often cruel.

'I don't like the guy,' Wilder said in a voice used to being listened to, even from a distance. 'But like that mean woman Monroe, he's cornered the whole damn market in what he does.'

Briskly, up and down, back and forth, he panther-paced his Oscar-lined office, six gold-plated monuments to yesterday's glories now dumbly mocking today's dilemma. Assistants suggested possible replacements and Wilder turned them all down without using big words or too much breath.

16

'There was only one Marilyn Monroe,' he said finally, his eyes small, distant, and uninviting behind strong optical lenses in heavy black frames, 'and, dammit, there's only one Peter Sellers.'

The wire services put out the Sellers collapse as a 'bulletin', a category reserved for the most important news stories, a category that rings a bell on tape machines in every newspaper office and television newsroom in the land.

Yet as the wire machines shrilled their front-page tidings that Monday afternoon, he was still in no apparent critical danger as he slept in suite 503 at the Cedars of Lebanon, checked every eight minutes by a nurse and each hour by a house physician.

On Tuesday morning, shortly after 2.30, the nurse urgently summoned the house doctor to Sellers. He found the actor 'unconscious with no blood pressure and no pulse'. He began immediate resuscitation and brought back a glimmer of life into the still body. He was swiftly moved to the Intensive Care Unit on the third floor, the department sometimes unnervingly known as the 11th Hour Ward.

Sellers' chauffeur, Bert Mortimer, who had taken the call from the hospital, woke Britt.

'You'd better get dressed and come to the hospital,' he said, and was surprised to hear himself whispering as if he were already in the presence of the dead. The thought made him angry and he said much louder, 'Wake up, Britt, be getting something on, I'll go and make some coffee to get the sleep out of your eyes.'

A few minutes later she came into the kitchen. He poured her coffee. It was almost finished before she realised it was six o'clock in the morning. 'Bert! It's the middle of the night. What has happened? It's Peter!'

'His condition has worsened,' he told her, nervous about the words to use. 'The hospital thinks you should be there. They're doing all they can but they think you should go along, just the same. You know, it'd be . . . better.'

A few minutes later her agent Dick Shepherd, summoned by Bert, arrived at the house. They drove to the hospital, neither saying much. The streets were empty and they drove fast.

'I just felt terribly numb,' she remembered later. 'The newspapers said I was near to hysterics. I was just numb.'

A nurse from the Intensive Care Unit was waiting. She made Britt sit on a bench before explaining precisely what was happening and what had happened.

'Your husband has had two massive coronary attacks,' she said in careful matter-of-fact tones, easing the impact of the news with precise technical data. 'The first attack came at 2.30 this morning. It was followed ninety minutes later by the second. He is now in our Intensive Care Unit. Everything humanly possible is being done for your husband, Mrs Sellers. But a few prayers would be very useful right now.'

The nurse gave her one of those practised professional smiles, one part sympathy, one part encouragement and one part pretence.

'Yes,' said Britt.

Dick Shepherd expected her to faint but she didn't faint. He arranged for her to have a private room next to her husband's and for six days and nights, except for two brief trips back to the house to collect fresh clothes, that is where she stayed.

The first thing she did at the hospital that morning was to telephone her mother in Stockholm. Only this time the call was brief and poignant. 'Mama,' she said, sensing the danger, 'Peter has maybe only an hour to live. Please pray for us. I'm so scared.'

The hospital issued a medical bulletin disclosing Sellers' critical condition. Unofficially, reporters were told there was no hope. 'It's amazing that a man of his age, with no previous record of heart malfunction, should suffer two such brutal attacks,' one doctor said then.

Yet those close to Sellers were not amazed, not even surprised, when they really thought about it.

There are some who insist he was infatuated with the

idea of death. Spike Milligan, perhaps the most original, egocentric, and brilliantly perceptive humourist in Britain, a man who grew up with and came close to Sellers during their radio Goon Show days in the early fifties, remembered:

'Years before he had this heart attack he always worried about it, was always searching for the bloody thing, as if it were a letter that he knew had been posted and hadn't arrived.'

On one occasion while they were driving to a BBC studio in London, Sellers suddenly jammed on the brakes of his car. 'Here,' he told the startled Milligan. 'Here, I've got a pain right here.'

His hand was pressing over his heart and his face had settled on an expression of terminal courage.

The drama lasted for several minutes before Milligan was able to convince him that he was suffering from nothing more serious than gas.

'He had,' Milligan said, 'about forty heart attacks before the real thing turned up.'

Now it was the real thing and Sellers was in the valley of death that he had casually joked about with his daughter Sarah so shortly before.

And while the doctors and the life-pumping Pacemaker machines worked to keep him from dying, the world of Peter Sellers trembled.

The people who loved and needed him, those who hated and depended upon him, the business associates, the mates and even monarchs waited for the news from California. Whether he lived or died would affect writers and directors, studios, producers, men in Wall Street and big financiers in the city of London, bankers in Zurich, and wheeler-dealers in every film capital in the world.

And in some way his life or death would touch, too, a million people in the world he never knew: the public – that anonymous, amorphous, vital mass of taste, humour, emotion, and temperament that, combined in the right, mysterious degrees, is the very alchemy that converts actors into stars and stars into superstars and superstars into shimmering, secular, celluloid gods.

Sellers was such a god and duly less than godlike: an earthly product that needed to be inflated and sold, traded, manipulated, bartered, and negotiated in the panelled, air-conditioned shrines of executive suites.

The true miracle of such twentieth-century gods is that when they sign deals in Hollywood or London or Rome you can hear the pen scratching through the canyons of Wall Street.

So the people prayed.

Some prayed for pity and some for his soul. And others for themselves.

Obituary

IF PETER SELLERS had been unduly apprehensive during the days before the coronary came, there was some cause. Only a week earlier he'd had a curious and disturbing encounter with the London clairvoyant Maurice Woodruff in the Beverly Hills Hotel.

A small, neat, and engaging man with remarkable powers, Woodruff had once had an astonishing influence on the actor's life (even predicting that he would meet and swiftly marry a woman with the initials B.E.), and there was a time when Sellers would not accept a film or sign a contract without first consulting him. Although the early enchantment was now wearing thin, Sellers still had enormous respect for him.

'Hello, Maurice, mate,' he had joked when they met, 'what's new with me?'

The clairvoyant, although impressed with Sellers' good physical shape and fresh California tan, felt there was 'something not quite right'. But the actor did not ask for a reading and they simply talked about mutual friends, what was happening in London, and their various plans.

Suddenly, Woodruff said: 'You're going to have a spot of bother, Pete.'

Remarkably, perhaps, neither man explored this extraordinary comment lobbed into the idle conversation, only to lie there, ticking.

But Sellers brooded over it, and that night asked Bert Mortimer to ring Woodruff and pursue it. 'Maurice,' said the chauffeur, coming straight to the point, 'how serious is that . . . bother?'

'I'm not sure, to tell you the truth,' said Woodruff, who had been expecting the call. 'But tell Pete everything will be fine, but he has to take care. It will come from within.

That is all I can tell you.' Later, when the obituary notices were being written around the world, Woodruff was one of the few people who insisted he would not die. It seemed an unlikely prediction in view of the bulletins coming out of the Cedars of Lebanon.

Within the business, the reaction to the news was mostly shock at the loss of a talent if not complete sadness for the death of a man.

Wolf Mankowitz, the writer and onetime partner in an ambitious but finally abandoned film enterprise, considered the Hollywood death drama with cynical disbelief. 'If he were dead in his coffin in this room now,' he said, 'I would first look around to see if there was a camera present.

'Then I would insist on every known medical test before I'd stir myself to attend the Archbishop of Canterbury's final epilogue for him.

'Sellers is inhuman and therefore definitely immortal.'

David Lodge broke down and cried when he heard the news on the set of *Guns of Batasi,* the film Britt had just quit. A character actor, he had been close to Sellers since their Royal Air Force days during the war and was best man at his wedding to Britt.

At his home in Virginia Water, an hour's car ride from London, Bryan Forbes had just finished lunch when the telephone rang. He was feeling spiky, having taken a chunk out of his leg with an axe while attempting to fell a tree that morning. Sellers, he was told, was likely to be dead before nightfall. As a director and an old friend could he write a tribute?

He was stunned. A few days before, he had talked to him on the telephone in California. He was then just off to Disneyland and sounded so bloody happy. Forbes, a small, intense man with the dark methodical good looks of a juvenile lead, which he once was, fed a sheet of paper into his typewritter and stared at it for a long time. Finally, he typed: 'Peter Sellers. It is impossible to believe. Like most public clowns he had a private and darker side to his moon.

'Sometimes it was as if he sensed he had an early appointment in Samarra – for he was a compulsive worker in the way that some people are compulsive eaters.'

He stopped typing. He stared at what he had written. He thought: 'Disneyland . . . for Samarra, read Disneyland.' He couldn't go on. Like many of the actor's friends and colleagues he was suddenly sickened by the idea of writing an obituary for a man who was yet to die, however tenuously he held on to life so far away.

He tore the paper out of his typewriter and crumpled it into a tight ball.

Later, he was to recall, his writer's natural sense of economy became too pressing and he retrieved the paper from his wastebin, smoothed it out, and returned it to a drawer.

'It was typed,' he says now, 'with a green ribbon – some passing affectation that perhaps concealed an omen, for I am not without my quota of superstitions.'

News agencies have no such superstitions or loyalties to get in the way of the news, and throughout the world the machines were relentlessly chattering out the obituaries in nervous staccato sentences:

> Sellers obit see embargo . . . in 1951 he married former Australian actress Anne Hayes . . . then perhaps better known than her husband . . . lasted eleven years . . . two children . . . he had owned more than seventy cars and spent thousands on beautiful homes . . . important see embargo, not to be published until death is announced . . . first major film success was *I'm All Right, Jack* . . . brilliant . . . married Swedish starlet Britt Ekland . . . always meant to take it easier . . . a genius, a tragic loss to the world of cinema . . . not to be released until death official . . . see embargo.

Caught on the hop, newspapermen preparing deadline tributes were frustrated to find that there was so little to bite on. 'It was,' said one, 'like writing an obit for an

23

apparition, trying to glue down a piece of smoke.' Said another: 'The only reality was what you saw up there on the screen. He came to life at twenty-four frames every second and disappeared when the film stopped.'

In London at the *Daily Express* I had to find the words to bury Sellers. Like Forbes I was distressed at the idea of writing him off while there was life left in him. Yet I had no choice. The presses were waiting with the saliva of ink.

'I don't think I've ever known a man chase happiness so hard and find it in such short moments,' I wrote.

It was only weeks since I'd broken the news that he was going to marry again, and we had gone out and celebrated in Dom Perignon '57 at the Carlton Tower Hotel. Now, tragically this:

'Sometimes the happiness came in the make-up of a new role, sometimes in the driving seat of a fast car, occasionally in the garden of a new home.'

Copy boys were waiting to snatch each page as I completed it. An hour later, the editor, Bob Edwards, came through to my office. He said, 'It looks as if we're going to have to use that stuff of yours tonight. The words are fine. We're making up pages four and five now. It looks very good but it's a bloody shame. The Foreign Desk's heard he can't last the night.'

I remembered again the night I reported his engagement. After dinner we'd gone back to the paper to watch the machines running off the story. He said then: 'Let's face it, luv, next time I get that kind of space I've at least got to peg out.'

I left the office and walked downstairs and took a taxi to the Savoy.

'Hollywood, what a place to live,' he'd told me on the phone a few days before when the tenderfooted servants had resigned because of the hard marble floors.

Hollywood, what a place to die, I thought. I remembered covering the Monroe funeral there and being somehow, unreasonably perhaps, offended by the undertakers with suntanned faces and capped teeth and sympathy, and polished fingernails. In the American Bar I had several large whiskies and wondered about the paths and the pressures that had taken Peter Sellers to Hollywood to die. Hollywood, once, a long time ago, the capital of his ambition.

Birth Pains

IT HAD BECOME a fashionable canard, perpetrated by newspapermen in a hurry, to say that Peter Sellers had no face, to charge that his countenance was merely an empty canvas on which he painted a different portrait for every part and occasion. When one London cartoonist, Jak, in the *Evening Standard,* drew him faceless at the breakfast table on the morning after he married Britt Ekland, with the caption: 'So that's what you really look like,' Sellers had smiled but was not really amused.

The face of Peter Sellers was strong. Although it had become too thin from the punishment of occasional starvation, it had an almost startling quality, fierce and bright and volatile in excitement and anger: sharp and inquisitive when his interest was aroused. Unguarded, the eyes, which were the colour of collection-plate pennies, revealed more than those of most men, and almost all actors, his feelings and moods to a telling degree.

In repose his face had a stillness and dignity, but there was a sadness there, too. A sadness that was not in the shape of features, not in any arrangement of expression, but seemed to be the legacy of centuries of suffering.

It was not a modern face at all and bore an almost startling likeness to that of an early ancestor named Daniel Mendoza.

His great-great-grandfather, Mendoza, was a famous Portuguese-Jewish bare-fisted prizefighter from Aldgate in the East End of London, who distinguished himself by becoming the heavyweight champion of England and giving lessons in the noble art to the Prince of Wales, later to become George IV. He was a *bon vivant* and a celebrity, whose volubility and boastfulness were legendary. Hostesses sought him out, restaurants and public houses fought for his noisy patronage, and even the hit parade of the day was seldom without a song in praise of his triumphs and adventures.

'He was,' said Sellers with satisfaction, 'the first pugilist to introduce science into boxing – probably because he reasoned it was more prudent than having the hell beaten out of him. Both Peg [he always called his mother by her first name] and I bear a most remarkable resemblance to him – it is almost uncanny.'

Yet Sellers was not at first prepared to make much of his ancestor. 'I don't believe he really understood the position old man Mendoza held in English history,' said Spike Milligan. 'He was never a very literate person, Sellers, not a great reader of books.

'Anyway, somebody sent him some etchings and as conversations went on it became clear that he had decided to recognise the old bloke.

'He started talking about him as if he were alive . . . which is one of the curious characteristics he had, talking about the dead as if they weren't.'

Sellers' maternal grandmother, the pugilist's grand-daughter, was an awesome lady named Welcome. She was to become professionally known as Ma Ray and spread her fame well beyond the narrow gas-lit back streets of Hackney in the East End of London, where the family had made its home despite the social upgrading of Daniel.

Even more than Daniel, the man adoring fans called the Light of Israel – but allowed to die broke – Welcome was the tough, uncompromising, and determined influence in the sturdy, close-knit family of Mendoza.

'Ma really ruled that roost,' recalled one Uncle Bert, the youngest of Ma's eight sons, shortly before his death in 1967.

At forty-four, roost-ruling Welcome, who had married a merchant named Solomon Marks, was widowed. 'Solly left me a big legacy,' she joked in better days, 'ten kids.'

Probably because the world wasn't ready for a female heavyweight boxing champion, she moved into show business, and launched what is generally regarded to be

27

the first travelling revue in Britain. She quickly established herself and became the unchallenged queen of spectacle around the provincial music-halls.

One of her favourite acts was built around a huge glass tank filled with coloured water and decorated with chorus girls in daring bathing suits. An aqua-act, incidentally, which frequently caused trouble, not to say havoc, with local Watch Committees, since some puritans felt that there was something indecent about ladies swimming in full view of the gallery.

The first revue, called *Splash Me,* came to an untimely end on one occasion when the tank burst in mid-performance and, according to family legend, all but drowned several elderly members of the orchestra playing Handel's *Water Music* (a bit of culture which Ma found helped to appease the more recalcitrant Watch Committees).

Undeterred, Ma promptly ordered another tank and the show went on, enhanced with a new speciality number in which a talented young lady ate a whole banana under water, a somewhat bizarre experiment in gastronomy that might have come straight out of 'The Goon Show', which was to make Sellers' name nearly fifty years later.

During the First World War the shows flourished. Peg sang patriotic numbers and the sentimental hits of the day and was generously applauded. With her mother she drove round the country in a magnificent scarlet Ford. It was the age of ragtime and syncopated music, life was sweet and the Depression was yet to come. The theatre boomed and Ma's shows were in demand, though, wisely perhaps, she never took them to London, a town probably not yet ready for subaqueous banana eaters.

But Peg had reached the age of twenty-four and Ma Ray worried about her unmarried daughter. 'Find yourself a nice boy, Peg. Get married, have little ones. You're not getting any younger, child. Is it an old maid you want to be?' Ma would chide with growing anxiety.

Peg, still an attractive woman in her prime, was obliged to give up her singing act for character parts. 'It is,' her mother told her, 'more dignified.'

One afternoon in the early autumn months of 1921, Ma had taken her latest show, *More Splashes,* to the King's Theatre in Portsmouth, a fairly regular venue, and between houses she heard a young piano player in a local café.

'He's very good for a café musician,' Peg said.

Ma was also impressed; but whether her interest was as impresario or potential mother-in-law is not altogether clear. When he had finished his stint for the afternoon tea customers, Ma called him over to their table.

'What's you name, son?' she asked.

'Bill Sellers.'

'Well, Bill, I need a piano player in my show,' she told him. 'If you want the job it's yours – if you can drive a motor car or are willing to learn pretty damn fast.'

'I can drive,' he said.

'And you can play the piano. Do you want the job or don't you?'

'Well, yes,' he said.

'Fine. It's a good car,' she said. 'A scarlet Ford. You'll like it. I'll pay you whatever you're getting here. We can discuss travelling expenses when the travelling begins. How's that suit you?'

'Fine, I reckon,' he said.

During this uncomplicated negotiation Peg had been watching the young man. He was blond, not too tall, and had the shy uncertain look of a man who might occasionally stutter. When he did speak his voice was pleasant, with traces of Yorkshire accent softening the words at the edges.

'Where did you play before this place?' Ma asked.

'I was assistant organist at the Bradford Cathedral,' he said. 'That's where I come from – Bradford.'

'At the Cathedral!' Ma said. 'Then you're not a Jewish boy.'

'A Protestant,' Bill Sellers told her, with a smile that Peg liked.

They were married at the Bloomsbury Registrar's

Office in London in 1923.

It was the romantic fusion of these unsettled talents that produced – on 8th September, 1925 – Peter Sellers. That he was not actually born in a trunk is testimony to his father's remarkable ability behind the wheel of the ageing scarlet Ford. Since times had been getting tougher, Peg had insisted on working until the last possible moment. Shortly after they made it back to Southsea Terrace from the King's Theatre in Portsmouth, a baby was being slapped to life by a tut-tutting Dr Little.

Two weeks later, Peter Sellers made his theatrical debut, carried on to the stage by the show's star comic Dickie Henderson, the father of the present English comedian.

'Here's little Peg Ray's son and heir,' he told the cooing audience. 'Good luck to him, I say. Let's all wish him well.' The audience sang 'For He's a Jolly Good Fellow' and Sellers, it has been reliably recorded, burst into tears, and for the first time in his life made an audience laugh.

For a while, the family lived in the small apartment where he was born, over a shop called Postcard Corner because it specialised, somewhat optimistically and ultimately disastrously, in selling postcard views of the local beauty spots and the dockyards of Portsmouth. Sellers' first memory reaches back to this place. It is of his father leaning over his cot with a gift: a pair of blue bunny-rabbit slippers.

'I remember the moment distinctly – the glow of the fire, the shadows on the ceiling, the furniture, and my dad peering into my cot and smiling. I was almost a year old,' Sellers had recalled.

What he doesn't remember is that he had already almost died.

A backstage baby, he had spent his earliest months touring with his parents. That winter, when they were playing the Hippodrome in Keighley, the bleak, raw-boned, Yorkshire town, he caught bronchial pneumonia. A Black doctor sat with him all through one night. 'The crisis is over,' he told Peg the next morning. 'He is a strong little chap, but I advise you to be watchful and not take any chances with his health.'

'He saved Peter's life, I'm sure of that,' recalled Peg later. 'Now I can't even think of his name.'

But if Peter Sellers grew up in the wings it was not in the wings of his mother's life. She doted on her son, the way one would expect a Jewish mother to dote on an only boy-child. Indeed, with an Auntie Cissie and Ma Ray also in admiring attendance at Postcard Corner, it became the considered opinion of at least one of the Ray uncles that young Peter was being dangerously spoiled.

Uncle Bert was among the unenamoured. 'If Peg had to go out of the room for a minute,' he recalled many years later with wonder still in his voice, 'he would set up a yell you could hear in the Portsmouth dockyards on pay day.' It would have been justifiable homicide, hinted another darkly, to have stangled the infant brat with his own bibstrings.

Of those early years Sellers vividly remembers standing on the side of the stage watching the acts, particularly his mother's. Fifty years later, with almost uncanny total recall, he could describe the act she was performing at the period.

Wearing white leotards she stood before a white screen on to which a magic lantern cast slide pictures of different costumes and backgrounds. Thus, in rapid succession, she became famous women through the ages: Britannia, Boadicea, Joan of Arc, Florence Nightingale, Queen Victoria.

The quick transformations fascinated the small boy watching from the side of the stage: witnessing his own beloved mother becoming so many different women, strangers, he didn't know. It wasn't his favourite act, but it held a kind of horrific spell for the child.

'Anyway, she looked so beautiful,' he remembered. 'And the applause, the applause warmed your whole life. To listen to audiences applauding my mother was one of the most memorable sounds of childhood, I think.'

Many years later, Harvey Orkin, who spent some years

as his agent before they fell out, was to remark: 'Sellers belongs to the stage, where he can get the applause at once. Making a film for him is like making love and not reaching a climax. He has to hear the sound of applause, the sound of acceptance and approval, immediately. It's practically useless if delayed.'

But at the beginning the stage did not appeal to the small child who could glean so much glorious and unforgettable pleasure from his mother's applause. 'I never liked the theatrical life. I still don't. To this day I can smell the smell of warm greasepaint melting beneath the hot spotlights, the smell of sweat and the dirt and the dust backstage, the stale air.'

Far worse than the smell of backstage was the smell of the boarding-houses. Slowly he learned to hate and despise the often dingy, back-street, lace-curtained, rule-ridden digs that catered to performers with frosted-over tolerance and little service. Later, he recalled mostly the smells of his childhood, for that seemed to be the sense most offended by his environment, perhaps because it was so unavoidably exposed, the least protected by his watchful mother.

The *smell* of the theatre, the *smell* of third-class carriages on trains, the *smell* of bus shelters at midnight, the *smell* of dressing rooms that nobody cared for.

But theatrical digs were the worst. They stank.

'They had a smell all of their own,' he said. 'A smell manufactured just for them. It was a mixture of cheap cooking fat and secondhand furniture and cold sheets that hadn't been aired, and cat food and boiled cabbage . . .'

He was not a docile lad, and had a fine streak of bravado with a certain charming defiance of authority. He conducted a most successful running skirmish with boarding-house keepers and their maids, and went to extraordinary lengths to triumph over them.

Particularly he hated to be called 'Sonny'. 'My name,' he would first reply with dignity and a warning measure of firmness in his voice, 'is not "Sonny". It's Peter.'

If, after that polite shot across the bows, they still called

32

him Sonny, battle would commence, Sellers playing his hand with saboteur's stealth. Only on one known occasion did he resort to open warfare.

Catching a particularly obnoxious Sonny-mouthing maid putting the regulation one lump of coal on the sitting-room fire, he placed his boot on her behind and pushed hard.

'She put her hands out to save herself and burnt them rather badly, I'm afraid,' he once recalled. It was an ugly wound that surprised rather than upset the swiftly apprehended assailant. For, as he pointed out in his defence, he had never been able to get much simple warmth out of the fire, let alone hand-scorching heat.

Despite this fast legal argument he was found guilty. Peg, on her return from the Wednesday matinée performance, was asked to find alternative digs immediately. Their bags had already been packed and were waiting in the hall.

'You might have waited,' she occasionally remonstrated in later years, 'until the last house on Saturday.'

By this time, at least temporarily, Peg had abandoned any notions of forcing her reluctant son into a theatrical career. When he was barely three, she had had a dressmaker make him up a splendid white-tie-and-tails outfit, complete with top hat and silver-topped cane. She then taught him to sing the old Albert Chevalier song 'My Old Dutch'. He was enrolled in a dancing school, and seemed locked into a theatrical future as securely as into a condemned cell.

'I pined for him to carry on the family tradition,' she said later. 'I wanted him to carry on where we left off.' When it became clear, even to Peg, that the child in the wings was not ambitious to take the stage, she felt cheated.

'It disappointed me, of course it did. What mother in her heart of hearts doesn't want a child prodigy? Something special from her son? But I wasn't going to force him. I think I knew it would happen one day, anyway. I think I always knew that.'

So Sellers got a reprieve from the sentence of his mother's ambition, but his life was not to change.

Peg and Bill never had another child. Sellers grew up in an adult world, largely without other children, without friends of his own age, without a single steady tree-climbing, apple pinching, hide-and-seeking, tin-can-kicking pal. He was a loner, caught in a world of grown-ups, a show business world of make-believe that was harder and tougher and more demanding and less certain than the real world outside the stage door.

'I suppose if I'd had more mates I would have been happier,' he reflected later. 'I never had any real set mates, no lasting companions. I'd make friends in one town for one week and then we'd move on again, it was always like that. You'd hope, if you played in that town again, perhaps a year later, that the friend you'd made would still be around; maybe if he was the landlady's son you'd be lucky. Then you'd hope that he'd remember you.

'I was never really lonely though,' he said. 'It wasn't something I was conscious of, anyway. Peg was marvellous company: she would always keep me entertained and was always great fun to be with, and I was treated more or less like an adult.

'I had quite a unique childhood. I'm sure it's stood me in good stead. I mean it encouraged the resilience, the durability; it forged the humour, I suppose, because without a sense of humour in those days we would have all gone under a dozen times a week.'

But the independence of those years, the life that went on without any sustained commitment to other people, gave him the beginnings of his later isolation, an isolation that was to become almost total after the death of Peg.

'Those years, those early, far-off years,' he said later, 'produced a strange hermit-like quality in me. Some people don't understand. But I can be on my own very easily. I never worry if I haven't got anyone with me. Often that is the best time. Alone.' (As he spoke those words his wife Britt was living less than a thousand yards away in their Mayfair apartment in Clarges Street, and

34

there was considerable speculation about the future of their marriage. The hermit time was with him.)

In 1933, when he was almost eight years old, Peg finally decided to give up touring the halls and make some kind of permanent home for her son.

Bill joined up with a ukelele player named Lewis and went on the road as a double act called Lewis and Sellers, a moderate down-the-bill fill-in that not many old pros can recall today. It meant long absences from home, and Bill Sellers' influence on his son, which had never been very strong, now became almost negligible.

Peg's parental autonomy was assured.

She took a house in Gloucester Crescent, near Regent's Park in London. And although she 'had to look at every penny', Sellers, as he had always done and would always do, attended a fee-paying private school: this time it was St Mark's Kindergarten.

'There never seemed to be any serious shortage of ice cream and I suppose that is how a boy judges his childhood fortunes,' he observed later.

At the time he was thankful to be away from the theatre and its attendant life. He felt nothing for it but a kind of loathing pity.

After a short time in Gloucester Crescent they moved to Highgate, where Peg opened a small antique shop. Sellers was enrolled at St Aloysius College in Hornsey Lane, a Catholic school run by the Brothers of Our Lady of Mercy. It was a decision that to the end Sellers, the son of a Protestant father and a Jewish mother, was unable to fathom.

'They seemed quite determined,' he once said, 'to make me a religious hybrid.'

His teacher was Brother Cornelius, 'I can't remember Peter at all as a child. He was just . . . average, not a memorable scholar, not a memorable athlete, no, nothing very outstanding at all,' he has since recalled.

But young Sellers must have made some kind of impression on at least one of the masters. Caned for some now-forgotten misdemeanour, he reported the incident to

Peg. The following morning she was at the school upbraiding the teacher, accusing him of sadistic tendencies and heartless insensitivity.

From that moment on, Sellers was the one boy in the school who was not permitted to be caned. For the rest of his truncated scholastic career he was punished with 'lines' – the repetitious writing of a single sentence in his best handwriting.

But now once again Peg felt the palm of her ambition beginning to itch. Tentatively but inexorably she again began to push her son toward a theatrical future. She got him a job modelling for Mazda electric light bulbs.

He was a good model and there was plenty of work. The Brothers of Our Lady of Mercy were frequently called upon to demonstrate their worthiness to their Order with displays of blessed tolerance toward his increasing absence from the classroom.

He was now thirteen. War with Nazi Germany was clearly coming, and Peg fretted for the safety of her son. Then, in the summer of 1939, while the British were digging their trenches and shelters in the towns, one of Peg's brothers, who was running a seaside theatre in the town of Ilfracombe, Devon, invited the family to stay with him.

Sellers was eager to go, having decided that show business, after all, had rather more to offer than scholastic endeavour at St Aloysius.

He never returned to school.

He was put to work in the theatre, doing whatever odd job the manager felt him capable of doing with the minimum disaster. From sweeping the stage to polishing the elaborate brass ornaments in the Victorian-plush, aspidistra-adorned foyer, Sellers moved on until he was actually trusted to operate the limes, the spotlights that can make or destroy an artist's act.

'I suppose by that time I really had the taste in my mouth,' he reflected later.

One evening as he moved the giant spotlights across the

36

stage with a professional, almost cocky air, he was curiously impressed with a transparently youthful actor playing an old man in a murder play. Later he consulted a programme to find out the actor's name. Paul Scofield, he read.

'Now I wouldn't mind being able to act like that bloke,' he told his mate on the limes.

War came. A German bomb put an end to their home, and Peg's shop, in Highgate. But the bomb changed nothing. Sellers was already sure what he wanted to do now: 'Very simply I wanted to be on the stage. Doing precisely what, I wasn't certain, except that I knew I had to perform.'

Now fourteen, he and a boy called Derek Altman were flushed with success, having won five pounds in a Sunday night talent competition singing a duet. Neither later recalled the name of the song, but there was some intelligent speculation that since they won the contest the number must have had a strongly patriotic flavour, a flavour not altogether unappreciated in England in 1940.

However, Sellers was shrewd enough to reason that his future in show business was not as a singer, patriotism being an uncertain emotion in peacetime. The answer to his future, he felt strongly, came one week when a gentleman known as Joe Daniels and his Hotshots arrived in Ilfracombe for a limited engagement at the Victoria Pavilion.

Mr Daniels was a spectacular drummer in the manner of Gene Krupa, and young Sellers fell instantly under the rhythmic spell of the drumbeat. After each night's performance, when Mr Daniels and all the Hotshots had departed and the theatre was dark, Sellers would come down from the lonely limes and attack the skins with fancied élan and a musicianship that was all imagination.

When he imparted his new ambition to his parents, a secondhand drum kit was swiftly acquired and lessons booked. Peg was overjoyed.

Yet, although none of them knew it then, it was already

too late to assume ambitions. For Sellers had unknowingly embarked several years earlier on his collision course with fame.

Ironically, perhaps, it was the death of Ma Ray, the family catalyst, that brought Sellers to the beginnings, the swaddlinged stirrings, of a career that was to make him a millionaire, a Companion of the British Empire, and, to many, a veritable genius.

When Ma died, the family fortunes, not helped by the creeping senility of British music-hall, slipped toward a nadir quite unforeseeable just a decade before. Peg had opened her modest antique shop in Highgate and to acquire stock she and Uncle Bert and, between engagements, Bill, would tour the country, door-to-door canvassing for old gold and silver and antique jewelry.

During school holidays, and not unoccasionally during school term, Sellers would accompany the trio on these gold-prospecting treks into the suburbs and the richer provinces beyond. 'They would split a district into three areas of attack,' Sellers explained later. 'My mother would do ten streets, my uncle would do ten streets and my dad would take on another ten. The patter was always exactly the same for all of them.

' "Good morning, madam," they would say. "I'm from the London Gold Refining Company and we are very interested in purchasing old gold or unwanted trinkets you may have. The London Gold Refining Company pays the very best prices, naturally." '

The pitch was not exactly computered psychology, but it was usually effective. 'My mother would almost invariably do the best business, because she was a woman and the old biddies were not so frightened of her. What usually happened was some old dear would say she had a load of stuff tucked away upstairs in the attic that belonged to her grandmother and if she could have time to sort it out . . .

'This was called a "call back", and they were usually very profitable. They'd pick up anything from gold watches to gold teeth: sometimes the gear was very good indeed. Actually, I learned a lot about gold during that period. I'm quite an expert on gold today.'

Often, while all this business was being conducted, Sellers would sit himself out of sight (he wasn't exactly good for the image of the London Gold Refining Company) under a nearby hedge or tree, preferably one bearing ripe and reachable fruit, and listen to all the chat, the hard, sly bargaining, the delicate negotiations over the price of an eighteen-carat molar or a silver snuff box.

While he listened, his childish imagination would idly create fantasies around the voices, giving them faces and shapes, until they became eccentric scientists, mad inventors, kind, dotty old aunts, or querulous colonels. It was a child's game, innocent and simple, but unconsciously he was also beginning to assimilate and store in his mind all the accents and tones and vocal mannerisms and idiosyncrasies he heard drifting across fences and over the manicured privets from the world of fly, if not always high, finance conducted on the doorsteps of Britain.

When Sellers created a role it was the voice he had to crack first – a singular approach to acting, as one American critic once observed, akin to a smile giving birth to a Cheshire cat.

That period when Sellers was towed about the country by the representatives of the mythical London Gold Refining Company is significant for quite another reason, too. For it was during this time that the seeds were sown for his latter-day automania, his relentless and passionate search for the perfect car, a search that took him through more than two hundred high-priced automobiles from the world's finest makers.

Several theories, mostly Freudian, have been advanced to account for this durable dream of the perfect car, but the most likely explanation is that it started sometime in the middle thirties with one Uncle Joe Barnet.

An occasional representative of the London Gold Refining Company, Uncle Joe had a car . . . and a bizarre passion for roadside hoardings. Indeed, he loved nothing better than to sing the slogans as they flashed by in a fashion that, again, was not unlike the Pop Art idiocy of the still-distant Goons:

'. . . the finest boot polish . . . keeps your hair in place all day . . . and free from night-time starvation . . . Esso . . . for faster relief . . . and deep refreshing . . . cat foot . . .'

And so on across the length and breadth of Britain.

On one occasion, Uncle Joe observed a lady cyclist and, temporarily bereft of any hoardings to orchestrate in his inimitable style, sang out: 'Oi Oi fat arse.' This fast, erotic thrust caused considerable mirth inside the speeding car and, it was generally agreed, the day was off to a fine start.

Later, when they met at a café rendezvous for tea and a show of fortune, Uncle Joe arrived in a state of considerable agitation, even shock. He was also soaking wet from head to foot. It turned out that he had had the misfortune to call at the home of the lady bicycle rider whose anatomy he found cause to criticise earlier that day. Recognising the caller from an upstairs window, she had deposited the entire contents of a household receptacle upon his head.

'You . . . you sex maniac,' she screamed at Uncle Joe as he retreated down the garden path, dripping.

'But,' concluded Sellers, retelling this story of his childhood, 'he did have a smashing car. That was really something in those days, having a car. We were never able to afford our own car, Peg and me. It would have been very useful, very nice. We would have had a better chance with a car of our own. I vowed then that one day I would own a car of my own, a great car, the best there was.'

So when the money came so did the cars – the Aston Martins, Ferraris, the Bentley Continentals, the Lancias, the flashing E-types from Jaguar – the recharging compensations for a childhood spent travelling in the back of other people's lives . . . if they had the room.

A compulsive nostaligic, Sellers was to make frequent pilgrimages to the past. 'I have a great yearning to go back to early places and beginnings and just wander around old haunts.'

In the sixties he went back to the very start, to Postcard Corner, now a café with a part of the premises in a state of disrepair. He asked to go over the house and walked from room to room. 'I knew where my cot was, the shape of the ceilings. It was uncanny, really uncanny. I felt exactly the same way you feel when you go into a room and think, "I've been here before", although you know you haven't or couldn't have been. I could identify every corner, the fireplace, the door, the windows. Only it all looked much smaller and older and sadder.'

One evening he was with Spike Milligan and, as often happened when they got together, they were discussing their early days, the hard times, the wild times, the giggles that echoed and grew louder down the years.

'I'm an old Irish nostalgic, Pete,' said Milligan, wiping the tears from his eyes. 'The past is so sweet and sad and beautiful for me.'

Sellers looked at him for a long silent moment, then with all the fun gone from his voice, leaving it tired and almost threadbare, he said: 'What do you mean the past, Spike? *Yesterday*. I get upset thinking about yesterday . . . because it's gone and it's so bloody buried, so irredeemable, and nobody seems to care. I can cry for yesterday.'

Milligan has thought about that remark a great deal since. He now believes Sellers yearned for the past not as a sentimentalist or a romanticist but simply as a kind of bereaved realist. 'The truth is,' he says, 'he knew that yesterday he was happier than he could ever be tomorrow.'

Yet Sellers believed that his search for the past had greater potential value than the generation of mere nostalgia and sadness and occasional tears, the stuff that Milligan mines and treasures with love. Sellers believed that somewhere buried in the past, even perhaps in the topsoil of yesterday, was a clue to what he was, a key to a

41

complex talent that was more than genetic genius, a success that was not merely managerial cunning.

'I'm anxious,' he once told me, 'to see and discover and taste the places that kicked me off, got me going. The beginnings, the very early days, square one. I want to see if I can find some element there, something that fed me, contributed to whatever it is I am now. I'm sure there is something there, and there must be a way of finding it. So I go back, I go back to old apartments, old homes, the boarding-houses I knew, searching, seeking for . . . I don't know, I honestly don't know what it is.'

Always the pattern was the same.

The Rolls (or the Cadillac or the Mercedes or the Lincoln Continental) arrived at some street in some town. The bespectacled occupant sat and watched the buildings, his eyes moving slowly, the eyes of a painter perhaps, measuring and absorbing and understanding.

After a time he climbed out and walked around the neighbourhood, occasionally entering shops, searching curtained windows and people's faces.

There was no hurry.

'Do you mind if I come in and look around? I used to live here. A long time ago,' he would say finally, zeroing in. Often it took him hours to knock on the old familiar door and introduce himself.

The reception was usually one of incredulous welcome and a certain amount of engaging trust: he often asked to be left alone, to wander through the rooms, standing, listening, looking at ceilings, now crouching child-high, touching the surfaces and door handles of those early years, sniffing the air with closed eyes shutting out the present in his pursuit of the past.

'Have you ever discovered anything important in any of these rooms?' I once asked him.

'No. I've only discovered that none of them was big enough for me,' he said and did not smile.

The Impersonator

THE NEED TO live a part, any part other than that of Peter Sellers, began to make itself felt most forcefully very early in his life. At the age of fifteen, with his good friend Derek Altman – the first friendship he had experienced that was not short-lived – he came under the powerful influence of Dashiell Hammett and the whole private-eye school.

The ambitious duo decided to open up their own detective agency.

Calling cards were printed, Selman Investigations, but business was – not unexpectedly – slow in the sleepy seaside town of Ilfracombe, especially during the off season in wartime Britain.

Not so much as a missing dog case came their way during the first months of their enterprise: nobody wanted a tail on an erring wife, nobody wanted to wreak revenge on a corrupt policeman or a crooked lawyer, and there was a depressing shortage of rich customers wanting to enlist their aid in seeking Maltese falcons or even Persian pussycats.

Finally the pair found a use for their visiting cards. Young Mr Altman fell passionately in love from afar with a hotel chambermaid. Unable or unwilling to make direct contact with the lady himself, Altman was desolate. Then Sellers hit on an idea.

Sticking a false moustache on a lip that patently was not ready for the wispiest whisker, Sellers climbed into his Alan Ladd raincoat, went to the hotel where the chambermaid worked, and asked to see the manager.

Shown to his office, Sellers produced his visiting card and, in an accent which he imagined sounded like something from the pages of Raymond Chandler, demanded to see the girl.

'I've got reason to believe,' he said, straining for the low notes, 'she can help us with our enquiries.'

But the manager was nobody's fool. He leaned across his desk with a strange look that *was* something from the pages of Raymond Chandler. Then, very slowly, in one long movement, he proceeded to remove Sellers' moustache rather in the delicate manner of a devoted philatelist parting a rare old stamp from a fragile backing.

It hurt.

Man and undone youth faced each other across the desk and neither spoke for a long, pregnant moment. Sellers ransacked his brain for something from Hammett that would cover such an emergency. There was nothing that readily came to mind.

'Get out,' the manager finally said, in what Sellers was to recall in later years were the most villainous and chilling tones he had ever heard in his life. 'Get out and never come back here again unless you want your young arse kicked from this room to the end of the pier and back again.'

He also kept the moustache.

After one other equally joyless assignment, when they were hired by a frantic bandleader who was appearing at the Victoria Pavilion (his life was being threatened by a mysterious Greek oboe player from Soho, believed to be known as Moisha Winnick), the company quietly expired without a single shot being fired, case solved, client satisfied, or fee paid.

The endangered bandleader, it was later discovered, was a well-known compulsive practical joker. But for a while there wasn't a Greek oboe player in or out of Equity whose life and oboe were not suspect. Altman went on to become a very fine gentlemen's hairdresser.

But now these remnant days of Sellers' childhood were ending. His drumming lessons were successful and as the war progressed and grew more voracious, the need for civilian musicians grew acute among the bands. So, still too young for the services, Sellers found himself in some demand. For a time he played with Oscar Rabin, then with Henry Hall, both notable and successful broadcasting bandleaders in Britain at that time.

The endless travelling, however, the one-night stands in factory towns the colour of soot and as inviting as the breath of a polar bear with pyorrhoea, were darkly oppressive to him. He began to hate the whole business with a ferocity that never mellowed (although his old phobia about packing and unpacking his own suitcase, nurtured in those crowded, rushing, unhappy days, was later overcome).

The hatred came to a sudden boil when he was touring with Waldini and his Gypsy Band, a collection of ill-assorted, mostly elderly, crippled, or otherwise militarily exempt musicians.

Maestro Waldini, it should be recorded, had tenuous if not unlikely associations with the Romany race. Fussy genetics apart, his gypsy troubadours were gay and col-ourful, and there were plenty of bookings in a country where both colour and gaiety were being drained out almost by the hour.

But the travelling conditions were appalling. The war was at its grimmest stage in England, the blackout putting a stygian armour of darkness across the land, restricting transport, disrupting timetables, and often leading Mr Waldini and company into cul-de-sacs of chaos, stranding them at midnight in godforsaken hamlets in the rain or snow or fog. (At least, this is the vivid impression Peter Sellers carried with him all his life.)

It was during one such mishap, when the bedraggled gypsies found themselves in a mill town in Lancashire when they should have been in a mining town in Cumber-land, that Sellers handed in his bandanna and took the next train home.

But his motive was more honourable than mere pique. Now nearly eighteen, the military call-up age, he had decided to volunteer for flying duties, having been notably swayed by the patriotic propagation of the feats of such RAF aces as the legless Douglas Bader, Sailor Malan and

Cat's-eyes Cunningham. But, although a 20-20 visionary his optics were not so good. Declining an alternative offer of a rear-gunner's posting (the mortality rate among rear gunners was the highest of all and entrance examinations less stringent), he was eventually enlisted as a humble Airman Second Class.

After a not very distinguished few months as an armourer's assistant in England, he was posted as a 'general entertainer' to the RAF Gang Show run by Squadron Leader Ralph Reader, famous in peacetime Britain for his Boy Scout revues.

When he told Peg he was being sent overseas she was distraught and started an intensive campaign to persuade the Air Ministry that her only son was totally unsuited to any kind of military career.

'She tried every excuse in the book,' remembers Spike Milligan with affection for the old lady. 'She idolised that boy.

'She tried everything; she must have gone through the entire medical encyclopaedia to find a disease that would get Pete back into civvy street, back into her loving care and protection: "He's got flat feet, he's got a flat head, flat ears, he's even got flat teeth . . ." Poor, lovely, desperate Peg.'

Sellers stayed stubbornly healthy throughout a series of the most intimate, probing examinations by incredulous military doctors anxious to check out the man Peg insisted was a walking plague zone, a threat to humanity in general and the Allies in particular.

Unaware of his mother's persistent ploys to free him from the services, he was becoming increasingly unsettled by the frequency of the visits from the medical officers. But he was moving too fast to attempt to get to the bottom of the military's interest, indeed, fascination, in his health.

There was plenty for Peg to worry about. But the emphasis of her concern was wildly misplaced. Charades and not enemy shrapnel were her son's greatest hazard. The military career of Airman Sellers was seldom to rise above the parapet of class warfare. There would be many scenes like this:

The young flight lieutenant drinking gin and tonic in the officer's mess of a fighter squadron somewhere in India was new to the station. 'Straight from Blighty, judging by the white of his knees,' said a pilot officer, eyeing the newcomer from across the room. 'It'll mean we'll get some fresh conversation and a bit of up-to-date gossip,' said another before returning his attention to a three-week-old copy of *The Times*. 'Must have a snorter with him tomorrow night.'

But the newcomer with the pale knees was never there the following day to be politely interrogated by his brother officers. A fortuitous absence in view of the fact that the flight lieutenant was in reality 2223033 Airman Second Class Sellers, P.

Dissatisfied by his lowly and obstinate rank, Sellers relieved the tedium by a series of cool and incredible impersonations. In this he was aided and abetted by an admirable selection of uniforms kept in the wardrobe of the RAF Gang Show.

It was the swift pace of his existence that enabled him to carry out his impersonations almost throughout his entire air force career – a career in which he was to rise from the imaginary rank of flight lieutenant to the exalted and even more imaginary rank of air commodore before it was finished.

'We were shooting around from camp to camp giving these Gang Shows and quite honestly most of the time the arrangments were a complete bloody shambles,' he has recalled. 'Nobody quite knew who we were or what we were supposed to be doing. It really was quite a simple thing to borrow a uniform and have a pleasant, civilised evening in the old officers' mess . . . and, anyway, it was a pleasant sort of escape, an easy way out of a really awful, drab kind of existence.'

This escape route from reality once led him to dress up as a Sikh officer of the Indian Air Force: clearly the beginning of his fascination for Eastern characters, which was to culminate some seventeen years later in his role as the Indian doctor in *The Millionairess*.

Yet still to celebrate his twentieth birthday, he enjoyed one very pleasant Christmas Eve in an officers' mess dressed as an air commodore, a rank rarely achieved before middle age even in wartime: although this particular triumph of impersonation he later modestly attributed as much to the inebriation of the guests as to his own prowess as a character actor.

David Lodge remembers later impersonations in Europe with a sense of admiration and alarm and even, occasionally, delayed shock.

'The first time I ever saw him pull this stunt – and it was a very serious offence to impersonate an officer – was when he appeared in the uniform of a squadron leader at a place called Gütersloh, a former Luftwaffe camp in Germany,' he says.

The entertainers had little regard for military conformity by this time. Discipline was as relaxed as a piece of chewed string. They wore long hair, cutaway Van Heusen collars, and custom-tailored uniforms of the finer Royal Canadian Air Force material that was easily mistaken for British officer cloth: a sartorial confusion that particularly appealed to Sellers. There was no serious respect for rank among the troupe and they enjoyed a freedom unparalleled in the history of the British armed forces. But the freedom was never quite enough for Peter Sellers.

On this occasion, dressed as a squadron leader at Camp Gütersloh, he announced he was going to inspect the airmen's quarters.

'Don't be bloody barmy, Pete,' warned Lodge, who had become something of a father figure to Sellers since saving him from a threatened barrack-room brawl some months before. 'They'll spot you a mile off.'

'Nobody is going to spot me, don't worry, boy,' Sellers assured him.

He parted his hair in the middle, slicking it down hard until it was stuck flat against his head. He put on a large false moustache and greyed his temples with talcum powder.

Watching this careful performance, Lodge was astonished at the gradual transformation in his friend. He wasn't merely dressing up, he remembers now, he was actually becoming a squadron leader. His stance stiffened; his walk, his eyes, his voice, and even his vocabulary changed.

The disguise complete, Sellers went out to tour the depressed camp: there had been severe flooding in the area and there was now a shortage of fresh water and decent food. The troops were fed up and decidely on edge that afternoon.

It was Sunday. The troops were lying about their billets in various stages of gloom, a mood concocted of Saturday night's hangover, Sunday's boredom, and the prospect of Monday's reveille that would start the tedious unmerry-go-round all over again. As Sellers walked into each hut, the reaction was the same. An airman, less somnolent than the rest, would spot the imposing figure of the officer.

"Tention. Stand by your beds. Officer present.'

Sellers waited while the men scrambled off their beds and out of their dreams, waited while the radios were silenced and the card games stopped.

Then, 'That's all right, chaps, stand easy. This is an informal visit. I simply want to tell you that I have arrived with a splendid show for you, absolutely tophole stuff,' he informed them, burning a low-voltage smile in his mouth, the nearest British officers get to informality with the ranks.

His performances on these occasions, recalls one witness, contained always the slyest hint of mockery at the expense of authority and the Establishment. His accent was Evelyn Waugh-to-Waugh at its most nasal. It was as if he were trying to see how satirically outrageous he could be without being less than convincing, without being unmasked. It was a dangerous game.

'I have also been instructed by the Air Ministry in London to enquire into your welfare here. Now, then, one at a time, any little grumbles?'

49

They complained about late mail, the water shortage, the food, the boredom. He listened, nodding solemn concern, giving muttered assurances of his personal determination to investigate further, to see that something was done to improve their welfare.

But David Lodge, who had followed Sellers on his rounds at Camp Gütersloh, was most concerned for his welfare.

'If those blokes had ever discovered he was just a plain ordinary airman like themselves, an actor having a bit of a giggle, they would have skinned him alive,' he asserts today.

After Sellers had toured several of the huts, repeating the performance, Lodge insisted he end the perilous charade. 'But I'm doing these fellas a favour,' Sellers said, surprised at Lodge's attitude. 'Now they really believe somebody cares about them.'

'And I care about you,' Lodge told him. 'So pack it in now.'

An hour later, demoted, detalcumed, and demoustached, he was in line in the airmen's mess collecting the same lousy food he had been hearing about all afternoon.

'The extraordinary thing was,' says Lodge, 'nobody ever saw through him.'

The more successful he became with these risky impersonations, the bolder he became. 'All the time it was as if he was seeing how far he could go, what he could get away with next,' Lodge recalls.

One evening, after a particularly well received show, the cast was invited back to the sergeants' mess for supper. 'It was a marvellous party, plenty of booze and some dolly WRAF sergeants to liven up the scene,' says Lodge. His contentment, however, was to be abruptly and sorrowfully shattered.

Sellers arrived. His temples grey, the moustache luxuriant, and the squadron leader's uniform immaculately pressed. Within minutes he was being entertained by a flattery of gin-pressing sergeants. It was not, perhaps, saying a great deal for the perception of the noncommissioned officers of His Majesty's Royal Air Force. In the opinion of Mr Lodge, 'Any idiot with half an eye and a skinful must have known it was the same bloke who was playing the drums in the show not an hour earlier.'

The deception, he was certain, could not last long, and the sight and sound of Sellers sobered him immediately. 'I just knew I had to get him out of there,' he recalls.

But before he could begin the delicate business of removing him from the danger zone, Sellers noticed him and said, 'Ah, young Lodge, dear boy. One of my best chappies. Do come here and sit yourself down, there's a good lad, don't be shy.'

For a moment, Lodge knew the cold sensation of having the steel muzzle of a Mauser kissing the nape of his neck. The awesome hosts dutifully made room for him. 'Just having a jar or two with these good gentlemen, Lodge,' said Sellers grandly. 'What'll you have, eh?'

Not one to miss such an opportunity, even under such trying conditions, Lodge ordered a large Scotch and prayed it would steady his nerves. But his nerves were not soothed during the long German night, as Sellers entertained and enthralled the sergeants around him, accepting their generous hospitality in return for his impressions of famous comics of the day, various celebrated military leaders, and even the camp commandant.

At an opportune moment, Lodge whispered: 'You've gone too bleedin' far this time, mate. The sooner we make tracks out of here the better for all of us.'

Sellers saw the light which, by now, was looking suspiciously like the dawn. 'Well, gentlemen,' he said, getting to his feet with the weary reluctance of a man who has drunk deeply the good life, 'time marches on and we must, alas, away. Good night to you and God bless you all.'

The speech, remembers Lodge, sounded slightly royal.

The senior warrant officer made a small emotional speech thanking the 'most civilised, intelligent and witty officer' for the honour of his company. Then the sergeants' mess gave three cheers.

51

'If you ever do that again,' Lodge told him as they walked across the barrack square, 'I'll belt you one, so help me, I'll belt you.'

Sellers, who will probably never know the icy touch of mythical Mausers, looked hurt. 'What's the matter? It was a perfectly splendid evening, dear Lodge. Now there's a good fellow, beddy-byes, we have to be early birds tomorrow and away.'

'I'm ready to leave right now,' Lodge told him with feeling.

'I do believe,' says Lodge today, 'that he was still living the part. He was too involved by then, I suppose, to unwind that easily.'

But if Peter Sellers managed to survive the war undetected in his various high-ranking performances – which, despite Peg's unrelenting fear, was to be the closest he came to real danger – he quickly came to grief when the war ended and he was once again thrown into the rough and tumble of show business.

Things were really hard in the first months of his demobilisation. When he was offered work in a fairground in Norwich as a barker for various sideshows, he went with alacrity. It was not a propitious beginning and his heart was made even heavier when he arrived in Norwich, a pleasant city just over one hundred miles from London. For the place, for some extraordinary reason he cannot explain to this day, was full to capacity.

Unable to acquire a room anywhere as Peter Sellers, he decided to simply become somebody else, somebody more impressive, more influential.

So: 'It's the Earl of Beaconsfield's secretary here,' he announced on the telephone. 'The Earl requires a single room for this evening only.'

'Lord Beaconsfield' did the trick. A room was found. When Sellers arrived at the hotel, the staff fell about to serve his lordly needs with a great deal of bowing and scraping and forelock touching.

The social elevation was short-lived.

It was quite a different mood pervading the hotel on his

return after an evening of hard spieling in the fairground; no bowing, no scraping, and not a single forelock was touched as he swept in with his assumed grand majesty.

The manager, a greal deal of the grease taken out of his voice, which was now as flat as the Norfolk Broads where it had been bred, informed Sellers that there were two gentlemen who would like to talk to him for a moment.

'Not in the lounge, if you don't mind. In my office,' the manager informed him.

At the sight of the gentlemen, Sellers' spirits sank like the *Titantic,* and his blood, appropriately, turned to ice. They were all too clearly military policemen in plain clothes. He took in their overpolished boots and belted military-issue raincoats, the short prickly-necked haircuts. For the first time in his life Peter Sellers had given a less than convincing performance. But just where had he gone wrong?

'Lord Beaconsfield?' asked the larger of the two men, his lip reaching for a sneer.

'Yes, rather,' said Sellers, game to the end.

'Not, uh, 2223033 ACI Sellers, recently demobilised from the Royal Air Force?'

'Well, yes, that too, actually,' said Sellers, dismay bleeping twitches in his face like unanswered May Day signals.

The game, then, was up.

But the failure of his impersonation was not due to any flaw in Sellers' masquerade, but merely to his manifestly impecunious circumstances. There was, for example, the packet of Woodbines, a most unaristocratic brand of cheap cigarettes, discovered in his case which, because of his phobia about packing and unpacking, had had to be unpacked by a porter.

The Woodbines, of course, might have been just a noble lord's idiosyncrasy. But the address in the visitors' book – 211b High Road East Finchley (where he lived with his parents) – although written with some flourish, did not seem at all appropriate for the nobility of England, even allowing for the most punitive death duties levied on the rich. Hence the call for the police. The police, suspecting he might be a deserter, had informed the military police.

Satisfied that he had been legally and honourably demobilised, they did not press charges. Sellers got his night's lodging, paid the bill, and left the following morning.

Nobody waved goodbye.

Dying the Death

THE EARLY DAYS after the war were the worst. The excitement of battle had gone and left only the angry frustration of victory: the shortages, rationing, queues. The lights of London had come on again only to light up the misery and the scars.

It was a bad time for Sellers.

The anonymity of civilian life was infinitely more oppressive than even the demeaning regimentation of the services. For a time he strangely missed the camaraderie of the barrack room and the masquerades which had so enlivened and dangerously extended his existence.

Now he was another uncertain civilian. His free government-issue 'demob' suit fitted him far less comfortably than those counterfeit officers' tunics he had worn with such dash. It was a three-buttoned, single-breasted, blue serge, pinstripe suit and he wore it like a straitjacket.

He was finding it almost impossible to pick up the threads of his career. The world, it seemed, was populated with drummers, and all far better at the game than he could ever be. A period of intense brooding and long depressions set in. Only the loyal and badgering encouragement of Peg kept him from abandoning the business altogether.

Still unable to afford a car of his own, he was finding his drum kit an overwhelming transport problem. When he did get work he was thrown on the mercy of car-owning musicians willing to give him and his load a ride to whatever engagement had been secured. He estimated once that he lost more than a third of his bookings because he was unable to find transport for his equipment. It was, in fact, a time when his childhood must have loomed touchingly close, a reminder of when he and Peg depended on more affluent relatives to give them rides on their gold-hunting treks to the provinces and suburbs of England.

Very soon he decided to give up the drums. He would develop his talent as a mimic and comedian. If anything, that market was even more competitive, but he had at last 'achieved mobility', he pointed out. He purchased a ukelele, and his father, who had toured the halls with a ukuelele-and-patter routine during the crumbling thirties, began to teach him the rudiments of the instrument.

If there was a time when father and son came close, that was it. For it was perhaps the first time in his life that Bill Sellers felt he had something worthwhile to offer his son beyond the generous reach and influence of Peg. His son was a good pupil and learned fast. But, ironically, his swift success as a tutor was a Pyrrhic victory for Bill Sellers, for it meant that their time of closeness was soon to pass; it would never come again.

Yet still the work was slow. Sellers talked more and more about becoming a professional photographer. It was talk that secretly worried Peg sick. The self-appointed custodian of his future, she still carried the bulk of her son's ambition. 'Peter,' she would tell him, 'the hard times are put here for a reason, son. Wait, you'll see.'

Peg worried too much. For Sellers had an instinctive flair for survival and despite the melancholy in his make-up he knew the score. A man who helped with the counting in those early days was Dennis Selinger, who remained his agent for almost twenty years and a friend all his life.

Sellers had just lost his job as the entertainments manager of a holiday camp in Jersey when they first met. Peg, who had been trying to persuade an agent to represent her son for months, finally arrived at Selinger's poky Soho office late one Friday afternoon.

'Mr Selinger,' she said, 'we want a good agent to look after the affairs of my son. Handled properly he will be very big.'

Selinger, himself just out of the army and struggling to

establish himself in the agency business, looked at the fleshy young man sitting opposite him. His unparted, over-greased, wavy hair was piled precariously high over four fingers of forehead. He smiled nervously and wore the overvaleted suit of a man who doesn't have a spare. His main concern during the entire interview, Selinger recalls, seemed to be with the immaculate crease in his trousers or, alternatively, with the leather gloves he carried in his lap.

He cleared his throat a great deal as if about to say something but rarely did. Peg did most of the talking during the first meeting and Selinger, accurately, got the impression that Sellers was an immensely shy young man, inclined to be dominated by his mother, but without resentment or objection.

'In fact,' says Selinger today, 'I was more impressed with Peg than with Pete at the first meeting.'

But he knew nobody can judge talent across a desk. And although Sellers was somewhat short of the kind of personality that wins friends and impresses agents, Dennis Selinger liked him well enough to agree to represent him.

'You are,' said Peg seriously, 'a very fortunate young man, Mr Selinger. My son is going to be worth a lot of money in this business one day. Listen to an old woman who knows.'

The sense of relief she must have felt at finally getting her son professionally represented was carefully camouflaged. It was not the end of her worries, she knew that, for work would still be hard to find.

As the days became weeks and weeks made months and seasons, Peg and Bill continued to support their only child, hoping that their endless enthusiasm hid their growing and natural anxiety.

But all the time, Peg contained a fear she could unburden to nobody. It was the unexpected influence that her husband was now having on their son. As the two men, teacher and pupil, locked themselves away day after day, the hesitant thin sound of the ukulele grew stronger and more threatening.

Yet it was not the thought that she was losing control that troubled her; the fear was more benevolent and more human than that. She lived with failure most of her married life, and now it seemed to her that she was destined to watch her beloved son follow in the plodding, undistinguished footsteps of her husband.

'Peter,' she finally told her younger brother Bert, 'is worth so much more than that.' And later he was to say, 'I reckon those first years after the war, when Peter was having such a lean time of it, aged Peg twenty years.'

But at the time she hid her anxiety well. For his part, Sellers hid the worst of his disappointments and setbacks from his parents. The nadir of his ill-fortune came in one of the poorer music-halls in Peterborough, the market town about eighty miles outside London with a population of sixty thousand people – every one of them, it seemed to him then, a critic.

Certainly, the audience at the first house on Monday evening, was not, to put it delicately, sympathetic. Indeed, some members in the balcony expressed themselves rather well on the matter. Others were less erudite but more colourful. Such was the reception that other performers on the bill began crowding into the wings to see what was causing so much ill-tempered commotion. On stage, without the experience to adapt his dying act, Sellers doggedly stuck to his set routine, helpless. 'I was shaking but it wasn't only fear, there was a lot of anger there too,' he said afterward.

Between shows the manager went to the small communal dressing room that Sellers shared with a dog act, a Hungarian acrobat and a blind piano-accordion player. He handed him a cheque for £15 – his week's salary. The pay-off.

'Sorry, old sport,' the manager told him as the other performers looked on in embarrassed silence, relieved it wasn't happening to them. 'Peterborough isn't your kind of town. It happens once in a while, so don't let it get you down. No hard feelings, I hope, sport.'

But Sellers, even at that joyless moment, was not

without his goodly share of fortune. Dorothy Squires, the English singer who was then topping variety bills throughout the country singing sobbing sentimental ballads, felt sorry for the young comic. When the manager returned to his office she was waiting for him.

'I hear you've fired the comic,' she said. 'I'd like you to keep him on. You know Monday's always a bad audience, and I think he is very funny.'

The manager, unwilling to displease his star, a lady who was undoubtedly a big success with the tough audiences of Peterborough, reluctantly agreed.

'You've got a very funny sense of humour, Miss Squires,' he told her. 'He must be the worse comic in the world.'

Privately, she was not entirely convinced that she did disagree with the manager. After the show that night she invited Sellers to her dressing room. She talked to him about his act, the presentation, advising what to dump, what to build, what to change.

'I don't think,' she has admitted since, 'I ever saw any great hidden depths of talent in him. No, he was just another struggling kid, fresh out of the services, very lonely and very scared. I would have done the same for anyone in his position.'

So he survived the week at Peterborough, but the failure was to fester. The word got around in the parochial and parroting world of agents and bookers and work became as regular as reunions of Kamikaze veterans. The months more than ever became pyramids of desperation, as quiet as any man's.

Then one afternoon he met by chance a press agent he knew who had been drinking with some musician friends in Archer Street, Soho. 'The boys tells me you've quit the business,' he said.

'I've packed in the drums,' Sellers told him. 'I've got a comedy routine together. Some impersonations, funny voices, you know.'

'How's it going?'

The resistance to the show business ritual of exaggerating one's own success was always strong in Sellers. He said simply that he was having a lean time.

'Have you tried Van Damm? He's looking for a new comic,' the agent told him.

Vivian Van Damm ran The Windmill, a nonstop strip-tease emporium just a grind and bump from Piccadilly Circus. The press agent offered to get him an audition.

'It was,' Sellers later observed, 'manna from heaven.'

If not quite that, it was most certainly a crucial turning point in his career.

Between the regular peeling acts Mr Van Damm slotted an occasional comedian, not so much to add variety to his bill as to enable the girls to recover their robes. It was a policy that mostly agitated the regular connoisseurs of the ecdysiastic art, and many of them used up the dead time of the comic's act jockeying for a seat closer to the stage.

Mr Van Damm auditioned Sellers the next afternoon in his office above the theatre and, suitably impressed (which was not necessarily the most carefully considered endorsement of a man's talent), agreed to hire him at £31 a week.

'Just keep it loud and going and you'll do fine,' he said.

'I will,' said Sellers.

'When can you start?' asked Mr Van Damm.

'Whenever you say,' said Sellers.

'Now,' said Mr Van Damm, who did not waste words nor time.

The engagement lasted for six weeks before the audience's consistent nonchalance caused Mr Van Damm to terminate the contract. Yet he was more than satisfied with the unknown comic's performance. When Sellers had finished his final act on a Saturday night in that spring of 1948, he went backstage to congratulate him.

'You're a trouper, sir,' he said. 'What are your plans now?'

'Well, I'd like to do straight stuff, one day,' Sellers said.

'Do it,' said Van Damm.

The following Monday morning the old impresario ordered that Sellers' name be immediately added to the theatre's bronze wall-plaque headed: Stars Of Today Who

Started Their Careers In This Theatre.

His manager was hesitant. 'Mr Van Damm, we usually wait until the end of the year before deciding who to add to the plaque,' he reminded him.

'I want it there now,' said Van Damm. 'And at the end of the year remind me to say I told you so!'

Sellers' name came after Harry Secombe's. He had never heard of him then, but they were soon to begin a close and vital friendship.

His six-week survival at The Windmill, sometimes known as the comic's Dunkirk, was enough to instil a brand of confidence he had hitherto lacked. He had hardly been the main attraction, but there was a certain durability about his performance and he was determined not to let this moment recede without some effort to capitalise on it.

So once more Peter Sellers was thrown back on an illicit impersonation to get what he wanted. Originally, he planned to telephone Roy Speer, a top radio producer at the BBC, and boldly ask for an audition on the strength of his stint at The Windmill. But when he was put through to the producer's office his nerve failed him. 'Mr Speer's office,' said the cool efficient voice of a woman who had clearly reached the age when she was pleased to have paid into the superannuation fund. Sellers knew that voice well. It was polite, impersonal, and as impenetrable as ice.

'Mr Speer's office,' she repeated.

He made up his mind in a moment.

'This is Kenneth Horne,' he said, slipping into the unmistakable tankard-ale voice of the well-known radio comic. 'Is Roy there, dear?'

The sound barrier was pierced, the voice lost its antiseptic flavour, asked him to please hold one moment Mr Horne, I hope you are well, I can put you through now Mr Horne.

'Ken,' said Speer, 'how are you?'

'Roy,' Sellers said, Horne-like, 'I saw a marvellous young comic at The Windmill the other night. Name of Peter Sellers. You should take a look at him. He has an original brilliance. I'm sure you could use him in one of your shows.'

He added that Richard Murdoch, who had also seen the act, wanted a word. Sellers switched voices, and comic Murdoch's light, distinctive tones assured Speer of Sellers' talent.

The unsolicited testimonies from such case-hardened professionals impressed Speer. 'Well, I've got to see him, haven't I?' he said.

'What about this afternoon then?' Sellers said in his own voice, a voice now tinged with nervousness lest the brazen cheek of his gamble anger the busy producer.

'Who the hell is that?' asked Speer, surprised at the strange voice on the line.

'My name is Peter Sellers, actually,' said Sellers, and waited for the make-or-break reaction, measuring the seconds with heartbeats.

'You cheeky bastard,' Speer said, after a tattoo of time had beaten a bruised feeling in the actor's chest. 'That's probably a criminal offence you've just committed. Get round here before you break any more laws.'

It was a remarkable incident, and one that Spike Milligan finds wholly significant and basic to the understanding of Peter Sellers.

'He was never able to sell himself, you see. To make money out of himself as himself he wouldn't get to first base. He was just a nice, very quiet, and very complex simpleton. He was the most complex simpleton in the entire world.'

It was the same telephone call to Speer that put Sellers on the route to Milligan and the climacteric Goon Show. The producer was taken with the comic's talent and quickly found him a five-minute spot in a popular radio variety show called 'Show Time'. Sellers did a series of amusing impersonations (including, for good measure, Horne and Murdoch) that delighted Leslie Ayre, the radio critic of the London *Evening News*, and on Saturday, 10th July, 1948, Peter Sellers had his first press notice to paste into his first green rexine volume of his cuttings books.

'O. Henry,' wrote Ayre, 'once spoke of an actor who did "impersonations of well-known impersonators". Certainly many mimics give too little study to their originals. Peter Cavanagh [then reigning "monarch of mimics" in Britain] is an exception.

'And now, in Peter Sellers, radio brings us another really conscientious and excellent artist and a genuine rival to Cav.

'Tall, good-looking, 22, Sellers was born in Portsmouth of a theatrical family. Entertaining in the war days, he was carefully studying famous radio voices. His first broadcast in "Show Time" recently brought a scurry of agents and he's already fixed up a long series of Sunday concerts all over the country; and Roy Speer immediately booked him for the first available return date in "Show Time".'

The article was headlined, This Mimic Is Tops.

Peg immediately recognised it for the omen of fame she had so long been waiting for and promptly had it framed. It stayed on her wall until the day she died. Dennis Selinger has also kept his snippet, now a treasured clipping the colour of pale whisky and crisp at the edges. Not many agents are so sentimental, especially about ex-clients. But at the time, that review had more than mere sentimental value.

Selinger smartly had it reproduced as a three-column £40 advertisement in the English theatrical trade paper *The Stage*. But at Sellers' suggestion the advertisement contained a significant omission of six words: 'and a genuine rival to Cav' had been painted out.

It was an improvement over the first advertisement Sellers had taken in that paper a few months earlier. That had concluded with the kind of pleading availability of all small-time performers anxious for work:

Available for production and Sunday concerts, all coms.: 211b High Road, East Finchley, London N2 Phone: Tudor 7621

63

The accompanying photograph showed an almost pretty young man with too much high wavy hair and full cheeks posing in a coyly theatrical three-quarter profile shot much favoured in the Ivor Novello-John Barrymore era of delicate masculine beauty.

A great deal had happened between these two advertisements. The radio dates were accumulating nicely and, being the big thing in England in 1948, radio begat variety bookings and Sunday concerts and a modestly enriching supply of private cabaret work and after-dinner shows. He also began playing small but increasingly noticed comedy character parts – with such excruciating names as Crystal Jollybottom – in 'Ray's a Laugh', starring the late Ted Ray.

His confidence was 'growing with every performance', said Peg. The work was now pouring in. He started his automania, buying and selling four cars in twelve months. During that time he also made over one hundred broadcasts and in October 1949 he was signed to play the London Palladium, then at its zenith of postwar prestige.

His act, called 'Speaking for the Stars', supported Gracie Fields and got scant attention from the press; several of the critics believed it to be his first music-hall appearance, and they were not corrected.

Yet eight months earlier he had topped a variety bill, 'Radio's Latest Sensation!' at the Plaza in West Bromwich. He collected a brace of very respectable notices from the local press. 'A wonderful display of mimicry,' wrote one. Said another, 'A brilliant young impersonator.'

The fact was, deep down Sellers didn't care what the press thought of his variety performances. His childhood hatred of vaudeville was turning to a quietly raging contempt. It was simply a hurdle he had to take on his way to 'the straight stuff' he was now more than ever determined to achieve.

Enter the Goons (and a wife)

IT WAS DURING this hectic yet curiously empty period that Peter Sellers met Harry Secombe, the comic whose name he had first seen above his own on the honours plaque outside The Windmill. A small, friendly, myopic Humpty Dumpty Welshman with a taste for milk and brandy and an engaging tendency to giggle with maniacal nervousness, he was immediately appreciated by Sellers.

'Do you know Spike Milligan?' Secombe asked one evening soon after they'd met.

'No,' said Sellers, 'but I like that name.'

'Oh, you'll like him, too, mate. He's one of us. A first-generation comic. He doesn't give a pig's eye about all that greasepaint aristocracy. The only trouble is,' and here Secombe became unusually serious, 'I should warn you, he is quite mad.'

There was reasonable cause for this private certification. Secombe had already become an authority on the life and mad times of Milligan. They had first met in North Africa in 1943 when a detachment of the Eighth Army was trying to dislodge a particularly anstubborn German gun emplacement at a place called Medjez-el-Bab. After several costly and unsuccessful attacks, a message was sent to Tunisia for a couple of persuasive 7·2 howitzers to help soften up the German defence. Gunner Milligan was part of the artillery detachment.

The guns were set up on top of a high wadi during the night but unfortunately, due to the haste and strict blackout in which the operation was necessarily conducted, Milligan's howitzer was placed too close to the far edge and not sufficiently well dug in. The direct consequence of this military oversight was that when the first shot was fired the gun recoiled with unexpected belligerence and toppled backward over the wadi to land dangerously close to the truck in which Private Secombe was sheltering.

'Hello,' said the bemused Secombe, observing the shattered gun at his feet, 'the bastards are *throwing* their guns at us now.'

A few minutes later Milligan – who had not actually seen the going of his gun since his eyes were screwed protectively tight at the time – appeared on the scene.

'Has anybody seen my gun?' His voice brimmed with the melancholy of a man who has just suffered yet another unreasonable blow in a life of unreasonable blows he knows will never be explained. 'I had it a minute ago,' he added, as if accusing the capriciousness of fate for his extraordinary loss.

The meeting between Peter Sellers and Spike Milligan occurred, less dramatically, during the autumn months of 1949 at the old Bedford Theatre in Camden Town. Secombe was selfconsciously appearing in an all-male ex-service revue called *Soldiers in Skirts*. They met backstage together with another young comic named Michael Bentine.

On the face of it, Bentine was the odd man out. A bearded, onetime Shakespearean actor, he came from a somewhat exotic background: born in Watford, he had a Peruvian scientist for a father, an Eton education, and an accent you didn't hear too often in working men's clubs.

With the strange surrealistic, anarchic Milligan, a tall, lean, and tormented man with a face that was soon to age with brilliant madness and a puzzled pity for humanity, the quartet at best seemed unlikely. But Harry Secombe was the catalyst and humour was their happy denominator.

After the show at the Bedford Theatre, it was suggested that they repair to a tavern in Victoria run by Jimmy Grafton, a scriptwriter and former war hero who had been decorated with the Military Cross at the battle of Arnhem in 1944. Milligan was lodging with Grafton, occupying an attic room just large enough to cope with his meagre possessions that included a sleeping bag, a framed photograph of a gentleman popularly believed to be Franz Kafka, or, alternatively, Milligan's maternal grandfather, and an antique typewriter that he operated with two-finger dexterity to the great insomniac depression of the resident mice.

A few weeks after meeting Sellers, Milligan vacated these cramped quarters in favour of a room offered at Peg's. It was the genesis of his durable fascination for the man he at first thought was abysmally average. His first impression is still vivid: 'He struck me as rather pudgy-looking Jewish boy who was as well dressed as he could be on £10 a week. He wore a raincoat and a good quality trilby hat and a pair of leather gloves for driving which he kept in his left hand. He looked like a nervous insurance salesman.'

The back room of Jimmy Grafton's pub remained the favourite meeting place of the four young comics and there they began to sharpen and channel their ad-lib humour toward a more lucrative script form. Hearing the results one night, Grafton predicted he would soon be losing 'the best free pub show in town'. Milligan was less certain. Nobody, he said, would 'have the nerve to buy this brillant rubbish for at least twenty years'.

Nevertheless, after a while they made an acetate recording (on a secondhand machine bought by Sellers, already the most affluent of the quartet, and his still-doting parents) and invited a BBC producer named Pat Dixon to listen to it. Dixon was amused but unencouraging about its chances on the then staid and cautious channels of the BBC. 'It's too far out,' he warned them. But, sympathetic, he promised to see if he could persuade 'one of the more daring souls' at Broadcasting House to give it a trial airing in some quiet hour.

The new kind of wild, near-nihilistic humour they were developing appealed to Sellers and began to unleash in him a case of bizarre voices fit for Milligan's sometimes professorial, often delirious, dialogue.

He was now frequently working twelve hours a day,

seven days a week. But he did not neglect the pleasures of his private life. He was an active amorist. he had just suffered a disastrous first love affair, one he would never quite forget, and one close acquaintance of those days recalls that 'he seemed to have an angry and compulsive need to play the field'.

'Certainly,' says Dennis Selinger, 'he had his share.'

Graham Stark, an actor who was to become a faithful and loyal friend and peripheral Goon, was a frequent team-mate in the pursuit of the fair game. He remembers their amorous adventures now with affection. And if their seductions lacked sophistication, they were not without a fine measure of scientific calculation. Indeed, their findings, but for the advance of phonograph technology, might have been of incalculable value to future lovers.

'Peter,' he says, 'had the first automatic record-changer I'd ever seen. He was mad for the latest gadgets even then. When his mum and dad were out, we'd go back to the flat in Finchley Road with a couple of dollies.

'The trick was to make your date before the last record ended because if you hadn't got anywhere by then you'd had it. The whole mood was broken if you had to leap up and put another eight records on.'

After a time they knew precisely how far they had to progress with each record if they were to achieve complete and final success. But the wooing time was not generous. The records were, in those pre-album days, 78 rpm – or a total of some twenty-four minutes from start to finish.

It took considerably less time than that for Peter Sellers to fall in love with Anne Hayes, a young actress from Melbourne, Australia. She had been living for some years with her parents in Hendon and had become almost indelibly British.

She was nineteen, a student at the Royal Academy of Dramatic Art. She had already appeared in one film, a small role in *Anna Karenina* for the lateAlexander Korda, and impressed several people in the business as a very promising actress. She was blonde with the pretty, econo-

68

mical good looks that would improve with age, and possessed a poise that was more than an actressy acquirement.

Elocution lessons had removed most traces of her Australian accent. She came from the anonymous centre of the middle class, and a sensible education had enabled her to become acceptably classless just as Sellers with his mobile theatrical education was classless.

Dennis Selinger had known her for some years and watched her career with interest, although a rival agent, Al Parker, had her under contract. Whenever Selinger wanted an elegant, attractive, and comfortable companion for an occasion it was often Anne he chose.

In the early winter of 1949 Selinger was to attend the Water Rats' Ball, a society of British vaudeville artists, at the Dorchester Hotel. Anne was to be his date. But he had a couple of spare tickets and offered them to Sellers.

'I think you should start going to these occasions,' Selinger told him. 'A lot of important people go and you should be seen around, get to know a few people.'

Sellers agreed, but was stuck for a suitable date. Selinger asked Anne and she suggested a friend called June Marlowe, who was to become the first Mrs Spike Milligan. But from the moment the four met it was obvious, at least to Selinger, that Anne and Sellers were interested only in each other.

'I'd never seen it happen before – or since – but it was, I'm convinced now, love at first sight. For the pair of them,' says Selinger. 'It was as fast and as equal as that. They were both among my dearest friends and I couldn't have been more delighted.'

Anne Hayes told June Marlowe that night, 'He has the most incredible eyes. They seem to see through and through you.'

Selinger was right. But Sellers was almost sullen with guilt. Certain that he had somehow stolen Selinger's girl, he avoided his agent as much as possible and kept their romance a secret for nearly three months. Selinger, who was kept well informed about the growing relationship, mostly from Anne herself, was secretly and hugely amused.

'He genuinely believed it would break my heart,' says Selinger. 'The poor love must have been going through torments.'

Although Anne had pleaded with Selinger not to raise the matter until Sellers told him personally, he felt the unnecessary game had lasted too long. One morning he telephoned his client: 'Look, Pete, I know you've been seeing a lot of Anne and I'm delighted you're hitting it off. Now can we stop this nonsense and all have some dinner together one night?'

They dined that evening.

But Sellers' concern for Selinger's feelings were almost certainly only part of his need for secrecy. For he was also much concerned for Peg's feelings. She was, he well knew, anxious to see him an established success before he slipped away from her potent influence.

But, with all the sharp protective instincts of the Jewish mother, Peg was quickly aware that Anne was to be taken more seriously than the other women in her son's life. At first she piously protested on the grounds that Anne was non-Jewish – an argument that lost some of its force in the cold light of her own marriage to Bill Sellers, a Protestant and a former cathedral organist at that.

'Peg never really accepted Anne. She considered her a premature intruder in their lives and never completely forgave her,' reckons one close friend of the family. 'When Peter came out and insisted he was going to marry Anne anyway I think it was the hardest decision he ever made as a son – and perhaps in all his life.'

'It was a terrible shame,' says Selinger, 'because Peg was basically an adoring mum who believed that nobody could love him or look after him the way she could.'

On 26th April, 1950, they officially announced their engagement. Beneath an inside page photograph of them both, in the old London *Star* – cut down to a single column picture of only Anne in later editions – the caption read:

'Her man's a scream. Twenty-year-old Melbourne actress Anne Hayes, who lives now in Hendon with her mother, has become engaged to radio comedian Peter Sellers, whose "You old saucebox!" is one of the screams of "Ray's a Laugh". Here they are at Mr Sellers' Finchley home.'

Peg's adamant disapproval was the singular force that kept them from marrying almost immediately. It was to be almost eighteen months, on 15th September, 1951, before they married at Caxton Hall in London.

For eleven years Anne Sellers was to exert a calm yet formidable influence over her husband, an influence that Peg both resented and was thankful for. 'I won't always be around,' she was frequently to admit during the good years of that first marriage, 'and Anne is strong and he needs that.'

Meanwhile the launching of the radio project hatched in the backroom of Grafton's pub had been a lot easier than anybody dared hope for. Less than a month after producer Pat Dixon had taken it to the 'more daring' but mysterious 'souls' at the BBC, a series had been approved. After a few skirmishes over the title, it was agreed that it should be known as *The Goon Show,* after an absurdly dim character in the old Popeye cartoons beloved by Milligan. The first show went out on 28th May, 1951.

The series set a frantic pace in lunatic humour, covering such high adventures as climbing Mount Everest from the inside, sabotaging a haddock-stretching factory behind the Iron Curtain, and smuggling dynamite into the Hungarian football team's boots. The purpose of any Goon adventure was always veiled in a secrecy that even the writers seemed unable to penetrate.

A slow starter, the audience at first unable to keep up with the show's urgent pursuit of the illogical, it finally caught on and became the in-thing among students and the young, who enjoyed the sharp anti-Establishment tang that often bordered on sheer anarchy.

There was a fashionable delight, too, in the unbelievably idiotic, sometimes cornball, exchanges delivered and abandoned with breathless speed:

'Here's my visiting card, sir.'

'But it's blank.'

'I know. Business is bad.'

Soon the cast of characters, with such unlikely and unlovely names as Henry Crunn, Major Bloodnock, William McGoonagle, Miss Minnie Bannister, Bluebottle, Neddy Seagoon, and Eccles, became a national addiction. Humour was being stretched to limits undreamed of by most people in that golden age of the stand-up patter comic.

But Sellers was not content with merely exploring the new and exciting limits of this humour. He wanted to push toward the frontiers of *believability* as well. More than either Secombe or Milligan (Michael Bentine left the team comparatively early in its life – 'I was always a breakaway Goon with an urge to apply my logical nonsense as opposed to their nosensical logic,' he said later) Sellers wanted to create an air of utter conviction about the world of the Goons.

'They weren't just funny voices for Pete,' says one veteran of those radio days. 'They were living, breathing, laughing, crying people with pain and joy and all the emotions and feelings God ever invented. Of course, it was a marvellous giggle and Pete was having his share of the ball, but he did take it terribly seriously. I think the human folly those early Milligan scripts exposed really got to him.'

The success of the Goon Show brought a surge of new interest from the music-halls, and Milligan, Secombe, and Sellers embarked on a tour that was not entirely successful despite their new fame. In Coventry, Milligan and Sellers were going through a particularly bad patch of audience hostility which only occasionally softened to glorious indifference.

The impact on Spike Milligan, a sensitive and most vulnerable man, was intensely disturbing, and the events in that town foreshadowed the nervous breakdowns and bouts of melancholia that were to plague him to this day.

Early in the run of the show at the Hippodrome, both Sellers and Secombe became concerned at the growing isolation of Milligan, who had been under intense pressure writing as well as appearing in the weekly Goon Show. In Coventry, his act was built around some slightly esoteric comedy routines and a trumpet solo that did nothing to endanger Mr Harry James' domination in the field at that time. One evening when his act was suffering an abnormally bad reception, he walked to the front of the stage and said:

'You hate me, don't you?'

The response was an overwhelming confirmation of his suspicions. He threw his trumpet to the stage and proceeded to jump up and down on it until it was irreparably crushed. This sadly desperate act only succeeded in moving the Coventry audience to appreciative applause. Milligan stalked off the stage in a terrible temper and locked himself in his dressing room.

Scared that he might try to commit suicide (always an avid collector of macabre trivia, he had only recently purchased a hangman's leather noose) Sellers and Secombe were obliged to smash down the door to comfort him.

It was a strangely grotesque yet ridiculous scene.

Sellers and Secombe had just finished a sketch called the East Acton Stick Dancers Festival – a send-up of national folk dancing contests – and they were wearing Cockney cheese-cutter caps with small silver bells, patched road menders' trousers with string tied below the knees and more silver bells, and large boots.

'I couldn't stop giggling, to be honest,' says Secombe, 'and old Pete was pushing me forward to break down the door because he was really scared to do it himself. Everytime we charged the door it sounded as if every church tower in the land was having a nightmare.'

They found Milligan crouching in a corner.

'It was awful. Poor old Spike was in a very bad way.'

It was the collapse of Spike Milligan that convinced

Peter Sellers that he had finally to get out of the mesh of music-halls. He had already appeared briefly in a few low-budget comedies including *Orders Are Orders,* an army farce in which, according to the English trade paper *Today's Cinema* (forerunner of *Screen Inernational*), he 'scored heavily as a guileful mess orderly'.

'I'm going into films,' he told Dennis Selinger the next day. 'Not as a sideline, Den, but all the way. Let's really work on it now, because this life is too bloody impossible. It'll kill me if I don't get out now.'

It was December 1954.

Sleigh Ride in August

PETER SELLERS FINALLY had too much strength, too much springback, to be destroyed the way Spike Milligan had been destroyed. And during that evenful and ill-starred run in Coventry – one of the rare times that Secombe, Sellers, and Milligan actually appeared together outside 'The Goon Show' – he was to demonstrate his bristling defiance of an audience unwilling or unable to reach for his brand of humour.

Angered and shaken by Milligan's public humiliation, he was at first inclined to back out of the rest of the show's run. Then, in a furious declaration, he decided to stay right where he was and 'fight the bastards on their own ground'.

The following morning, after Selinger had returned to London to work on 'the film career', Sellers went out and bought an album of conductor Wally Stott's Christmas melodies and a record player. At the next performance, he appeared on stage dressed in the baggy, leopard-skin tights that he wore for the distinctly unpoised balancing act he did with Secombe and Milligan, and aptly named Les Trois Charleys. It was a matinée largely frequented by old-age pensioners, admitted at reduced prices.

'Good afternoon, brethren,' he intoned as he began setting up his equipment with the care of a polytechnic lecturer. 'I want to play you some quite lovely melodies this afternoon. They are particularly endearing to me and I hope you will find them enjoyable also.'

The audience watched in puzzled silence as the man in bulging tights and heavy horn-rimmed glasses switched on the turntable and placed the needle upon the disc, a small, loving smile just melting the grim lines of his mouth. The sounds of Wally Stott's orchestra and chorus rendering

'White Christmas' filled the theatre. Sellers, his head bowed in deep meditation in a pose that Auguste Rodin would have loved to sculpt, watched the spinning disc until the last pure note, then politely applauded the machine. The audience, after a moment's hesitation and glanced consultation with their neighbours, also politely applauded.

The next number, 'Jingle Bells', began and a hush fell over the auditorium as Sellers fell into his waiting-for-Rodin pose. When the number had finished, he again led the applause, which was both polite and reverent.

After the third number, he packed up the equipment, bowed graciously to the audience, and left the stage in a stiffly official walk. Nobody laughed, he recalled.

But he probably got more applause, albeit puzzled applause, for that extraordinary performance than he had managed to accumulate during his entire run at the Hippodrome. The management, however, was not so easily satisfied, and certainly not at all amused.

Not, apparently, getting too much sense out of Sellers, Sam Newsome, a theatrical magnate of some power in the provinces, a man not to cross, telephoned Dennis Selinger in London and demanded his immediate presence. Selinger took the next train. The film plans would have to wait.

The general theme of Newsome's grievance was that Sellers had broken his contract by not performing his act 'as known'. This is a show-business term written into all contracts which obliges the artist to conform to a recognised routine. True, Newsome conceded, Peter Sellers was known as a comic, but playing a phonograph while wearing an ill-fitting loincloth was bordering on the indecent and was not his idea of humour and, even if it was, it certainly didn't make the old-age pensioners laugh.

Selinger agreed that Newsome had some justification and promised that his client would not depart from his established routine again. 'Although God knows how I ever expected to make Pete promise that,' he has reflected since. 'I think I must have prayed a lot.'

Harry Secombe, who had watched the entire performance with a kind of horrified hysteria, was enormously impressed with Sellers' courage: 'He was brave, you see. He would do new things, he was never afraid to experiment. It was very exciting working with him because out of sheer boredom, or defiance, like then, he was likely to do *anything,* even knowing the consequences.'

It was the most impressive performance that Secombe had ever seen from Sellers. 'After poor old Spike's collapse, let's be honest now, we were all a bit scared, most performers would have knuckled down and accepted the brute supremacy of that audience. But Pete went out and gave them merry hell. It took guts. I couldn't have done it mate.'

On stage Sellers had a courage that had always matched his talent. In the early months of 1958, the time his career was beginning to take the shape of things to come, he was appearing for the first time in a legitimate stage play.

It was called *Brouhaha,* and at the same time he was making the film *The Mouse That Roared.* It was the time, too, when he was markedly under the influence of Alec Guinness, an actor he grew to admire and occasionally imitate after appearing with him in *The Ladykillers* some three years earlier.

They had become good friends, and when Guinness was knighted he invited Sellers, whom he regarded as something of a protégé – he is known to have recommended him eagerly to the attention of at least one critic – to his celebration party.

It was a most convivial occasion which lasted long into the night and which, for Sellers, was followed by a hard day at the studios. The Morning After was a protracted affair and, indeed, was not entirely over when Sellers walked on to the stage at the Aldwych Theatre in London that evening.

A short time after the play began, to the fury of theatrical purists, he interrupted the performance to announce: 'I'm sloshed.' Further, he offered to relinquish the role for the evening and allow his understudy to take over.

But he had come a long way since Peterborough and the audience had paid good money to see *him*. The offer was rejected with flattering finality from the stalls to the farthest reaches of the gods. 'I can't remember too much about it after my confession – which was all too super-fluous – but I'm told it was a memorable evening,' he said later.

Yet it was something more than the groundwork for an amusing anecdote to be told and retold and embellished in the future. His career was then at a critical stage, and that reckless confession of alcoholic exhaustion might well have severely damaged his reputation with not a few theatrical angels, who are notoriously wary of investing in the vicinity of drunken actors. Some of his closest friends and most trusted advisers implored him to announce the next day – following the inevitable morning rash of Drunken-Star-Confesses headlines – that the episode was a joke or a publicity stunt for the play.

He refused.

The humour of the situation probably overcame his sense of self-preservation. And certainly at that time, with his career swiftly gaining momentum and his first marriage still a bedrock of security, he was enjoying life with a passion he never knew before and would never achieve again.

But, even then, there were a few who believed the pleasure was illusory and bound to be brief. 'There was far too much hysteria in his need to work,' explains a writer who moved in and out of the Sellers circle down the years.

Admittedly, since that December night in Coventry when Sellers had set his course with Selinger, both men had worked hard. In those early days there was almost nothing the actor would not do to work in a film studio.

He impersonated an absent Humphrey Bogart when John Huston needed some new dialogue in *Beat the Devil,* was the off-screen voice for Winston Churchill in *The Man Who Never Was,* and even supplied the voice of a parrot in *Our Girl Friday.* He dubbed voices for Mexicans, Chinese bandits, American gangsters, and was constantly on hand with a range of English accents from the aristocracy to Cockney. One possibly exaggerated but persistent legend has it that for a film called *Malaga* he provided every voice with the notable exception of the leading lady's.

When he was in some danger of becoming a vocal odd-job man around the studios, he landed his first good role. The film was the Ealing comedy *The Ladykillers;* it was 1955. Selinger had originally sent him to the director, Alexander Mackendrick, to read for another and more important role, but he lost it to Danny Green, a capable veteran character actor. Yet Mackendrick was impressed with Sellers and, a few weeks later, offered him a smaller part he had failed to cast: a fat-slob Teddy Boy aide to Alec Guinness.

He was on his way.

They were the last of the good old days, the best days, says Spike Milligan. The days between obscurity and the lonely tenancy in that empty bubble of fame. The time when all their humour was too much to contain on a stage and too pressing to purvey only for the loot and the glory.

'We had a lot of wonderful jokes – Peter was mad on jokes,' recalls Milligan, his voice distant, his head shaking in small, sad, reverent movements. There is silence while he rummages around in those dark corners of the past for some memory to help explain what it was all about.

'We bought this car, a 1929 Austin Seven, a Tin Lizzie, convertible. A great old car. We used to drive her through London right in the middle of the rush hour at about twelve miles an hour, top speed. But we'd be wearing crash helmets and these ludicrous goggles and leather overcoats like old pioneer flyers. And we'd cry out in pitiful strangulated voices these lunatic pleas for help.'

Down the dark tunnels of time you can hear their voices echoing in your mind, the voices of Eccles and Blood-knock, of Minnie Bannister and Henry Crunn:

'For God's sake, no man can live with this speed I tell you, steady I say, for the sake of all that is sane and British cease this reckless abandon or we'll all be goners before nightfall.'

79

The voice of Milligan interrupts: 'Oh, it was a marvellous, hilarious, silly, beautiful, pointless time . . . yesterday.'

On another yesterday, they purchased the sledge that actor John Mills used in the film *Scott of the Antarctic*. They loaded it with garbage pails, phonographs, a dog kennel containing one mongrel bitch, assorted boots, a stuffed parrot and a tattered Union Jack – and proceeded to haul it down Regent Street. It was a hot summer day.

'Of course,' explains Milligan, doing a lightning sketch of a smile on his face like a nervous pavement artist watching for the law, 'we wore full furs and threw up pieces of paper-snow to help create the right atmosphere.' Then the sketched-in smile is gone, rubbed out without a trace.

There was never any commercial angle to these exploits; more often than not they left the still less than affluent adventurers considerably out-of-pocket. 'We just did it for kicks,' says Milligan.

In these last of the good days, too, Sellers and Milligan lived opposite each other in an apartment block in Highgate, a neighbourhood in North London then much favoured by advertising men on their way up. Milligan, who had now married June Marlowe, was feeling restive. It was shortly after his crack-up on the stage of the Hippodrome in Coventry. 'I'd just come out of the mental home having written myself stupid, you know what writing can do to you, and I needed to do something funny.'

He telephoned Sellers: 'Peter,' he said, his voice conspiratorial, 'I'm sending across a Swedish bloke I know who's in the lumber business. I think we can buy into something good.'

Milligan put on the oldest and most disreputable suit he owned and a raincoat unlikely to repel a good cry. He laid out a series of used matchsticks on a tray and marked each one with a price, according to its unburnt length, from a penny to a shilling. Unshaven for eight days, he looked like a tramp in search of a sandwichboard as he shuffled across the hall and tapped on Sellers' door.

For a long time he listened to the sound of bolts and locks and chains being manipulated.

Sellers had always been very security-minded. While using his bed during one of his absences, Milligan pulled what he believed to be a light switch; nothing happened until the sudden arrival of a dozen police. The switch was a direct burglar alarm to the police station and Milligan, in his usual state of dishevelment, in somebody else's bed, and, for reasons that are now obscure, fully clothed, was intensely suspect for some hours.

Now the last bolt was drawn, the last lock undone, and Sellers opened the door.

He was quite naked except for a coloured woollen scarf around his neck and a pair of army boots on his feet.

The pair stared at each other across the threshold. Neither giving an inch of batted eyelid.

'I'm sorry, dear boy,' Sellers finally intoned in his finest George Sanders voice. 'I've had a very bad year.'

Milligan smiled at the memory.

'The bastard,' he said. 'That was the kind of rapport we had. Bloody marvellous. He was the only guy in the world who could top me at that kind of thing, you know. The only one, God bless him.'

Jack

In 1958 THE sleigh-ride-in-August days were coming to an end. Peter Sellers was now conscious of a vehement, almost violent, dissatisfaction with himself, and there was the first evidence of the strange uncertainy even of his own identity.

He had made some half-dozen good films now, including *The Smallest Show on Earth,* playing an ancient broken-down cinema projectionist; *tom thumb,* in which he was an obese knockabout villain, an Oliver Hardy to Terry-Thomas' Stan Laurel; and his first multiple-role appearance in *The Naked Truth.*

His professional confidence was growing and, although still desperately ambitious, he was slowly developing a reputation for being 'difficult'. The ruthless selectivity and fickle pirouetting around a decision, later to enrage producers who suspected temperament or the victimising vanity of stardom, was already an integral part of his suspicious, self-protective instincts.

At this time agent John Redway, Dennis Selinger's partner, was urging the Boulting brothers to look at his client. He was more than a 'funny voice' now, he insisted. Finally he extracted a reluctant promise from John Boulting to watch a television show Sellers was doing.

The director remembers seeing a plump, short man playing a schoolmaster in a very inferior sketch, but:

'All I can say is that watching it I thought, my God, this is a brilliant artist, this man is a wonderful actor.'

Redway had not told Sellers that Boulting would be watching the show that night; it may have been the actor's instinctive genius or simply his sheer good luck that he was in such fine form despite his poor material.

Boulting was not the only viewer impressed that night. Graham Stark claims the impact on him was cataclysmic. 'It suddenly hit me that Pete was more than just a cut above the average. Watching him that night I knew I wasn't watching a comic any more; I was watching a sensational acting performance. That was the time I began to value Pete for what he was.'

John Boulting immediately telephoned his twin brother who was dining in Soho. 'Redway is quite right about this man Sellers,' he said. 'He's more than a mimic, he's a bloody marvellous actor, Roy. I think we've found our Kite.'

The following morning they telephoned John Redway and asked him to bring Sellers around to their office for a meeting. The same afternoon they outlined the role of Fred Kite, the shop steward in *I'm All Right, Jack,* to Sellers. He was, according to the Boultings, 'excited beyond belief'. Feeling that the matter was settled, they began to tailor the part for him.

A few weeks later a copy of the finished script was sent to him. Peter Sellers read it and promptly turned it down.

John Boulting was at first 'bloody furious'. But his fury soon turned to fascination for the man, still little more than a small-part actor, who could refuse a starring role in a major production.

The difficulty was, he reasons now, the script had no ordinarily funny lines, only lines that were funny 'in character and situation'. It was something Sellers was not yet fully trained to recognise. 'He wanted the jokes, the obvious belly laughs, and they just weren't there,' he says.

Redway told the Boultings that Sellers felt that he wasn't yet 'actor enough to cope with Kite'. But by now John Boulting was convinced he was the *only* actor for Kite. He launched a campaign of sweet persuasion to build his confidence and convince him that the ageing shop steward was well within his dramatic range. He invited Sellers to his home to discuss the subject.

The actor arrived shortly before 7.0 p.m. The two men

talked through dinner, through brandy, and through the night. At the end, Sellers was still unconvinced and uncommitted. Boulting, whose blue eyes burn with hope during the worst fuel crisis, suggested another date the following evening; in the film business even a war of attrition can be conducted in well-fed luxury.

The next meeting began on what seemed a hopeless note. He wanted, Sellers told him with some finality, to 'make my mark' in films, and Fred Kite is 'a second-rate part'. Curiously, John Boulting felt that even this determined refusal contained a trapdoor. 'Peter,' he said with a voice that can beg most elegantly, 'I implore you not to dismiss this, because I promise you Kite is *the* part.

'It may not be much in terms of size but in terms of *impact,* in terms of *dimension* . . . the film will be yours, my dear fellow.'

For hours they covered the same ground, fought the same battles. Then suddenly, without warning, Sellers capitulated.

'Let's test,' he said.

'I give you my solemn word, dear chap, you won't regret this,' John Boulting told him.

The major obstacle was over. Boulting now knew he could win, but still his nerves jangled: 'Until we had the test in the can he was quite capable at any moment of walking out on the whole project . . .'

Boulting knew he had only worn this man down and not won him over: he had to work fast. The following afternoon they went to Bermans, the film costumiers close to Leicester Square, and searched the racks for a suit for Kite; they found a lumpy, grey, double-breasted suit that just didn't quite fit anywhere.

Sellers next had his hair cut in a severe short-back-and-sides style, and grew a square moustache.

And for a week he worked on the voice.

'Once he got the voice,' recalls Boulting, 'his confidence started to tick over.'

'Christ!' exclaimed the director one evening when Sellers took him some possible Kite voices on tape, 'that's it, that one, it's bloody marvellous, it's perfect.'

'Are you *sure*, Johnny?' Sellers asked.

'Certain,' said Boulting, surprised at the actor's doubt. Boulting arranged for him to study 'several hours' of television and cinema newsreel interviews with strike leaders, strikers, and union officials. Two days later they went on the floor at Shepperton Studios for the crucial test – a remarkable occasion, since it was a test to convince a supporting actor, and not an undecided producer, that he was capable of the role. It was the first time that Sellers had come together with the complete Kite outfit; until that moment they had experimented with the suit, the voice, the mannerisms separately.

Boulting recalls a feeling of genuine shock. 'It was,' he says, 'an incredible transformation, yet apart from that hideous haircut and the moustache, he wore hardly a piece of make-up.'

More important than the impact on Boulting was the effect it had on the actor himself: 'He looked at himself and he couldn't recognise himself. He was totally different, he wasn't Peter Sellers at all. It wasn't merely the physical appearance, it was the . . . attitude. He was a man called Kite.'

The man had disappeared inside the actor's disguise to such a degree that even as he walked to the studio restaurant that day his gait, it was noticed, had a hint of stiff, self-conscious officialdom, and his eyes stayed as steadfastly ignorant as those of a gazing bull.

The test was already superfluous. The moment the stage-hands heard him speak his success was assured. 'They were dead silent – then giggled like schoolboys,' recalls Boulting. They had recognised Sellers' unsuspecting model, 'a man quite well known in studio union politics', it was widely claimed later.

At the end of the test, people in the studio applauded. 'We didn't have to wait for the results of that test,' said Boulting. 'Peter was satisfied he had the measure of Kite.'

John Boulting had not let him down in his estimation of that role's potential: it won Peter Sellers the British Academy Award in a year when Sir Laurence Olivier, Richard Burton, and Peter Finch were considered to be the hot contenders.

Whetstone Was a Long Time Ago

AT THE END of the fifties Peter Sellers was living in Whetstone, a fingertip suburb of North London clawing for the open countryside of Hertfordshire. He had bought a solid £10,000 family house in Oakleigh Avenue, a pleasant, tree-lined road with predictable, snug, secure rooms behind polished windows which gloriously contained Vote Conservative posters during election times. The Sellers' front garden was locally renowned for its tulips.

Sellers, recalls one neighbour, 'was our anonymous celebrity'. He was the 'actor chap' always doing something new to his house with 'builders in and out' all the time; and didn't he 'jump up in the world' with a Rolls-Royce, 'secondhand probably but very smart', and a man to clean it for him 'sometimes twice a week'. But he was 'quite nice when you met him' and not a bit 'what you'd call actory'; *she* never had a lot to say for herself, 'no, not stuck up' but 'kept herself to herself', and the children were well behaved and 'always very well dressed'.

'He was personally concerned, personally involved with that house,' says Herbert Kretzmer, a fine writer and fair critic whose large rustic appearance is urbanised by a gracile moustache. 'He was happy, I think, then. He knew what he was about, he had an image of himself that was real and as accurate as any man can expect.'

But, perhaps corroded by the fast chemicals of fame, it was not to last, and 'when he lost that, the less environment seemed to affect him or even matter', believes Kretzmer.

In 1959, at the height of his acclaim for his prize-winning performance in *I'm All Right, Jack,* he left the refuge of Oakleigh Avenue. He bought a manor house at

Chipperfield, twenty-three miles from London on the 'rich and desirable' Hertfordshire-Buckinghamshire borders. Part Tudor and part Queen Anne, it contained ten principal bedrooms, five acres of garden, stables, tennis courts, and much wooded domain, a £4,000 swimming pool, and two tithe barns. Overnight Anne Sellers, now the thoroughly domesticated mother of two children – he had firmly insisted she abandon her career when they married – found herself mistress of a household that included a nanny, a butler, valet, groom, two gardeners, one goose, four dogs, as many cats, a canary, countless tropical fish and an expanding aviary of erotic doves, five hundred feet of model railway, and a life-size mechanical elephant.

'Whetstone,' Sellers was to observe soon after moving in, 'was a long time ago.'

It was, like Postcard Corner, behind him, on the far safe side of the iron railings surrounding his new manorial home, a piece of the past perhaps to be revisited and excavated in future searches for himself.

There was some slightly mocking comment on this self-propelled elevation to the landed gentry. Less hostile and certainly less envious, Spike Milligan was to say, 'Peter has always overspent himself. He realised early on that he was never going to be happy unless he spent and spent and still had money left over, and this must always be part of his pattern.'

Sellers had a more simple explanation for the flight to Chipperfield. 'I wanted a place I could walk around without crossing any streets,' he said. 'It is a very civilised exile.'

But he could not exile his emotions, and Chipperfield did not give him the peace nor the solace he sought. His marriage, he had already confessed to John Boulting, was not going at all well, and his move to the country was almost certainly part of an intuitive plan to re-create a more satisfactory persona. Boulting was in fact amused and astonished to discover on his first visit to the manor house that Sellers had seriously adopted 'the full country squire' outfit complete with deer-stalker hat and shooting stick.

It was mere imposture and inevitably failed; Chipperfield closed in on him, in many ways becoming more suffocating than the claustrophobic poverty of his travelling past.

By 1960 he had made a dozen films. Anne Sellers had grown used to the peculiar and growing demands the parts made on him. But the last film had put a strain on their already rickety relationship quite unlike anything that had gone before. He was playing Lionel Meadows, a ruthless and sadistic racketeer (whose carnal rages were cut by at least one local licensing committee not entirely satisfied with the 'X' adults-only certificate the picture was given by the British Board of Film Censors) in a thriller called *Never Let Go*. Overly concerned with extending his range and versatility, he had, according to one family friend, 'immersed himself in the part' far beyond even his own extraordinary limits. He found it uncommonly hard to unwind from the role: a dinner guest at Chipperfield during this time was 'frightfully appalled by his table manners; he was an uncouth stranger' and 'you were pleased to leave'.

Anne betrayed her unhappy concern to few friends, but there were few who did not know and did not feel for her. Later, although usually intelligently reticent about discussing their private life together, she was to tell a woman journalist, 'The trouble with Peter is that he really lives these characters. The worst time was when he was making *Never Let Go*. He would come back from the studios each night and shout at us in a nasty way.' She added loyally, 'Until he relaxed into his normal self.'

Thomas Wiseman, English novelist and former show-business writer, found himself unduly fascinated by the actor at that time and was to write, 'His character creations serve as vessels into which he can siphon off his own unwanted or undesirable emotions and attitudes.' It was, he added, an 'ingenious form of psychological buck-passing' and 'his characters when the occasion required

89

were lascivious, egotistical, ruthless, prejudiced'. He added, not quite accurately, 'their creator remained pure and colourless'.

It was not an isolated opinion even then, and more and more people were coming to recognise, as Herbert Kretzmer put it, 'a revealing link between the roles he chose to play and the state of his emotional life'. *Never Let Go* must have expressed some deep need at that time 'because what other reason was there for him to choose a picture so out of tune, so out of character with anything he has ever done?' It was a poor, unimaginative script enacted without style; the result was a film now generally counted among his most unsuccessful and least memorable. 'I think he did it,' says Kretzmer, 'because his life was wrong and he felt violent and needed to play a violent man.'

His next film was *The Millionairess* with Sophia Loren. During the production I went to dinner at Chipperfield. It was a pleasant, quiet evening, with Sellers still very much in his part as the Indian doctor; he was gentle, a considerate host, and his accent was consistently Eastern. But there seemed to be a sadness about Anne, a remoteness that was alien to her usual warmth.

'You're very quiet this evening,' I said as we walked back from an inspection of the pool and tennis courts. 'With all this you should be bubbling with excitement.'

'Bubble-bubble,' she said. 'Isn't that the noise people make when they're drowning?'

Peter Sellers had fallen in love with his leading lady. 'It was the very last thing I thought would happen. This was my first really big international film [his price had risen from around a steady £16,000 to £47,000 for this film] Sophia Loren was the biggest star I'd been cast with,' he was to tell me in another time. 'I was genuinely scared . . . overwhelmed, really, is the word.'

There was no hint of the coming crush at their first meeting. 'I was just hoping,' said Sellers, 'for a good professional relationship, you know – what else, man? I was two stone overweight. I wasn't the most attractive man in the world, let's face it. Then it just happened. I think she must have liked the fact that I was so unassuming. She liked my simplicity. I made her laugh. We were very happy together.'

He talked simply about the time that was to be so finally hurtful. He talked with affection for Loren, recalling, without embarrassment and with an honesty that few men ever achieve, especially when talking to other men about women, that 'I was absolutely around the bend about her at times'.

But precisely how deep Sophia Loren's involvement went has remained questionable. At that time, with his own marriage so unhappy, he was vulnerable and probably unconsciously something of a romantic fantasist. It could well have been that Sophia Loren's natural, warm Neapolitan generosity misled him. Certainly she had a keen perception of him that caused her concern: 'Peter,' she once asked, 'have you ever sat down and said to yourself, "Today I am really happy"?' He was surprised at the question, more surprised at his answer. 'No,' he told her.

That they were close friends is evident; when she was robbed of nearly £82,000 worth of jewels during the making of that film, Sellers gave her a valuable Eastern ring 'to launch a new collection'.

Sellers' love for his leading lady became common knowledge on the set of *The Millionairess*. One of the first men to know exactly how far it had gone, at least for Sellers, was Wolf Mankowitz, the writer, whose erratic relationship with the actor was then enjoying one of its warmer spells. Driving home from the studio one evening Sellers stopped the car and pointedly informed Mankowitz of his love for Loren. He added that he was about to tell his wife 'everything'.

Mankowitz is a phlegmatic, cultivated East End Jew whose bulk lends his look of supine disdain a threatening authority. His face, even in repose, seems a network of subtle sneers, and one easily imagines he collects more confessions than confidences. It adds up to the same thing, of course: Wolf Mankowitz is *informed*. He received this particular piece of information with a rigid control over his nervous system, although he now recalls brushing a sudden avalanche of cigarette ash from his lapel.

Sellers touched a button and a window closed with the sound of tearing silk, shutting out the noise of passing cars until there was just the sound of two men breathing. Mankowitz asked whether he planned to leave Anne. Sellers answered he hadn't considered it and 'sounded surprised' at the question.

'Then why say anything to Anne?' counselled Mankowitz. 'What do you want her to do? Walk out on you?'

'I want her,' said Sellers simply, 'to understand.'

The two men talked in the car for a long time, backward and forward, until Mankowitz was 'pretty convinced' he had persuaded him not to reveal the situation to Anne. (Mankowitz's concern for maintaining the status quo may not have been entirely philanthropic. Embarking on an ambitious partnership with the actor, he naturally did not want Sellers' emotional equilibrium troubled by domestic pressures.) 'But the next thing I heard he had told Anne everything,' he recalled later. 'I guess she probably knew anyway, but he didn't have to . . . tell her. It must have been a lousy time for the pair of them, and so bloody pointless.'

Later I asked Sellers why he felt so compelled to tell his wife when his future with Loren was so problematical. He still seemed surprised at the question. 'Because,' he said, 'I don't believe in hiding anything like that.' He put a full stop at the end of the sentence that you couldn't trespass beyond. Although another time he was to say, 'It all happened during that awful time in our marriage, a time that happens in all marriages I suppose, when we had fallen out of love with each other. Looking back now, if Anne and I had hung on we would have survived and it would have been very, very good.'

For a while they both worked to keep the marriage going. Bored with Chipperfield, or otherwise disappointed, he moved the entire household to the Carlton

Tower Hotel in Belgravia.

The swiftness of his decision may be gauged by Peg's total astonishment, even disbelief, at the news of the evacuation. When a columnist on the London *Daily Mail* telephoned and asked whether it could be true, she told him with chatty confidence, 'I'm sure it can't be right. Peter rings me up nearly every night for a mother-and-son heart-to-heart. And he hasn't mentioned anything to me about moving.'

In November 1961 Chipperfield was sold for nearly £41,000 and it was clear to most people that the couple were having serious matrimonial difficulties: the press was becoming increasingly inquisitive. Sellers blamed the move on 'staff problems'.

Meanwhile, an unexpected shift of emotions was taking place: as Sellers grew more confident and certain that there would be no divorce the choice was slipping inexorably away from him. By the time he had 'grown in love' with his wife again the malicious fates had rallied against him. Anne Sellers was falling in love with someone else . . .

Altogether it was a hard, bleak, poignant time. His success – he was voted the film actor of the year in 1960 by the Variety Club of Great Britain (for *The Millionairess, The Mouse That Roared, Two-Way Stretch,* and *Never let Go*) – was overshadowed by his disintegrating marriage, an unrewarded love affair, and the death of his father from a heart attack.

Sellers was perhaps guiltily aware that he had not shown his father the love and gratitude he might have. That he had allowed him to fade too easily into the background of his affection was evident, and the depth of his grief when the old man died surprised those who knew the relationship.

After the mourning Sellers was left with a reawakened awareness of his old fears of heart failure; yet, instead of caution, he worked with a 'madman's zest', in Spike Milligan's words. His appetite for work, always voracious, had become obsessive; he barely finished one film before

93

the next studio set was klieg-bright, an enticement and an escape.

Only in work could he lose himself and lose himself more exhaustively than most actors who submerge their own identities in new roles; for Peter Sellers it meant almost literally becoming another man, a man with a new set of problems, ideals, friends, goals. Between *The Millionairess* in 1960 and *Doctor Strangelove* three years later, he made no less than eight major pictures, including *Lolita, Only Two Can Play, Waltz of the Toreadors,* and *The Pink Panther.* He also starred in and directed *Mr Topaze,* retitled *I Love Money* in the US. During this needfully arduous period he amazingly advanced both his critical and his popular reputations. 'I think,' he was to tell one critic, 'I sometimes work better under pressure.' Whether he was referring to his schedule or a more impalpable, painful force is obscure.

His driving sense of insecurity too was evident in a casual remark to Graham Stark at that time. 'It can still jump either way, luv,' he said. The success of *I'm All Right, Jack* would bring him at least 'two years of good offers', but the public, he knew too, is fickle, and he still seriously suspected the stability of his star rating (this despite the curious new and romantic tone of his fan mail following *The Millionairess;* it amused and flattered him, but according to one associate, 'there was little real reassurance there'). He was not, he believed, the stuff of romantic heroes. 'If I'm going to survive in any worthwhile sense,' he said, 'I'll have to survive as a character actor.'

In a sense he was right, although his character roles were to take on the glow of stardom. With Kite in *I'm All Right, Jack* he had laid down a formula that the fans were eager to encourage at the box office and the critics willing to praise with almost unanimous enthusiasm.

In seriocomic vein, in global-ranging accents, he embarked on his great exploration of the 'little man' – with humour, compassion, and a painful, insightful truth. He had finally reached 'the straight stuff' he had always ached for. Only a very small handful of critics, and the public not at all, were uneasy with this apparent obsession for playing such undynamic men 'too small for comfort'. By trying to be 'subtle and discreet', wrote one critic, 'he frequently tends to efface himself . . .'

His performance as a naval officer in *Up the Creek,* rebuked a writer in the London *Times,* 'was so believable, so minutely observed that he never quite fitted into this broadly farcical' film.

But Sellers did not intend to disappear into his own myth. He was carefully plotting his future career with something more than an actor's optimism or conceit. In early 1960 he was moving with apparent ease into a production partnership with Wolf Mankowitz: Sellers-Mankowitz Productions Limited. The aim: to produce a series of films which Mankowitz would write and/or produce with Sellers starring and/or directing. In the spring of that year Sellers, Mankowitz, and agent Leslie Linder outlined plans to free themselves from the Front Office tycoons. It was, they said, to be an operation not unlike the early United Artists deal. (In 1919 Douglas Fairbanks Snr, Mary Pickford, Charlie Chaplin, and director D.W. Griffith formed United Artists to gain more profits by pitting their glamour and box-office potency against the complicity of the cinema chains in America.) Actress Diane Cilento was to be put under contract and would star with Sellers in *Memoirs of a Cross-Eyed Man.*

The involved process of formulating the company went its way through the winter and spring months and into the summer of 1960. But still the contracts between the writer and Sellers were not finalised, and signs of agitation began to creep into Mankowitz's correspondence with Sellers' business manager Bill Wills. 'I can't understand why Peter's and my contracts with one another are taking so long to draw up . . . I really think we ought to push them through and get them signed as soon as possible, especially as we are now entering into various commitments which are predicated by the existence of these contracts between us . . . If you will thump your solicitor I will keep on thumping mine . . . Do let's get it signed up . . .'

On 30th August, 1960, the morning that Wolf Mankowitz was due to meet a group of financiers willing to back the company for £124,000, he received a hand-delivered letter from Sellers. In six paragraphs he said he could not go through with the partnership.

He wrote that he wanted to concentrate on acting and could not afford to take on any responsibility that might conflict with his career. Adding that he valued their association and wanted to keep it 'free from complications', he closed with the simple Yiddish endearment, *Muzzel.*

It was a tremendous blow to Mankowitz. In one moment, and at the eleventh hour, his dreams of a small Byzantine Empire were crushed. He went to the meeting of financiers and in a flat voice read them the letter *in toto.* 'Gentlemen,' he concluded, 'in the circumstances I think you will agree it is pointless to capitalise the company now. Sellers was the major asset and most of our activities were related to him or around him. I think you should put your money back in your pockets.'

Nobody argued.

He left the meeting and walked back to his office. There he wrote a series of bleak notes, the last as a director of Sellers-Mankowitz Productions Limited. 'I'm sorry to have to report the company is now virtually kaput . . . I fear that I lack some finally essential quality necessary to a producer . . . This dissolution has not been of my seeking . . . Since all my production plans this year hinged on the partnership with Sellers, my situation is currently chaotic, [adding with wry humour] in fact back to normal.'

Some fifty days after the partnership failed the news was broken in the English press. Sellers, now surprisingly removing the cellophane gloss from his earlier explanatory letter to Mankowitz, told a reporter: 'In my opinion – although I doubt whether he will much value it – Mr Mankowitz has too much on his plate. He is a very strange person with so many things on his mind. He should concentrate more on one thing, like screen writing, and leave the impresario business alone.'

But if he was sincere in his original letter to Mankowitz, and he undoubtedly was, why this belated attack?

Reckoned an agent who knew something of their original plans, 'I suspect that at the time Pete really didn't know that he was suddenly big enough to cause real havoc in other people's lives with his whims. When it finally hit him he felt bloody guilty and he needed an excuse for his behaviour.'

Mankowitz himself replied with a kind of forlorn honesty rare in a business where face-saving is practised in Mount Rushmore proportions. 'The truth is,' he said, 'he has taken over Sellers-Mankowitz completely, and I leave it to you to guess who got pushed.'

Almost immediately after this abrasive and unpleasant break-up Sellers declared he was going to make *Mr Topaze* – as star *and* director.

Re-vamped from Marcel Pagnol's pre-war play about a shy, honest, idealistic French provincial schoolteacher corrupted by a crooked financier who hires him as an innocent front-man for his organisation, the picture flopped badly. Neither critics nor audiences cared for it at all. In the spring of 1961 the writing was clearly on the wall. The British trade paper *Kinematograph Weekly* published its epitaph: 'I'm afraid there's little chance of *Mr Topaze* making the grade. The comedy drama has its moments and is delightfully staged but for some reason or other Peter Sellers fans are just not interested in his latest.' It coincided with the news that *The Millionairess* was faring badly in America, surviving for less than two weeks in New York.

It was a blow to both his ego and his pride, and it came at a time when there was only the bare bones of comfort to be found in his private life. The executive suite view was that 'Sellers has thrown the big one and lost' and 'now perhaps he's got the big-I-am ideas out of his system'.

Even Sellers suspected that his 'two years of good

offers' were nearing their end. 'It takes just three bad pictures in a row and it's all over, you're finished in the big league,' he repeated again and again. Professionally it was his darkest hour since those early post-war days when he was scratching a meagre living around the hostile British music-halls.

Then Stanley Kubrick, still deeply and particularly impressed by his earlier, more stylised, bravura performances (*The Naked Truth*, *The Ladykillers*), invited him to play Clare Quilty in *Lolita*. Sellers accepted, and made what was to be an astonishing and emphatic return to the macabre, wilful, *comédie noire* of his formative years with the Goons. Appearing in a series of preposterously eccentric impersonations (a neurotic policeman, a masochistic voyeur, a German psychiatrist) he made author Vladimir Nabokov's evil-minded Quilty, with his unwholesome designs on Lolita, almost enchanting; almost, thought some critics, 'the real hero' of the piece. The notices returned mostly to their old adulatory tone, '. . . he reduces us to a state of delighted bewilderment with his virtuosity . . .' (The prototype for Quilty's voice was Norman Granz, the jazz impresario. Granz read sections of the script into a tape recorder for Sellers to study and develop.)

His ailing stock was revived. Kubrick did not hesitate for a moment. Although *Doctor Strangelove*, full of its megaton risk in asking audiences to laugh at their own threatened annihilation, was still some two years away, he invited Sellers to play 'the lead and the lead and the lead'.

Sellers was at first hesitant. 'It's going to look like a gimmick,' he told Kubrick. 'I think another multiple-role assignment would be wrong.'

Kubrick was gently persuasive. 'It's not a gimmick, Peter, if I can't find any other actors who could play these roles better or at least as well as you could play them.' The director's admiration for Sellers after *Lolita* was sincere and professionally boundless. 'He was the hardest worker I knew,' he said. 'I'd come into the studio at seven o'clock in the morning and there would be Peter Sellers. Waiting, ready. Full of ideas.'

(Kubrick declined to be interviewed about Sellers. 'I love Peter,' he wrote. 'I think he's a great actor, but I am never any good on this sort of thing. I'm terribly inhibited about discussing an artist like Peter . . . I'm peculiar about this, but it's a very personal relationship you have with an actor.' He offered to 'cautiously torture out' a comment and finally wrote: 'When you are inspired and professionally accomplished as Peter, the only limit to the importance of your work is your willingness to take chances. I believe Peter will take the most incredible chances with a characterisation, and he is receptive to comic ideas most of his contemporaries would think unfunny and meaningless. This has, in my view, made his best work absolutely unique and important.')

Since working with John Boulting some four years before, this was the closest and most profitable relationship Sellers had had with a director: he trusted him – with good reason. For there were moments on *Lolita,* he was later to confess, when he felt he 'had gone too far' and feared 'nobody will ever believe this'. Yet all the time Kubrick pushed him firmly 'to the limits of the nightmarish' Quilty, assuring him that the essential 'reality was there', only 'larger and not smaller than life'.

Nevertheless, after *Lolita* was completed Sellers scurried back to his imaginative but safer pursuit of the Little Man in his various disguises: in Kingsley Amis' *Only Two Can Play,* as the philandering, underpaid, resentful Welsh librarian; *The Dock Brief,* as the lonely defeated lawyer hired to defend a self-confessed wife murderer; *Waltz of the Toreadors,* as the ageing, imperious, hollow lecher; *Heavens Above,* as the far-too-Christian priest.

But, it seemed, the once satisfying and perhaps remedial role of the Little Man was losing its kick: far from choosing that classic comedic genre he now felt 'trapped' into it by a natural conspiracy of unimaginative producers. In April 1962 he expressed some of his serious dissatisfaction to Joseph Morgenstern in the old New York *Herald Tribune.* 'Everyone,' he lamented, 'says the same thing,

99

"Peter, I've got a lovely Little Man part for you, nice and down-trodden". I invariably say that I want to do other things, and they say, "But, Peter, don't fall into the trap", the trap being in their estimation that maybe I was cut out by nature to be a little man and am in mortal danger of eluding my destiny.'

He told Morgenstern – who felt Sellers could use a bit more arrogance 'to protect himself from his own humility' – that he had nothing against little men, but simply found 'the roles unsatisfying'. Then, 'Producers are always striving to capture the Chaplin bit, but short of putting on baggy pants and wearing a cane, it's difficult to do. I'm not the one for that sort of physical humour.'

(One can measure from this statement the constancy of Peter Sellers' world: within a year he was to embark on the *very* physical humour of Inspector Jacques Clouseau, a character in the Chaplin mould.)

That Sellers was deeply troubled about the direction his career was taking is obvious; that it reflected an even deeper concern with his private life and affairs and standing is more than probable.

His fundamental isolation grew more acute during this time. His marriage was not to be salvaged, despite his efforts to save it, and by the end of 1962 he admitted it was 'a write-off'. Anne had fallen in love with a South African architect named Elias Levy, the man Sellers had hired to decorate their new penthouse home on the slopes of Hampstead. His private life was 'a mess' and 'a bloody shambles'. Paradoxically, that year Hollywood, carefully forgetting the expensive failures of *Mr Topaze* and *The Millionairess,* offered him no less than twenty-one major films. He had time for only one before embarking on the longstanding *Doctor Strangelove* for Stanley Kubrick. Perhaps as a precautionary ballast against the dangerous, defiantly shocking humour of that movie – explaining his final acceptance later he said: 'Some forms of reality are so horrible we refuse to face them unless we are trapped into it by comedy. Anyway, to label any subject unsuitable for comedy is to admit defeat' – he decided to make

100

The Pink Panther for Blake Edwards.

The role of Inspector Clouseau, a pathologically acci-
dent-prone French detective, appealed to Sellers (as 'a bit
of a giggle'), and something that would not overtax his
emotions before the inevitable strain of the now certain
divorce and *Doctor Strangelove*. It was not the principal
role; David Niven (as a lordly international jewel thief
continually eluding Sellers), Capucine (Sellers' two-timing
wife), and Claudia Cardinale were far more heavily
involved in the plot. Yet it was to be this performance that
convinced a few of his more aggressive critics that he was
more than just a funny face, an accomplished impersonator, a mimic. The wide-ranging and swift portrayals from
Kite to Quilty to Clouseau could not be excused as
anything but the work of a great actor.

The Pink Panther script, by Blake Edwards and
Maurice Richlin, was amusing, elegant, literate, but not
unduly original. Sellers gave it a new shape, often blatant-
ly banana-skinned, and created in the process his first
memorable performance as a visual screen comic in the
Chaplin-Keaton tradition and class: he waves a solemn
finger of caution and it becomes stuck in somebody's
nostril; he casually rests a hand on a large globe and it
spins him to the floor; he attempts to kiss his disdainful
wife and she slides elegantly off the bed between his legs
and he kisses the cold pillow.

Against the background of his unhappy homelife his
performance became more and more therapeutic; it was
one of the happiest and easiest films he ever made.
Clouseau, to be gloriously and more fully repeated less
than two years later in *A Shot in the Dark,* became a man
you cared about and laughed at, but compassionately, for
the world was a malevolent conspiracy to deflate his
dignity.

In the second film he has only to step out of his car to
land in an ornamental goldfish pond. Will he catch
pneumonia? 'I probably will,' he answers with unshake-
able aplomb, 'but it's all part of life's rich pageant.'
Having given Elke Sommer a light, he returns the burning

cigarette lighter to his pocket and sets himself on fire.

But emotionally this was to be a less happy liaison with Blake Edwards, and for a time the pair fell out. But that was after *Doctor Strangelove* and his divorce and the therapy of Clouseau was no longer enough.

'I desperately wanted Anne back,' he told one friend. 'The days were all right. The days I worked. At night . . . I would sit at home, alone, for hour after hour, just going over my childhood mostly, trying to fathom it all out.'

But he didn't really have to go back that far, not this time, for the familial stability he wanted and needed so much had begun to spoil the day he left the calmative Whetstone – 'his last real habitat', Milligan was to call it – on the final run to the brilliant, consuming fame of the twentieth century: stardom. It would take him to the edge of death and make him a fortune to pay for the return journey.

Aftermath

IT WAS A backstage party, noisy, with models and actresses and slumming socialites, frozen elegance balanced on the tips of their expensive nose-jobs. But one guest, Janette Scott, a former English child star, did not feel particularly beautiful that night. Although few people knew it then, her marriage to Canadian singer Jackie Rae was over. She was depressed, and recalls being unusually upset by the gossip of the evening, by the sound of reputations suffocating beneath the satin slander of the trade. It was too loud and the teeth were too large in the smiles.

She was looking for the nearest exit when she realised that she was being watched. Unable to find Dennis Selinger, who had taken her to the party, she retreated to a quiet corner and waited. In a moment she knew that the man watching her was Peter Sellers. His interest might have pleased. Instead it made her 'bloody uncomfortable and a bit angry'.

Later she was to articulate her first reaction to Sellers' scrutiny. 'His interest seemed to lack warmth', was void of sensuality, and 'was not a flirtation but an examination'. Later still she was to tell a friend: 'He was staring in a way that made me feel like a specimen and not a woman.'

When Selinger finally came for Janette Scott, Sellers approached her. The agent introduced them, and almost immediately, in a voice 'so soft he was almost inaudible', Sellers asked whether he might telephone her sometime to invite her to dinner.

She said yes.

At 7.30 the following morning Selinger was on the telephone. 'Jan, luv,' he said, and there was a still a lot of sleep in his voice, 'I'm sorry to wake you so early, but I've had Peter Sellers on and he's in a bit of a two-and-eight.'

Sellers, he said, wanted to know whether she 'really meant it' the previous evening when she agreed to have dinner with him.

'I've told him I'm sure it's okay, but he's insisted I call you and confirm it, because he has to know right away.'

She confirmed the arrangement.

Minutes later Sellers called and they made a date for dinner that night.

Janette Scott had a great deal in common with Sellers. She, too, was born into a show business family. Her mother, Thora Hird, was the compelling force in her early years. Yet, like Sellers, she had inherited a kind of suppressed shyness from her father, Jimmy Scott, a businessman. Each was an only child. And each was emerging from the debris of a broken marriage.

Perhaps the most significant difference in their circumstances then was that Peter Sellers was riding the crest of a career wave while Janette Scott had reached something of an impasse. Among the most durable and talented child stars in Britain, she was at that time trying to bridge that gap between pigtails and cocktails that has bedevilled every 'movie moppet' since Shirley Temple. Despite a couple of well-reported romances, a few good adult roles, and even a marriage to an older man, she remained a child of pristine innocence in the eyes of the public, a freckled girl-child forbidden to grow up. For an ageing child star is a too traumatic reminder that time is passing, and it is a psychological fact that audiences resist such fundamental biological progress to the last seat in the circle.

One might speculate what it was that Peter Sellers saw in this haplessly enforced professional virgin figure. She was the complete antithesis of the sophisticated women he had been seeing since his marriage to Anne had gone wrong. He had become one of the most peripatetic playboys in London, a city where the competition is fierce. Harvey Orkin, a former comedy writer turned New York agent, was working in London then and spent a great deal of time with Sellers, watching the women walking into his life and right out the other side.

'The problem with Peter,' Orkin was to explain much later, 'was that he could never like a girl who liked him. It was the old Groucho Marx routine about not wanting to join any club that was willing to accept him as a member.'

Yet women were genuinely fond of him. 'Not because he was a big-deal actor, but because he was a pretty nice guy they could get along with without too much effort, at least on a casual basis. He could never believe that.'

Such is the insecurity of Peter Sellers that his *affaire de cœur* with one of the most beautiful and tantalising women in the cinema, a woman who could match his fortune and his fame, seemed no longer to count. He believed with flinty conviction that women found him 'just about tolerable' because of his vogue and riches.

'It bugged him,' said Harvey Orkin, his face a small landslide of sadness that could no longer be propped up with his shafts of cynical humour.

Still more punishing to Sellers at that moment was the three stone he had shed since the divorce. He became hooked on one crash diet after another in a frenetic bid to ward off middle age as he approached his fortieth birthday. Like all actors he had a highly developed and understandable preoccupation with himself and that was a time of some stringent stock-taking.

It was also the time he was preparing *Doctor Strangelove, or How I Learned to Stop Worrying and Love the Bomb*. (His fee was now in the million-dollar class; of his multiple performance in *Strangelove* Kubrick was to observe wryly: 'We got three for the price of six.') Originally he was to play four roles: the Nazi-bred, crippled, sieg-heiling scientist; the bald American President Muffley; the English RAF Group Captain Mandrake; and a gum-chewing Texan bomber pilot called Major 'King' Kong. It was the latter role that was causing him most concern.

The evening he met Janette Scott for dinner he was particularly on edge. He told her about his dilemma and the strain he was under. She understood. Like all actors touched with genius he was obviously going to be restless and worried so soon before such a major undertaking.

But even so she did not realise just how deeply disturbed he was, nor was she prepared for what happened next. Perhaps unusually moved by her sympathy and understanding with an actor's neurosis at such times, Sellers began to weep. Everybody, he told her, 'expects so much, so bloody much'.

Greatly moved, she pleaded with him not to play the fourth role, the Texan pilot, whose voice and characterisation he couldn't yet crack. (Fate intervened anyway: Sellers broke his ankle and Slim Pickens was hired for the part.)

Janette Scott was unprepared for and fascinated by the deep, unpredictable actor. Soon she was seeing him almost every evening; she found her growing concern for him helping her through her own not untroubled time and, concedes now, was 'not entirely unselfishly motivated' in her devotion.

Yet he was still stubbornly living in the unhappy Hampstead penthouse that Levy had designed and decorated while falling in love with Anne Sellers. Janette Scott was dismayed and perplexed by his refusal to leave.

'It was tearing him into little pieces living there,' she recalled. 'Every time he showed it to his friends you can imagine the agony . . . every word of praise would plunge into him like a knife.'

Yet he stayed.

Several times he threatened to commit suicide by throwing himself from the balcony. He was convinced that his anguish was greater than any man had ever known: 'Why should I have to go on putting up with this, remembering. To be dead is nothing', he said again and again.

Bert Mortimer was convinced that he meant to do away with himself. For weeks he followed Sellers around the apartment: 'scared stiff to let him out of my sight', he told Janette Scott, 'because he meant it, this time he could have jumped at any minute.'

Toward the end of *Strangelove* their affair had reached the question of marriage. But by this time Janette Scott knew that she could 'never live with Pete'. One morning, without too much preparation, she packed her bags and left for New York, later to meet and marry and divorce Mel Torme.

'During the months I was with Peter he had become totally impossible, a really different man,' she said. More and more, he failed to turn up for dates or was late for dinner parties she had arranged days before for their friends at the penthouse. He became elusive, evasive, and his appearance grew more 'maddeningly erratic'.

Finally, days would pass without a word. Then, 'Bert would phone at four o'clock in the morning and ask me to rush over because Pete was in a state, or locked in the bathroom, threatening to do himself in. I mean, who needs it? I thought I knew him very well and, of course, I didn't really know him at all.'

Britt

THE END OF his marriage – he finally sued Anne for adultery with Levy – followed by the sudden embarkation to New York of the consoling Janette Scott could hardly have had a reassuring effect on Peter Sellers' ailing ego. Again he was thrown into a state of lonely, sometimes savage, confusion, and melancholy rejection (aggravated by the news that Anne, now married to Levy, was pregnant) which he once more attempted to relieve in brief moments with some of the most beautiful though not always most eligible women on the London scene at that time.

But if he was gaining a certain amusing notoriety as a rake and a womaniser, it was in direct contrast to his marathon pursuit through psychiatrists' offices of a real, durable, but damnably elusive solace.

By this time he had taken Janette Scott's reiterated advice, and moved out of the penthouse with its morbid memories, and taken up residence at the Dorchester Hotel. It was an interesting choice of abode and maybe a significant one.

The Oliver Messel suite, which he finally settled on, then cost £400 a week to rent; and you had to dig deeper than your small change for the extras. It is a spacious apartment that tries hard not to look like a hotel suite and ends up looking exactly like a hotel suite, albeit with an elaborate pedigree. People who claimed to know Peter Sellers well have observed that he was only at home in hotels, and this address seemed to accommodate him best of all. It was not a flattering assertion.

The Oliver Messel suite is pretty, delicate, and so precious that even the television set masquerades as a miniature theatre with Victorian red velvet and gold

108

tasselled drapes. On the dawn-grey walls of the sitting room are paintings by designer Messel of eighteenth-century English garden scenes set in lattice-work frames. Long French windows with English chintz curtains open onto the garden terrace. The carpet, morning-haze green, is woven in a design of flower beds, a wheelbarrow, and a swan swimming with elegance in a pond. The master bedroom walls are hung with yellow corded silk, the colour of crocus, and Mr Messel's original sketches for the ballet *Sleeping Beauty* are hung from sashes of mulberry silk. The bathroom, beneath a canopied ceiling, has a mirror display to reflect every inch of your anatomy with no stress to your eyeballs or imagination.

It is a rich man's waiting room, a transit lounge for a VIP traveller.

('Since Whetstone I have never been inside a Sellers home and recognised Peter,' said Herbert Kretzmer, his South African speech rhythm giving his words a sympathy the words alone do not convey. 'I don't recognise him in the furniture, in the design, in anything. He has *House and Garden* ready-mades and just moves in.')

Sellers was living in the Oliver Messel suite when he first met Britt Ekland. She was buying magazines from the bookstand in the lobby and looking, he recalled, 'sensational'. Who, he wanted to know immediately, is *that*? He was told that she was 'the new Swedish bird' 20th Century-Fox had just signed for *Guns of Batasi*. Britt Ekland.

Sellers was in an especially vulnerable mood at that time. 'He was actually still talking about getting Annie back', remembers Dennis Selinger. 'It was crazy talk. Annie was married to Levy, she was pregnant – and Pete was going on about a reconciliation!'

Selinger finally talked him out of this freakish idea. He persuaded Sellers that he really did have to accept that his marriage to Anne was finished.

'You've got to look to the future now', the agent told him with genuine concern.

'I met a great TWA bird', Sellers said. 'I'll give her a call and get her over.'

'That's the ticket, Pete', Selinger said, relieved, thinking: if he can't have love, a bit of lechery won't do him any harm. 'Where is she, this TWA lady?'

'New York.'

Selinger was appalled.

'You'll spend a fortune flying her over and within twenty-four hours you'll be trying to give her the elbow. Can't you call somebody a bit closer to home?'

Finally a friend called somebody at a London club. One of the hostesses comforted Sellers that night.

But he could not get out of his mind the blonde he had seen buying magazines in the lobby. Britt Ekland. It was not too surprising. Less than six months before, Maurice Woodruff, the clairvoyant, had predicted he would meet and marry a woman with the initials B.E.

Within six days he was telling Roderick Mann, the *Sunday Express* columnist, 'I really believe this may be more than just a casual relationship. Funny, isn't it? I keep saying to you I'll never get hooked again; that I'm tired of having my heart bleed; but here I am, waiting to be hooked.

'My trouble, I suppose, is that I can only be attracted to pretty girls. And that's courting disaster from the start. Especially if you tend to be jealous, like me.'

Yet, they were both to admit later, it was not 'love at first sight' – as it had been between Sellers and Anne a dozen years before – but incipient infatuation.

Britt was in the shower when the bell of her small one-roomed apartment at the Dorchester sounded. She took the bath towel and wrapped it around herself and answered the door. She felt, she has since recalled, 'very much like a Hollywood film star: a little wicked – but a little nervous too'.

The caller was Bert Mortimer. The sight of the betowelled Britt momentarily overturned his poise. For a few seconds, she recalled, he seemed lost for words, although his mouth dutifully went through the motions of opening and closing. Finally he succeeded in explaining that he was Peter Sellers' valet and his master would like to photo-

110

graph her at some mutually convenient time. He assumed she would know who Peter Sellers was, but he had assumed wrong. Hiding her ignorance well, she answered coolly that she would give the matter some thought and let him know.

She telephoned the studio and asked whether a 'freelance photographer' named Peter Sellers was bona fide and whether he was 'any good at photographing women'. She was assured that he was a reputable and talented photographer, and incidentally, 'quite a good actor, too'.

But wary of men who send young girls invitations through their valets, she wore 'a blouse up to *here* and a sweater on top of that and boots you tied with laces to the knees'. She was, she calculated, 'physically unassailable'. Later she was to view the scene with humour: 'It was very funny. I was so determined not to be carried off to the boudoir by some dark-haired gentleman just because he was a film star that I have never been so uncomfortably dressed in my life.'

After the photographic session, which was not by all accounts very successful ('he was as nervous and shy as I was'), Sellers invited her to go to the cinema to see *The Pink Panther* which had just opened in London. It was the first Sellers film she had ever seen and she was hugely impressed. Afterward they returned to the hotel and smoked marijuana. Britt said it was her first joint.

According to Sellers they made love. Britt says her memory of what happened is hazy, except that she was suddenly in Sellers' arms and he was kissing her. She woke in her own room with a hangover from Dom Perignon and Acapulco Gold.

The following morning she received a large and beautiful bouquet of flowers, swiftly followed by another bouquet and another and another. None of them came with a card. Miss Ekland was delighted but not particularly puzzled, believing they merely reflected her star status.

'I had just signed the deal with 20th Century-Fox, had spent a marvellous evening with a famous actor, seen my pictures in all the newspapers. So suddenly in my childish

111

mind I was a film star . . . and film stars are always sent flowers.'

But the maid continued to arrive with more flowers, and very soon even the sanguine Miss Ekland grew curiously apprehensive; it didn't seem 'lawful', she thought, surveying what was rapidly becoming in her mind a kind of botanical speakeasy. But when the final bouquet came it contained a card which simply said, *Peter*. 'I was astonished and a bit ashamed, because I didn't even think of him. I thought they had to be from *dozens* of admirers. I really believed that was what people did.'

The flowers were not merely an example of Sellers' overkill. They reflected his genuine remorse. He was convinced at that time that he had seduced a credulous inexperienced girl. 'He really did believe that he was first', Maurice Woodruff recalled. Sellers had called the clairvoyant early the following morning to tell him that he had met the girl with the initials Woodruff had foretold.

'He was sort of cock-a-hoop and sort of stricken too', Woodruff said. 'He wanted to believe in her innocence. He was a great romantic. But if Britt had been a virgin so was my aunt Fanny.'

A homosexual, a misogynist with a waspish humour, Woodruff had an instinct that transcended clairvoyancy.

The following night Britt was having dinner with Harvey Orkin at Ronnie Scott's Jazz Club in Soho when Sellers arrived. She was just finishing the last of her chicken kiev.

'Have you had dinner?' Sellers asked.

'No,' she lied.

'I know a marvellous Italian restaurant called The Tiberio. Would you like to have dinner with me?'

Despite the alacrity – and not a little digestive inconvenience – with which she accompanied him, Sellers felt despondent. 'I suddenly thought that night there was no chance and that was it, you were just going to be another girl,' he was to tell her later.

Certainly, at The Tiberio – a high-priced, low-lit Mayfair establishment where the waiters are as discreet as

112

Venetian blinds – she outlined a personal philosophy that must have severely cramped his optimism.

'I have a suitcase, a passport, and a good contract with Fox,' she told him. 'The last thing I want right now is a husband to mess it all up.'

In the expensive gloom she could not see his face too well but he said, 'Well, I know this isn't going to lead to anything, but it's nice having dinner with you.'

But Britt Ekland was feeling a growing affection for the man that her cool Swedish exterior did not show. 'He seemed to get more shy and more charming all the time', she noticed. That night they returned to the Dorchester and made love. This time Britt was clear about what happened. She told Sellers that she had had several affairs. He pressed her for details. After losing her virginity at seventeen to her unofficial fiancé in Stockholm, she told him, there had been a Russian ballet dancer, a piano-player, a film director, an Italian playboy, and an American student in St. Moritz.

Sellers appeared to take the confession in his stride. The following morning he was on the phone to Woodruff. 'She's not the virgin Swede I thought she was, Maurice. She's been around a bit.'

He wanted Woodruff's advice.

Woodruff told him, 'You should be flattered that she's been so honest with you, Pete. She had no obligation to put all her cards on the table like that.'

'That's right, that's right', Sellers said, clearly delighted with the idea.

Privately, Woodruff was not so certain.

'She was a very silly girl telling a man like Pete so much, even if he was pushing her. If she had been a bit more reticent, more discreet, they could have avoided all that heartache and suspicion in Hollywood. Her past preyed on his mind, you know. It was eating him up.'

('Every man's dream is still, I'm sure, finding a virgin. That's why marriage has gone on the rocks,' he told writer Helen Lawrenson in 1970. 'The original idea was that the girl had never been with anyone else, and it was so pure.

So I came to this conclusion that to be in love with the girl of one's dreams – who if possible was a virgin – was the ultimate happiness. I still want to keep the ideal situation where I can discover the ideal woman and undress her, reveal her, in this fantasy of mine.')

For the next few days in London, Britt and Sellers were inseparable. When she finally had to fly to New York, he was inconsolable. The following night he telephoned her via the Telstar satellite and proposed; she accepted.

On 12th February, 1964 she returned to England and at London Airport he placed a century-old engagement ring (six rubies, six diamonds, six emeralds, noted the press) on her finger. It was a popular, romantic affair and, like all the important relationships in his life, happened swiftly.

But many of his closet friends were dismayed; one even telephoned Janette Scott in New York and pleaded with her to return and 'talk some sense into this smitten lunatic'. He was almost forty years old, she pointed out, and quite old enough to know his own mind.

Peg gave her blessing, saying only that she was 'a little apprehensive' at the speed they were going; but there were no signs of the obstinate objections she had raised to the first marriage.

On 19th February, by candelight, in a ten-minute ceremony in a Guildford register office with five hundred people outside, they were married. It was snowing.

A few days before the wedding they had invited me down to Elstead for dinner. On the mantelpiece, with dozens of other cables congratulating them on their engagement, was one from Spike Milligan: 'You swine, Bluebottle. Give me back my ring.' It was signed 'Eccles'.

She asked what it meant and Sellers explained 'The Goon Show', using all the old wild voices. She laughed and reacted like a small child hearing a nursery rhyme for the first time. When he went outside to fetch some logs for the fire, she said, 'He is a marvellous man, isn't he? Most of the time since we met he has been so happy. But I know he can be very depressed too.'

114

She talked about her time in Rome the previous year, when she was starting her career: 'I almost wanted to die,' she told me, her accent pleasantly removing the uglier sounds of self-pity.

'I would stay at home at night, not seeing anyone, just eating and eating and eating. I put on ten pounds in a month. I know something about depression, believe me.'

I said I hoped so, because she was probably going to see a lot of it before she was through. 'Yes, I know,' she answered. 'But don't worry. About either of us. I can look after myself now, and I will learn to look after Peter.'

Sellers came in with the logs and put them on the fire. 'You know,' he said, watching them catch and crackle, 'I lasted nine months as a bachelor. But a man has to have roots. He has to have roots before he can grow again.'

That night in Sweden, Britt's parents and her small brother Carl went to the local cinema to see the man they would soon have in their family. 'Our daughter seems to have chosen a nice young man,' said Sven Ecklund on the way home.

But Britt Ekland was not to fall in love with Sellers until 6th April – the day he was admitted to the Cedars of Lebanon, the day she sat on the bed and wept.

'If there was a precise time when I really fell in love with Sellers,' she was to tell me later, using her husband's surname in the affected manner of young European actresses, 'that was it, alone in the house, that morning. Certainly I never loved him when we married. And I don't believed he loved me. We were both intoxicated with the *idea* of love. But that was all. I remember feeling both very guilty and very pleased that day I cried in Hollywood. Guilty because I had not loved him – and pleased because I knew that I finally did.'

But, ironically, while Britt was discovering for the first time that she was in love with her husband, she was in danger of losing him forever. Less than two months after their wedding in London, Peter Sellers was dying in Los Angeles.

115

Get Them Out-of-Range

BUT SELLERS DID not die that time, at least not on any permanent basis. His death, like so many things in his life, was for a limited engagement only. But he had heard the world mourn him, if not the angels sing, and the sound was profoundly disturbing.

He genuinely felt it was without justification, somehow without merit.

He had died eight times and eight times the doctors had brought him back. Yet there was no sense of achievement or adventure within himself, only a sense of gratitude and a sense of shock. Gratitude toward God and the doctors and those who waited and prayed. Shock because he had tasted his mortality and the taste was neither bitter nor sweet, as he had believed and expected; it was a dreamless sleep, deep and untroubled.

'I remember', he was to recall later, 'saying goodbye to Michael and Sarah. I remember going to the hospital and going into the private room and being dumped on the bed. I remember going to sleep. The next definite thing I can remember was being awakened with a violent jolt and seeing a great flash of white light.

'Between sleeping and waking I had died. And there was nothing in between.' (Much later his memory improved remarkably. Peg, he said, had come to him and, taking his hand, led him back to life.)

On 21st April, 1964 Sellers, now out of the Intensive Care Unit and off the front pages, wrote to me from the Cedars of Lebanon that he was feeling 'almost like my old self'. He said that if he took it easy for about six months the doctors expected him to be as fit as he ever was. 'At any rate,' he added, 'I don't intend to work until February or March next year, so I shall just laze around.'

Yet already, between dictating such reassuring letters to friends, he was prowling the hospital, amusing other patients, visiting children, studying the equipment that helped to save his life, spending demanding hours on the transatlantic telephone, and both confounding, and displeasing the doctors – a dangerous displeasure since, like Saki's dressmaker, when a doctor loses his temper one tends to find it on the bill. (His final medical reckoning was considerable; excluding the cost of any lost tempers, he later put it at more than £12,000.)

Until February or March, or perhaps May, 'work is out of the question', he vowed in various notes. Most of his friends knew that he was incapable of holding still that long. But how long he could or would remain inactive was the kind of question you could collect 64,000 dollars for answering on television.

The informed betting was that he couldn't sustain the part of Peter Sellers – 'it's too damn dull, deadening, anonymous', reasoned one sporting producer – for more than three months without running for the chameleon cover of a film role.

But he was alive and he had been dead. It was this singular, recurring, awesome thought that at first pleased and comforted him, then grew cold to haunt him. That he was soon putting on a special performance for the outside world is now without question. Privately he was becoming more morose, difficult, and disillusioned with each passing day.

'He was unbelievably sensitive and very touchy,' recalls Britt Ekland. In four eventful months she had seen their relationship completely reshape itself: the infatuation had gone and there was now a satisfactory mutual love, yet it had brought Britt, at twenty-one, responsibilities she was hardly prepared for. Her role became increasingly that of protector, guardian, and nurse. She worked fiercely and with devotion, but 'quietly fretted' over a career that seemed to be burnt out on the ground.

'I had to watch him all the time, calming him, seeing that he wasn't irritated or annoyed. He could get terribly upset at the slightest thing. If somebody came over to the house and mentioned they'd caught a fly on their windscreen it would practically plunge him into despair.'

Although the real torment was well hidden from outsiders during those early weeks of his recovery, there were those who spitefully suggested that the moment he knew he wasn't going to die he cast himself in 'the leading role of resurrected hero'. That he had not 'created a more Christ-like image', chided an actor, 'was probably due more to religious considerations than modesty'.

Such remarks were glib, cheap, and without appreciable humour, yet curiously they did reflect a growing suspicion in Hollywood.

'Peter,' said Britt, 'had changed.' But outside the obvious and expected pattern of his post-coronary depression she was unable to explain the change; she simply felt 'it was somehow like being with another person, fundamentally, yet not a stranger'.

Two months and one day after his 90-second excursion to eternity, Peter Sellers returned to Britain, looking 'bronzed and ebullient' and with 'a merry quip on his lips'. He told reporters at Heathrow Airport: 'Having died for a minute and a half I suppose I am one of those believe-it-or-not Ripley characters. I will now have to alter my whole way of life. If I don't there won't be a Peter Sellers around much longer.'

Precisely what changes he planned were unspecified. Moreover, whether his intent was at that time very serious became questionable three days later when he ordered a new car – his eighty-third – an £8,500, 150 mph Ferrari 330. 'I suffer,' he apologised, 'from a prolonged mechanical adolescence.'

During his airport interview, however, he mentioned that he preferred working in Britain or on the Continent. 'I'm not mad about the atmosphere in Hollywood,' he said. 'I think the thing is that if you don't like it you should leave.'

In Hollywood this casual remark was regarded as 'very ungrateful'. When he amplified it a few days later in an

118

interview with Alexander Walker, the film critic of the London *Evening Standard,* it created an incident that was to sharpen that resolve to change in at least one respect.

What he told Walker was this: 'I've had Hollywood in a big way, luv. America I would go back to gladly tomorrow, but as far as film-land is concerned I've taken the round trip for good. The noise and, to coin a phrase, the people. At the studios they give you every creature comfort except the satisfaction of being able to get the best work out of yourself.

'I used to go down to film *Kiss Me Stupid* with Billy Wilder and find a Cooks Tour of hangers-on and sightseers standing just off the set right in my line of vision. Friends and relatives of people in the Front Office come to kibitz on Peter Sellers, actor.'

When he complained to Wilder that he could not work with so many strangers on the set he recalled (slipping into Doctor Strangelove's Prussian accent) that Wilder told him: 'Peter, be like Jack Lemmon. Whenever he starts a scene he shuts his eyes and says to himself, "It's magic time!" And then forgets about everything else.'

Sellers, astonished at this remark, replied that he couldn't work that way either. He told Walker: 'I should have ridden on to the set on horseback, perhaps, with a brass telescope to my eye and bawled out [this time he slipped into his *Waltz of the Toreadors* voice] "Who are these damned civilians? Get them out of range of my cannons." '

Alexander Walker confessed, unnecessarily you might think, that he 'got the impression Peter Sellers no longer has the enthusiasm he took to Hollywood for director Billy Wilder'.

A few days after this interview appeared, Sellers received this cable: 'Talk about unprofessional rat finks.' It was signed by Wilder and the cast of *Kiss Me Stupid,* including Dean Martin and Kim Novak. The contents were mysteriously released to the press before Sellers had even received it.

Such an attack, with the political weight of Wilder

behind it, could have proved professionally catastrophic to a lesser talent and, indeed, many attributed the contents solely to Wilder, who had reason to feel particularly maligned by Sellers' remarks.

'I don't believe another actor without considerable encouragement would have gone that far,' says a writer who was close to the scene at the time. 'It was a pretty mean trick to aggravate a guy still as sick as Sellers had to be. Wilder can be a most malevolent power when he wants to turn up the voltage.' It was, insists Wilder, 'a short collaborative effort'.

Yet perhaps that cable was the one thing that Peter Sellers needed to dispel any lingering thoughts of self-pity. Certainly it came at a time of epochal introspection.

'That illness gave me a lot of time to rethink my life and my attitudes. Attitudes I hadn't bothered to examine for twenty years,' he was to say later. 'I mean, Billy Wilder was one of my idols and I suppose I just automatically accepted that he would be great for me. Well, he wasn't.

'I still have a few idols but now I consider them no more infallible than the man next door. "Okay," I say to them, "now prove you're as great as I think you are." Now the responsibility is all theirs. I made the mistake of expecting Wilder to mould me. Now I know it's me who should be doing the moulding. That was another thing I learned during those months, boy – confidence. Now I know I've got at least as much talent as any of them. I have.'

On paper the words look more brazen, less pleasant, than Sellers made them sound. His voice, quiet and occasionally indistinct, stripped such statements of conceit, varnished over the vanity with a kind of unspoken appeal for understanding.

Yet the Rat Fink cable rankled. Sellers felt deeply that the attack was unfair, and on 1st July, he bought a full-page advertisement in *Variety,* the influential show business newspaper, to dispel the feeling that 'I am an ungrateful Limey or rat fink who has been abusing everything in Hollywood behind its back'. He said, 'I did not go to Hollywood to be ill. I went there to work and found, regrettably, that the creative side in me couldn't accept the sort of conditions under which work had to be carried out. This is a personal matter. I have no criticism of Hollywood as a place, only as a place to work in. The atmosphere is wrong for me. At the same time anyone is at liberty to say that I am wrong.'

The advertisement, which cost about £250, went on to thank Doctor Rexford Kennamer and the staff at the Cedars of Lebanon 'who saved my life. For all these things and many others I could never be ungrateful.'

The somewhat squalid misunderstanding was over.

It is now interesting to contemplate the consequences of that unfortunate encounter with Wilder. If the director could teach him little about acting, he was perhaps to teach him a great deal about in-fighting; many believed he became 'an inflammatory influence' in shaping Sellers' hard and often dictatorial line on the set in pictures to come (although to deny more than a hint of its presence prior to this would be absurdly ill-informed).

His former agent Dennis Selinger, who has the sad face of a sleeping Basset hound on which someone has pencilled a moustache, certainly noticed 'quite some change'. But, cautiously, he says, 'I think he became markedly unapproachable after the Hollywood business, but how much was due to his illness and how much to Wilder and how much to his growing maturity both as a man and an actor I don't claim to know. But he did change, and for the better. When I say that, of course, I mean for the better from his point of view and not necessarily for those around him.'

Through May and June and July of that year Peter Sellers rested in his fashion. He took up photography again, did some bicycle riding, got hooked on archery and played for hours with his model railway set at Brookfield, his sixteenth-century home in the Surrey countryside; Britt was pregnant with Victoria, born the following January. 'He had enough on his plate to occupy ten men,' said one producer, 'yet he was restless as hell.' Indeed, the nervous agitation was becoming severe and, feared his doctors, alarming.

In late August, some five months after he had suffered that fierce multiple coronary attack, and still more than half a year away from the time he vowed he would begin acting again, his physicians called it a day. He was ordered to return to work. In early October he flew to New York to play a small three-day role in 'Carol for Another Christmas', a television production in aid of UNO.

'The inactivity was killing me,' he said. 'The old adrenalin was rushing around again and I was full of energy and there was nothing burning it up.'

At that time producer Charles Feldman was setting up a comedy called *What's New, Pussycat?* in Paris and was searching for an actor to play a psychotic psychiatrist to whom Peter O'Toole, as a girl-crazy magazine editor, foolishly entrusts his complexes. It was a small but vital role of co-starring status and Feldman invited Sellers to play it.

It was an invitation of considerable boldness. Sellers, for reasons both emotional and economic, wasn't exactly in the hot-cake category. 'Nobody wanted him, including United Artists,' Feldman recalled. 'He was considered too much of a health risk and no insurance company was willing to underwrite him at anything near a viable premium.'

Calculating that he could get him through his role in sixteen days, Feldman underwrote the liability himself. 'I figured if anything went wrong the very most it could cost us would be £149,000,' he was to explain later. Sellers signed for £124,000 plus ten per cent of the producer's gross. It was less than the money he was getting just prior to his illness but still impressive. Again it would seem that somebody up there was definitely looking out for Peter Sellers. The film, which had turned up at such an auspicious moment, might have been written for him: a very modern farce with a hint of pure anarchy about the acting, the dialogue, the humour, and the direction by Clive Donner.

Sellers threw himself into the film with an unguarded

enthusiasm that occasionally unnerved those around him and certainly caused some divided loyalties in the heart of Mr Feldman, who found himself in the dangerously unique position of being his own benefactor, beneficiary, broker, claims clerk, and investigator.

But his trust was not ill-placed. 'He was terrific,' he reported afterwards. 'His contribution to that picture was beyond calculation.'

Wearing a black wig that gave him the appearance of a hippie Mozart on marijuana, he turned in one of the most impressively spontaneous performances of his career. Delighted and relieved at the end of the film, Mr Feldman gave him a present. 'A token of my appreciation,' he modestly called it. It was a Rolls-Royce.

Yet even during the making of *Pussycat*, which was to be a huge hit, Sellers knew for certain the line he had to take. Certainly Peter O'Toole recognised the signs. 'Peter,' he says, 'taught me to be ruthless.'

On one occasion, after long delays on a particularly involved scene, Sellers removed his wig and placed it on director Clive Donner's head. 'When you're absolutely sure you're ready I'll be at the hotel,' he told him and left.

'He did it,' says O'Toole, 'very nicely. No fuss, no noisy tantrums. Polite and firm and swift as a dart.'

Talking to a newspaperman in Paris at that time, he said, 'The only thing I've been told is that I mustn't get into any arguments while filming. It'll make me too nervous. I just have to shut up and walk away. But in six months' time I can tell them all what I think of them, the swine.' There was plenty of Goonish humour in his voice, but not quite enough to drown the spirit of his real feelings.

Still the reports from the *Pussycat* set were impressive and encouraging. He was determined not to work so hard, he insisted to friends. He had found you cannot paper over the cracks in your life with Treasury bills, it seemed. But it is perhaps easy to see now that all the time he had been quietly sharpening the protective edge of his genius. And it would soon be clear to everyone that when he took his life apart and examined it so carefully and then put it together again he had left a few sharp edges where before there was only a bland finish.

One man who was then fervently hoping he had settled down into a less erratic pattern was John Bryan. A brilliant, English, Oscar-winning production designer turned producer, he had joined forces with Sellers shortly before his illness in a company called Brookfield, named after his country home. A calm, intelligent man with a relaxed, stylish sense of humour, he had been setting up *After the Fox,* which Sellers wanted Vittorio DeSica to direct.

At this time Sellers was obsessed with the idea of working for the famed Italian film-maker, a man in his short list of idols: 'He is the one man I've always wanted to direct me,' he told me one evening at supper on the outskirts of Paris. There was a large group of people there, including Harvey Orkin, Britt, Peter O'Toole, John Bryan and the guest of honour, DeSica.

The deal for him to make the film with Sellers had been completed that day, and he was holding forth in English that was barely held together with a great deal of Neapolitan patchwork. He dominated the evening, despite the presence of such rampant raconteurs as O'Toole and Orkin. Sellers, as he so often does on these occasions, quietly and steadily depressed himself into less than his usual dimensions. I felt an immediate anxiety for their future relationship. Another guest at that supper was to say later, 'Any idiot could have seen they were on a collision course. They may have admired each other's talent but they were totally incompatible as artists.'

It wasn't many days into *After the Fox* in Rome that the serious troubles started. Sellers was dissatisfied with his own performance. 'He knew he wasn't getting anywhere near to what he believed was possible,' said Bryan. 'He blamed DeSica's direction and he was probably right. DeSica simply didn't have the feel for this particular stuff.'

But worse, even at times embarrassing, was DeSica's natural, flamboyant tendency to pantomime the performance he wanted from Sellers. 'With the most disastrous results,' remembered Bryan. One could sense the horror that was still inside the producer when he talked of that time.

DeSica's English proved to be even less fluent than was at first thought possible; and his insistence on using his own Italian scriptwriter, who spoke even less English than he did, to work on Neil Simon's original screenplay, full of indigenous New York-Jewish humour, greatly burdened the atmosphere. Quite clearly there would soon have to be a showndown . . . and casualties.

Some three weeks into production Sellers wanted De-Sica removed from the picture. John Bryan, aware that a change of director at that stage might still further compli-cate the situation, strongly resisted the move.

When matters continued to deteriorate, 'Peter naturally blamed John for DeSica's survival,' related Judy Good-man, a production assistant and sometimes secretary to the actor. 'When a picture goes bad that's what happens. Everybody blames everybody else. It is a human chain-reaction. It is not unusual in the film industry.' At one stage Sellers, as much victim of as contributor to the ailing climate, even wanted to sack John Bryan, and complained bitterly to the Front Office in New York about his handling of the production.

(Sellers claimed his personal relationship with DeSica brightened considerably when he made it clear he was not impressed with the Italian's acting lessons; it said a great deal for their resilience and mutual respect that they survived the rigours of *After the Fox* to make a second picture together: *Woman Times Seven*.)

Precisely how desperately fragile the liaison between Sellers and Bryan had become can be judged from an episode that took place one weekend in Rome. It was a Saturday afternoon and the producer, as usual, was outlining the shooting schedule for the following week. Suddenly Sellers stopped him cold. 'Don't try to tell me what to do, John,' he told Bryan. 'Now you listen to me . . .'

'And please don't talk to me like that,' answered Bryan, uncommonly riled.

Sellers asked the producer to leave. He left without another word. The following afternoon he called Sellers again and suggested they meet for tea and sort out the situation. 'After all, we do have a picture to finish here, whatever happens between us,' he pointed out.

Sellers agreed, and the pair met and resolved, at least temporarily, their differences. But, still puzzled, when they had completed the work, Bryan asked what had set Sellers off the day before.

'Well,' said Sellers, clearly hurt, 'you *have* been giving me some very strange looks lately, John.'

It was an explanation that to the day he died John Bryan found somewhat odd if not downright incomprehensible. The partnership, once based on an ambitious six-picture foundation, ended immediately after they had completed *After the Fox,* their first film together.

'But you know,' said Bryan, 'with all the problems, all the difficulties and unhappiness there were between us, it would have been perfectly logical for Peter to call me at any time and suggest we do another picture together. And to be perfectly honest . . . I don't know what my answer would have been.'

Suspicions of a Solitaire-Player

AT THE COMPLETION of *After the Fox* in Rome and his cameo performance as the seedy alcoholic doctor in *The Wrong Box,* Sellers was definitely hot again. In December 1965 the well-informed London Bureau of the New York *Motion Picture Herald* published its annual survey of British box-office business. He was among the top ten stars, and his film *A Shot in the Dark,* completed before his Hollywood misadventure, was the fourth largest money-making picture in the country.

Still glowing from the success of *What's New, Pussycat?* – despite some appallingly rude notices – Charles Feldman produced a lucrative offer for him to play the bogus James Bond in *Casino Royale.* After a great deal of uncertainty, denials and agents' double-talk ('it was on and off twenty times before he finally said yes just three weeks before we started shooting', Feldman disclosed later), the picture started under a cloak of secrecy in London on 11th July, 1966. 'Feldman,' it was said, 'is producing *Casino Royale* like General Groves made the first atomic bomb.'

It was to be another unhappy argument-ridden picture for Peter Sellers. His acute sense of self-preservation, not to be despised, had now reached the stage where he might well worry about being double-crossed at solitaire. Lamented Britt, 'He is so insecure, he won't trust anyone.'

From the outset, then, it could be safely assumed he was going to be particularly wary of Mr Orson Welles. Indeed, anything less than extreme caution would have been most imprudent, for Welles is a scene-stealer of considerable note. In fact, 'scene-stealer' puts it rather mildly – akin, perhaps, to saying that Jack the Ripper was merely a misogynist. He has been suspected of performing

127

feats of grand larceny on entire pictures – as cool as Raffles, as bold as Rififi, and, when the spoils have been worth the effort, as brutal as Robespierre. Now, as Le Chiffre, the notorious gambling mastermind of SMERSH, the shadowy, infamous Russian intelligence network, he was to share the pivotal card-game sequence of the film with Peter Sellers.

'We've got to be very careful when Orson arrives, Joe,' Sellers told director Joe McGrath, implying that nothing short of a Red Alert vigilance would do. 'He might try to take over the film.' It was not, clearly, unfounded advice. And Sellers was almost certainly as much concerned for his protégé's welfare as he was for his own survival.

McGrath had never directed a major picture before (although he had worked to brilliant effect with Sellers in television and directed *The Running, Jumping and Standing Still Film,* an Oscar-nominated comedy short produced by Sellers) and might easily be prey to the legendary reputation of Mr Welles, a man of whom it has been said, 'There but for the grace of God goes God'. A view that Mr Welles has never seriously challenged, suspecting, perhaps, that time is on his side.

A small, inoffensive-looking Glasgow-born Scot who could pass for a strap-hanger in the rush hour of life, McGrath was in a supremely uncomfortable position. He was, to begin with, given the film only because Sellers had insisted, and producer Feldman wanted him desperately enough to go along with the star's apparent whim.

The daring of that decision to entrust an entire multi-million-dollar picture to a man who had made nothing more spectacular than a shoestring comedy, however fine that may have been, is to be admired. It nonetheless unsettled McGrath to know that his foundations were embedded in nothing more substantial than one man's whim and another man's ransom. When he invited Feldman to run some of his BBC shows, he was told, 'There's no real point in that, Joe. Sellers has director approval in his contract and he approves of you.'

And now McGrath was faced with his first big challenge

At nineteen in his first Ralph Reader Gang Show

Peg and Bill in later years

Peter at six

As a twelve-year-old

The Ladykillers with (r) director Alexander Mackendrick (1955) (EMI)

Kite, *I'm All Right, Jack* (1959) (EMI)

Carlton-Browne of the F.O. (1958) (EMI)

The Smallest Show on Earth (1957) with Bill Travers (EMI)

The Mouse That Roared
(1959) with (r)
William Hartnell
(COLUMBIA)

Heavens Above! (1963) (EMI)

The Millionairess (1961) with Sophia Loren (20th CENTURY FOX)

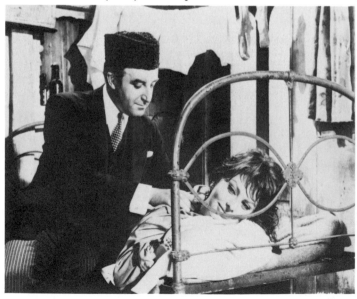

A classic Clouseau pose (UNITED ARTISTS) ▶

With Stanley Kubrick *(Dr Strangelove)* (1964) (COLUMBIA)

With Peter O'Toole *(What's New Pussycat)* (1965)
(UNITED ARTISTS)

The Bobo (1967)
(REX FEATURES)

As Queen Victoria in
The Great McGonagall,
with Spike Milligan
(1974) (REX FEATURES)

The Wrong Box (1966) (EMI)

There's A Girl in My Soup, (1970) with Goldie Hawn
(COLUMBIA)

The Optimist (1973) (SCOTIA BARBER)

Around the world in *Soft Beds, Hard Battles* (1973) (FOX-RANK)

Major Robinson

Gestapo chief Schroeder

Prince Kyoto

General Latour

The original *Picture Post* caption in 1951 said: 'After making good individually, four young comics – Michael Bentine, Harry Secombe, Spike Milligan and Peter Sellers –have got together on a radio programme. In "Crazy People" they put across their favoured kind of fun which they call "goonery". *Picture Post* cameraman, Charles Hewitt, photographs the goons at the Graftons' pub, Victoria, where they have rehearsed for years. (RADIO TIMES HULTON PICTURE LIBRARY)

A reunion special. The last Goon Show (1972). (SYNDICATION INTERNATIONAL)

Brief encounter: Liza Minnelli (1973)
(REX FEATURES)

Sellers v. Kramer
(1980)

With his last wife, Lynne (SYNDICATION INTERNATIONAL)

Chance, *Being There* (1980) (DDA)

Fu Manchu (1980)
with Helen Mirren
(ORION)

in the gentle art of directional diplomacy. On paper, certainly, the teaming of Sellers and Welles looked exciting. But an actor's ego is a time-bomb ticking away. On the studio floor, a no-man's-land between the idea and the screen, McGrath knew the whole idea could blow up very nastily in his face. 'He is going to try to take over the film,' he could hear Sellers' warning like a whining ricochet through his nervous system. 'We must be on our guard, Joe.'

Despite his loyalties to Sellers, his benefactor and friend, he believed it was both foolish and wrong to prejudge the man and the situation. Let Orson get here, he reasoned, and at least have a chance to show his true colours. Yet, sadly, he became increasingly convinced that Sellers had made an inflexible decision: he would not wait until Welles ran up the skull and crossbones.

He was right.

A few days before Welles was due, Sellers informed him that he did not 'think it necessary' to appear on the set with the American actor at all. Welles, he suggested, could play his scenes – mostly across the table from Sellers – on separate days. Technically this was possible and not unknown in a business where, after all, deception is fundamental; but it would create additional problems for McGrath. He would be deprived of an establishing master shot of the two actors together as well as the sharpened spontaneity their mutual presence would bring to the scene. (When an enthusiastic publicist suggested announcing Sellers and Welles as the 'most explosive casting chemistry of 1966' he was dissuaded. 'To get just a spark you have to rub two sticks together. These two characters aren't even going to meet,' he was advised.)

McGrath felt the warning tremors beneath his feet. 'You can't,' he argued, 'make a ten-million-dollar film, the high point of which is a card duel between two men, if those two men never appear together.' Sellers was not very impressed. He insisted the scene would play better if it were paced and intercut in the editing rooms.

What McGrath didn't know then was that apart from

any professional reservations Sellers may have had about the redoubtable Mr Welles as an actor (and the real reason for this seemingly blatant act of hostility is still uncertain), it was probable that he was already seriously disenchanted with him as a man. This feeling may or may not have stemmed from an occasion just prior to shooting when they met at the Dorchester Hotel.

Welles had spent a few days working on his portion of the script with Wolf Mankowitz, the fifth writer to tackle the screenplay – Ben Hecht, Michael Sayers, Terry Southern, and Billy Wilder had worked on the script at some time or another – and they had gone to Sellers' suite to discuss the changes and additional ideas. Both Welles and Mankowitz are very large men; they clearly enjoy the good life. In the words of Mr Mankowitz, this is what happened on the afternoon they visited Sellers.

'Orson and I are huge. Orson really huge and me just my ordinary huge. I suppose our joint displacement on that particular day must have been quite fantastic. Anyway, neither of us had seen Pete for quite a while and when he came sort of popping out like a sparrow, a very tough sparrow, I was astonished.'

He said, 'You've got very thin, Pete,' thinking that perhaps he had been ill again. Sellers, who was perfectly well, did not disguise his distaste for the heavyweight gourmets. 'Anyone,' he told them, 'can get slim if they have discipline.'

Welles and Mankowitz exchanged imprisoned smiles too guilty to leave their eyes. But while Welles may deplore his own Falstaffian vastness, he actually enjoys his gluttony on the principle that 'an awful lot of fun goes into committing it' and 'at least it celebrates some of the good things in life', a view he once set out in a candid *Playboy* interview.

On this occasion, Mankowitz went on, 'we had just had a few dozen oysters and a few odds and sods as a snack in his suite, and we were clearly very well fed. Because I should tell you, when you work with Orson that's the way it is; he has to work with an enormous amount of noshes during the day. And who am I to complain?'

After that meeting, which did not last longer than any of the participants considered strictly necessary, the sated pair left Sellers' suite. Going down in the lift, probably just that much faster than most people go down in lifts, Welles looked hard at himself in the mirror. Turning to his ample companion he grinned and said, 'Who is that skinny bastard anyway, Wolfie? Just another Metrecal actor.'

'I'm afraid,' Mankowitz was ruefully to admit later, 'their relationship never quite got off the ground after that unfortunate incident. I think Pete basically resented Orson's honest girth. Because you've got to understand that Sellers was really a fat man masquerading as a thin one. He must have been under constant strain.'

The strain during the making of *Casino Royale* was undeniably severe and it is appropriate and revealing to look closely at the whole erratic development of that extraordinary production, which more than any other film uncovered the eccentric pressures placed on a star of Peter Sellers' emotional calibre.

It was apparent at least to Joe McGrath that the days of the most extreme crisis would begin with the arrival of George Orson Welles, the man who still threw the awesome shadow of *Citizen Kane* wherever he went. 'Whatever attitude he might decide to adopt, bullying or benign,' reasoned McGrath, 'there had to be trouble.' Another well-placed observer of that scene was to say later, 'Welles couldn't win. He was the rogue elephant, an oversized virtuoso the pygmies either resented or feared. Add to that Sellers' curious reaction, his stubborn absence, and you'll get some idea of what the guy was up against.'

Unbothered by the close climate at the studio and Sellers' distant disapproval, Welles was satisfied to sit on the sidelines. He took an apartment above the Mirabelle, a rich and highly reputable gourmet restaurant in Mayfair. 'I don't at all mind waiting,' he told friends. 'The room-service is excellent.'

After a few days of fitful shooting at Shepperton

studios, naturally complicated by Peter Sellers' promised absenteeism – now sanctioned by Charlie Feldman – McGrath was convinced that Welles had abandoned or otherwise decided against anything more ambitious than petty larceny in a scene or two. 'And with Sellers not there to mind his own shop, who could blame him?' was one view. Otherwise, he was on his best behaviour with not a hint of the vast territorial demands he had been expected to make on the director's vulnerable patch. Perhaps because he was making his own film in Madrid at the time, he was content to shoot his sequence, take the money, and get back to Spain as quickly as possible.

Still, Sellers' attitude remained one of stealthy suspicion; and he was not without supporters. You mustn't trust appearances, he continued to caution McGrath, don't be taken for a ride. Unfortunately, the little Scotsman was finding Welles anything but a threat, and, thrown constantly into his company by the conspicuous absence of his own mentor, he was beginning to fall under the spell of the charming, gregarious, cigar-smoking, ageing *enfant terrible*. (Sellers' non-appearance during this period became so acute that designer Julie Harris had to fit several of his outfits on his stand-in. 'I've never in all my experience had to do that before with any star,' she said.)

'For five days Peter simply didn't turn up while Orson was on the set. So for five days I had to shoot on Orson. If I hadn't it would have been five days with nothing done,' McGrath said later. 'Peter just wasn't around.' Sellers' humour could not have been improved, he added, when Princess Margaret visited the studio immediately after Welles had finished his enforced five-day solo performance, in which he was obliged to fall back rather heavily on his old conjuring skills for something to do. 'They had to think fast,' it has been reported, 'or the picture would simply have ground to a halt.'

Invited to see the rushes before a Dom Perignon and caviar lunch provided by Sellers, she was duly impressed with the singular presence of Welles. Understandably, since her host did not appear at all in the scenes she was shown that day, the lunch talk tended to be centred on the brillance of the American actor.

Welles beamed graciously, especially, some thought, in the direction of Sellers.

'The important thing about that lunch is that it was the exact moment when Peter lost confidence in me,' McGrath calculated afterward.

Yet on the surface, helped by the fact that the set was locked tightly away from the press, all still seemed well. Only a perceptive report in the Paris edition of the New York *Herald Tribune* came close to the truth. 'Mr Sellers,' wrote columnist Mary Blume, 'has never looked better – slim, cool, and elegant enough to make Sean Connery seem straight out of Barney's Boys' Town. His manner is carefully easy; only the flatness of his smile suggests his tension.'

Some indication of the sense of mounting chaos on the picture was the unannounced arrival of Lord Snowdon on the set, 'climbing all over the place and photographing anything that moved'.

Wanting to get on with the film, but hardly knowing how to evict Princess Margaret's husband and Sellers' friend, McGrath telephoned Charles Feldman. 'Did you know that Tony Snowdon was coming today for *The Sunday Times?*' he asked, understandably piqued that he had not been let in on the secret. Feldman said he didn't know anything about it; he thought that Sellers must have arranged it 'privately', because the set was firmly closed to the press, wasn't it? 'Well,' asked McGrath, 'what do you want me to do? I can't shoot with him swarming everywhere. He's got more assistants and equipment than we've got.'

After a long pause that ended with a sigh, Charlie Feldman said, 'Let him take pictures, Joe.'

Certainly by this time Charlie Feldman, a handsome man once described as the boardroom's Clark Gable, was having very serious qualms about gambling so heavily on the inventive genius of Sellers. His decision to play the

133

role straight and 'practically legit just as if he were Sean Connery' was particularly disturbing the producer. He had anticipated and felt he had paid for another chameleon-wrapped cinematic *tour de force* from Sellers.

This was the real heart of the troubles on *Casino Royale*. For while Charlie Feldman felt, perhaps with some justification, that he was being short-changed, Sellers believed he was turning in a performance of considerable daring. That nobody seemed to understand *his* gamble was trying. Indeed, McGrath so misread the situation that later he said he believed that Sellers 'didn't know how to play Tremble' and 'he didn't know what he was going to do with the part'.

But Tremble, the small-time card-sharper hired to impersonate Bond, was simply unvarnished Sellers.

'Sellers tried to play Sellers the way Cary Grant plays Cary Grant, and there was nothing there,' observed one newspaper critic who is also a friend of the family. 'I'm surprised somebody didn't put a stop to it during the production. It was clearly going to be a performance in a paler shade of white.'

There seems little dispute about this now, and it does, at least in part, explain why Sellers was so reluctant to work with Welles. Indeed, it is almost farcically unfair that a man trying for the first time in his career to emerge from behind his protective make-up, bravely shedding all the paint and rubber citadels of his craft, should encounter an antagonist whose mesmeric theatrical presence and almost regal bulk (often creating an air of reigning rather than acting) is sufficient to cramp the style of the most assured performers. And more than that, a man whose immediate ambition, Sellers felt certain, was totally incompatible with his personal well-being on *Casino Royale*.

Long before this telling incident, Peter Sellers always reminded Roy Boulting of the gypsy matador Procuña whom he saw fight in Mexico City. For the first kill he collected two ears and the tail, 'but when the second bull came there was this extraordinary moment. The man and the beast faced each other for a long moment, then

134

Procuña turned and fled, the crowd hooting and jeering. But his gypsy instinct told him this bull was bad for him. I suspect that Sellers had a lot of this gypsy instinct in him. He saw somebody and had an immediate thing – good or bad – and either embraced them . . . or ran the other way.'

It is interesting that one who saw him often felt that because of his fascination for the occult and allied subjects it was 'entirely possible' that Orson Welles' reputedly exceptional clairvoyant powers 'might have been seriously upsetting Peter'. Sellers, he thought, might not have wanted to 'get too close to that particular influence which might have been malevolent and was certainly unfriendly'.

It was McGrath, however, who was the real casualty of the Sellers-Welles skirmish. He left the picture on a Friday night amid a noisy flurry of announcements that his 'segment' of the picture had been completed, and, in accordance with the 'multiple director policy' of the production, Robert Parrish would take over the following Monday.

One man who watched the drama unfold was Douglas Hayward, the London tailor who had been hired to make Sellers' suits for the picture. In early January 1966 he was working on a fitting when the original question of McGrath's appointment was being discussed. Sellers, he recalls, was 'resisting the view' that McGrath was not perhaps experienced enough to cope with a production of the size, cost and complexity of *Casino*. Fade Out.

Fade In. It is now February of the same year and Mr Hayward is working on the final fittings; he has just heard that Joe McGrath is to be replaced by Robert Parrish. 'It's a shame about poor old Joe getting the chop like that,' he says, thinking that some murmured consolation is in order in view of his client's original advocacy in the matter of his appointment. 'Yes,' Sellers answers, 'but he does lack experience in that class of picture.'

Later he wrote to the director, saying he was sorry the film had turned out the way that it had, and hoped they would have the chance to work together again one day. 'I don't know why he was sorry,' McGrath was to say in calmer days, but with a face like a jigsaw puzzle that somebody has forgotten to finish. 'It was obvious he had withdrawn his support. The reason I started the film was because Peter insisted. It must follow that the reason I was dropped was because . . . Peter insisted.'

This looming example of Sellers' ruthlessness is not without at least one ominous precedent before he had achieved the kind of status that makes suspect the motives of such defensive axe-wielding. 'There is no person I know that Peter would not sacrifice if he felt this a professional obligation,' said director Roy Boulting after *Carlton-Browne of the F O* (in which Sellers played a Machiavellian prime minister of a British banana colony) in 1959. 'There is nothing I know about Sellers that suggests he has ever had any great concern for people.' This harsh judgement was confirmed, he believed, two years later, when the actor unsuccessfully attempted to enlist John Boulting's influence in having Virginia Maskell removed from *Only Two Can Play*.

She was cast as his wife, and Sellers genuinely, deeply, felt that she was 'totally bloody wrong' for the role; he implored John Boulting to persuade Sidney Gilliat, who was to direct the picture for British Lion, a company they both were directors of, to replace her. Boulting refused.

Unaware of the moves to fire her, she gave a fine performance and collected excellent reviews. When she died at the age of thirty-one in January 1968, the London *Times* obituary notice particularly commented on that role as 'a moving and convincing performance as a young wife trapped by domestic drudgery'.

Sellers was so distressed by the final picture, however, that he sold his ten per cent interest to British Lion for less than £20,000. The sale, against the advice of the Boultings, demonstrated the depth of his despair. Up to 1967, the purchased percentage had earned the film company an estimated £89,000. Sellers never mentioned it again.

Sellers was not unaware of the unfriendly and implacable impression he created with these arbitrary acts. 'I know,' he once said, 'I have a reputation for being a shit, but it's a reputation mostly put about by those mediocre people who will always resent and try to cut down a man's talent. It's like Spike Milligan says, and God knows he's right, the world is full up with mediocrity and you find it everywhere, and when you brush with it you brush up venom.'

'He was ruthless, absolutely ruthless, as all great artists are, I suppose,' insisted Roy Boulting. 'Behind that soft exterior he had an obsessional impulse to get his way. He was a child in that sense.' John Boulting, closer than his brother to Sellers, agrees, but with a reservation that sheds light perhaps on Joe McGrath's swift downfall after his openly expressed admiration for Orson Welles. 'If it served Peter's purpose,' he says, 'he would be very unkind to me. But I say this – he would have had to persuade himself that I was a bastard before he would have performed a single act of disservice, of that I have no doubt at all. He would have needed to convince himself that I was an absolute shit – which I possibly am.'

There is enough circumstantial evidence at least to suppose that Sellers had convinced himself that Joe McGrath had failed him, and even in his liaison with Welles been disloyal; he was therefore no longer a contributory force, at least on *Casino Royale*.

That's What Life Is All About

CASINO ROYALE WAS finally premièred in London in April 1967, in aid of the 'hurt minds can be healed' mental health campaign, and was massacred by the critics. Peter Sellers did not attend the royal occasion 'in the presence of Her Royal Highness Princess Alexandra' and 'just about every star, socialite, and celebrity' in town. The following morning I flew to Monte Carlo, where Sellers was putting his new yacht *Bobo* through her sea trials in the Mediterranean. I had taken all the reviews from London, as he had asked, but by the time I arrived he knew the worst. His secretary, roused before breakfast, had read them to him over the telephone.

'How's Charlie taken it?' he asked.

Feldman, I told him, was pretty upset.

There was no love lost between them by the time they came to the end of the picture – indeed, Sellers never actually completed his role, a fact not quite disguised even by ingenious editing. (In the late extra editions of the London *Evening Standard* of 15th April, 1966, it was reported that Sellers' connection with the picture 'has ended without his part being completed'. When his contract expired, he was quoted: 'I was approached by the producer and asked if I would be prepared to continue and make what they called "a gesture". I was naturally anxious to see my part finished, as I have helped to write it and will be getting an author's screen credit. [He didn't.] So I told them, "All right, but we've got to get on with it." We were about to begin one week's extra work when they decided not to continue. It's all very strange . . . a gigantic puzzle, the whole film.') But he seemed genuinely concerned for the producer.

'This could kill him,' he said. 'A man like Charlie could

die after this, just to punish the world: "See what you've done to me? Now aren't you sorry?" I mean it. It's on the cards, man.' It was, alas, a most prophetic remark. Feldman, deeply hurt by reviews that had so scathingly diminished some two years of his life, never made another film and died almost exactly one year later in California.

It was late in the afternoon when Sellers finished showing me over the £100,000 boat. He was pleased and excited about his new possession; but there was something disturbing him. When we returned to the Hotel de Paris that day he telephoned Feldman in London. 'The notices are rough, Charlie,' he said, 'but so were a lot of *Pussycat's. Casino* could still surprise everybody.'

Sellers, oddly, was perhaps the one man in the world who could have consoled Feldman on that day of judgment. He had to swallow his pride to do it and he did. 'At the end of *Pussycat,*' a mutual friend was to say later, 'Charlie gave Sellers a Rolls. At the end of *Casino,* Sellers gave Charlie a kind word. They're square now.'

The following day, in that spring of 1967, the *Bobo* anchored off a small island not far from Cannes and, while Britt sunbathed on deck, we took the motor-boat and her Yorkshire terrier called Fred to the island. Sellers now had three consecutive tough films behind him: *After the Fox,* the notorious *Casino Royale,* and the troublesome but, he hoped, more rewarding *The Bobo.* He was convinced that he had finally embarked on his most productive decade; the important years had begun.

'The next ten years,' he said, 'will see the fruition of all my hopes. It's going to be a very exciting time, no more crap, nothing but what I really want to do.'

It was the first time I had heard him talk about the long-range future with so much genuine anticipation; and I wondered if he was finally learning to jettison the past. The tension had left his body and his face; he was looking fit, having put on six pounds and maybe more during the weeks he had spent on holiday in a small hotel near Arosa in Switzerland, recommended by Sophia Loren, who had surprisingly survived his first passion and become an understanding friend. He talked, often almost desultorily, about the peculiar trials and tribulations of the past few pictures, about his own highly developed self-protective instincts. Words do not come easily to Peter Sellers, except in real anger. Now he was not angry but forlornly puzzled.

'If you want to be known as a sweet guy, a lovely fella, never a hard word all day, arrives on the set on the dot and gets on with his job, does as he is told and goes home smiling polite good-nights to everyone, and have people say, "there goes Peter Sellers, sure he's all right as an actor – but what a sweet, lovely, gentle human being", fine, you know, if you want that, it's easy.

'You abdicate your responsibilities as an actor. I want to be something more than an "all right" actor. So I have to protect myself – from the vultures, from the morons, from the mediocre. Especially the mediocre. I know what's best for me. I do. And on that level, sure, I'm difficult. You bet I'm difficult.'

It was a long speech for Sellers. We walked on for a long time in silence after that. The sun was well up and hot. The paths were rough.

During such times one wondered about his heart, but he never seemed to give it a thought, occasionally scrambling and sliding off the track to crouch perilously on some rock-face to study an angle for a photograph. 'I'm a different fellow on the studio floor,' he said, returning to his self-exploratory theme as if there had been no inter-ruption at all. 'I'm a very quiet chap in private life, as you know, but when I'm working I'm a different cup of tea. Ruthless, yes. Ruthless. You have to be. No, not with fellow actors – unless they shouldn't be in the business anyway. I believe if you're in this overcrowded profession you should be fully equipped to cope and if you're not . . .' He lifted his eyebrows and shoulders and turned down the corners of his mouth; then his eyebrows and shoulders fell with the final condemnation of a guillotine blade. 'You must be ruthless just to survive. If I had a brother I would not use him in one of my pictures if he were wrong or incapable. I owe that much to myself. That's sense, isn't it? That's what life is all about – survival.'

It was a theme that Britt Ekland Sellers knew well. During the planning months of *The Bobo* she had been more than maritally close to Sellers, sharing his worries over the script, casting, locations. At that time he was going to direct the picture (although he had passionately vowed never to direct and star in another picture after the cool response to *Mr Topaze* in 1961) and was more than usually caught up in the preproduction vortex of a major film.

The greatest problem at that time was to find an actress to play Olimpia, a part that on paper at least was even larger than Sellers' own role. 'I didn't dream of playing Olimpia myself,' she has recalled. 'I was working steadily, doing a picture with Yul Brynner, and there was talk of a picture with Frank Sinatra to follow. I was very happy with the way things were going for me.'

On a Saturday morning towards the end of July 1966, after she had dutifully exhausted all her suggestions of actresses who might play the role, she was in the bath at their home in Elstead when Sellers walked in. For a long time he simply stared at her. At first she was pleased, even flattered, at her husband's interest. But too prolonged speculation, even by a husband, can finally unnerve the most sophisticated woman. 'I got mad. He wouldn't say a word, wouldn't answer my questions. I was upset because somehow, after a while, it was a horrible thing to be submitted to. I mean, if you have a man staring at you for such a long time without saying a single word and not listening to a word you are saying . . . it is not very polite.' She asked him to leave.

Later that morning he told her, 'You've got it.'

'Got what, for God's sake?'

'You're going to play Olimpia,' he said, adding that he had talked to the producer Elliot Kastner and it was all fixed.

'Elliot really wants me?' she asked.

'Yes.'

'But do *you* want me, Sellers?' she asked seriously.

'Yes,' he answered.

Within a week she left to complete the location-work for her film in Spain, feeling she had the world on a string, and not at all suspicious that perhaps the string was connected to her neck.

It was almost a month before they met again, and Sellers immediately informed her that he no longer wanted her in the picture.

'Okay,' she told him, making an effort to keep her voice and emotions on a straight course, 'I have other things to do.'

It was a sickening moment for her. 'I knew I had just lost the part of my life,' she told me later. 'But I knew Sellers too well to argue or to kick. I knew I had to play it cool.'

At seven o'clock the following morning, a favourite time for telephone calls, Sellers called producer Elliot Kastner and told him, 'She's out.' Kastner was shocked, and any resilience he might have had was hard to muster at that hour of the morning. Anyway, there was not a great deal he could do about it at any hour. Sellers had leading-lady approval in his contract and that applied no less when the leading lady happened to be his wife. Kastner called Britt and assured her he personally felt she was the best actress for the part and would resist her removal 'tooth and nail'. But, he warned her, don't be too hopeful because Sellers 'sounds damned determined that you should go'.

Meanwhile, her agent was growing uncomfortable; repeatedly she was asked whether she really believed she could cope with a role that size opposite an actor like her husband. 'If you don't feel ready for it,' she was told, 'it would do more harm than good to get it.'

'I'm ready,' she insisted, thinking, 'I really don't think I am. I don't know how I can possibly do this, but I must have the chance. I must con them into backing me.'

After a week they were no closer to finding a replacement for her, and her agent believed she would be offered the part again. Again she was warned of the possible consequences if Sellers felt his arm was being twisted. 'He may finally have to agree to take you,' she was told, 'but he could hate you for it.'

There was nothing anybody could tell her that she hadn't figured out for herself. 'I want that part,' she insisted, feeling 'pretty damned scared inside'.

Some weeks later she was told the part was hers again. But then a distinct chill began to seep into the marriage. 'From the outside looking in,' observed one associate close to them both, 'it looked cosy enough – except that there was frost on the windows.'

Said Britt, 'Sellers knew inside himself that he didn't want anybody but me. But he was furious with me just the same.'

As the starting date for the picture grew nearer Sellers grew more and more restless, the agitation propelling him around the apartment, around the block, around London, his face as friendly as a clenched fist.

Apart from anything else at that time, he was certainly deeply worried about finding the key to the role of Juan Bautista, the matador; the voice was still eluding him, and without the voice Sellers knew he had nothing.

'He started to talk about a separation,' Britt recalled in a happier time, but not quite hiding the old hurt. Scar tissues never tan. 'Then he left and went to Rome. Well, I was stuck in London feeling very ill and miserable. I had throat and nose and everything you want. I was in bed and the doctor came and gave me injections every day.'

Within a few days, shot through with penicillin and concentrated vitamin boosts, she was feeling considerably more lively than she should have felt. She decided the time for a showdown had come. At eleven o'clock on a Friday evening, three days before she was due to fly to Rome to start the picture, she telephoned London Airport and enquired about the next flight to that city.

'There is an all-tourist flight at three o'clock in the morning, madam,' she was told.

'Book me on that,' she said.

She got out of bed and drove herself to the airport in her Mercedes 230 SL. She arrived in Rome shortly before seven o'clock and took a taxi to Sellers' villa on the Appian Way.

It was Saturday, a 'beautiful morning', she later recalled. A fine mist stretched across the still-pale sun and the town seemed rinsed in a light the colour and warmth of iced sapphires. The villa looked 'as if it were sleeping and had been for a hundred years'. It was not to sleep for much longer. She rang the bell and, for good measure, beat the door with her bare hands.

The cook answered it.

'I'm Mrs Sellers,' Britt announced rather imperiously. 'Where is my husband? Which is his room, please?' The cook pointed out the fastest route to Signor Sellers' boudoir. Britt stormed in.

It was an anticlimax. Sellers was fast asleep. She watched him for a full minute, feeling the heat leaving her temper. When he finally woke she demanded, 'Well, Sellers?' uncorking a glower she knew had not travelled well. 'What do you really want? What is it all about? You can throw me out if you wish. But I must tell you I have no more taxi money and you will have to take me to the airport. But if you throw me out now I shall return to Rome in two days' time, I will stay at the Excelsior, and I will make this film with you and that is that.'

She had rehearsed that speech very carefully all the way from London, in her car to the airport, in the plane across the English Channel and high over Europe, in the taxi through the deserted streets of dawning Rome, and now that it was delivered she felt lost, bereft, even a little sheepish. What now? There was no follow-through and she could only wait for him to react. Would he yell at her? Be violent? Throw her out? Would he, perhaps – and this she feared most – retreat even deeper into his isolation?

'What's the bloody time?' he asked, finally, his voice grumpy with shattered sleep.

It was a ludicrous scene, and both appreciated the

humour of it. 'In a minute we were both giggling, then it was all sort of – mmm – cuddles and everything. We had breakfast, and I lay in the sun by the pool all day. It was lovely. Sellers didn't want me to return to London at all; but I had to go back to complete the dubbing on my picture.'

She returned finally early Monday morning and was back in Rome that night. Later she was to regard that flight to Rome as an important development in their love affair and also in the more basic foundation of their marriage. 'It was one of the things one has to be prepared to do with Sellers. I was lucky to have discovered it then,' she has reflected.

But it was a calculated gamble at a critical time, and does not fully answer the question why he had turned against her in the first place. Britt at least believes she knows. 'He got nervous. He panicked. It was a big part and he knew that if I failed, if I were bad, the whole film would suffer and perhaps fail. He didn't want to take that risk, especially not with me.'

There are less charitable interpretations of his quixotic behaviour at that time. 'But,' said one associate, 'it took more courage for him to blow her out than just let her walk into the part without a murmur. At least he raised the questions in people's minds, he made them think twice, and that was essential because, let's face it, nepotism begins at home. If she had just waltzed into that part and been lousy, people would have been damn quick to point the finger at him.' Moreover, Sellers must have been somewhat disquieted by a palm-reading by the cook, Assunta, in which she saw a third marriage in his future. When the production office discovered they had hired a clairvoyant cook for Sellers, whose belief in such things was no secret, the consternation was deep. Judy Goodman presented Assunta with the strictest instructions: she was not permitted to predict more children, sickness of any kind, unexpected travel, arguments and emotional disturbances or domestic mishaps. She was also asked to be 'particularly positive' about the happier aspects of the future. Meanwhile, the picture underwent several extensive script changes as well as the usual spontaneous studio developments, and finally there was rather less to be seen of Britt Ekland than was originally intended. The critics, however, found her performance 'fresh' and 'professional' and 'promising'. But it still wasn't the picture Peter Sellers expected it to be, the one to mark the start of his auspicious decade.

Peg

WHEN PETER SELLERS was moving precariously in and out of those unremembered mansions of death in California, Peg Sellers grieved guiltily in London, fearful that perhaps the side effects of her transplanted ambition had finally been too severe for her son. It was one of the rare occasions when she came near to revealing her concern – a concern that grew in proportion to his swelling success – at the force she had unleashed in her only child.

'Peter works too hard,' she told a reporter in what for her was a most untypical, semi-emotional outburst. 'But I can't stop him. He's only really completely happy when he is working.'

But more and more during her last years she suspected the realisation of one's dreams can be the beginning of sadness, and she shared uncomplainingly and unstintingly in what Spike Milligan was later to call 'the sorrow of his success'.

'The fine days,' she said, 'are very fine. But oh the other days, the bad days, they are very bad . . . poor Peter, people don't understand. I don't think that even Peter really understands.'

On the bad days, surely, Peg felt as culpable and dispirited as she felt justified and elated on the good days. For she never failed to acknowledge that however unwittingly, for better or for worse, she had brought his present life about.

Whenever he wavered, and he did, she was there to assure him that all would be well, boychik. Restlessly she schemed and plotted and pushed, developing as she went along the great influence on her son that he was not to break free from until well into his manhood and perhaps not even then.

147

During the making of *I'm All Right, Jack,* director John Boulting, who had become deeply fascinated by the complex actor, invited his father and the indomitable Peg to lunch.

'It was,' he recalled afterwards, 'a most startling and illuminating occasion. It was as if everything were being unscrambled and neatly packed into place for me. I suddenly thought: "My God, this explains everything, this is the complete answer to Sellers, it's so bloody simple." And it is.'

Bill Sellers, who had grown into a quietly graceful grey-haired man with sadly amused eyes, impressed the director as 'a most sweet, gentle, and engaging man, and probably fighting shyness'. He still carried occasional traces of a Bradfordian accent in his voice. He played the role of junior partner without fear and without apparent resentment, accepting Peg's bravura behaviour with mild humour, even affection.

Like sponge-covered granite, she seemed to have 'a hard masculine toughness' below the more obvious surface of her femininity, Boulting suspected. She looked, observed one acquaintance with admiration on another occasion, like a butterfly and worked like a bulldozer.

That Sellers was the complete amalgam of these two radically opposite people is unquestionable. On the day that John Boulting had contrived his enlightening lunch he was to tell his brother, Roy: 'I think I've come a long way on the road to understanding the fiendish Sellers today. His utter ruthlessness – that quality in him which says, "To hell with everybody, I'm going to be a success and nobody is going to get in my way" – comes straight from Peg.'

'And from his father he gets what?' asked Roy Boulting, who unlike his brother is sceptically inclined to believe there was little else in Sellers' character to mitigate the bile of this maternal inheritance.

'From his father he gets that rather kind and passive quality,' John Boulting told him, undeterred by his brother's cynicism. 'And these two extremes are constantly warring in him.

148

'I think this is the root cause of his agony today. These two people are there in him, so much a part of his make-up as a man, and they are quite totally incompatible.'

Roy Boulting was not impressed then and, he insists, has discovered nothing since about Peter Sellers to make him change his mind.

'In a way,' John Boulting said, 'Peter was a refugee from his mother. It might have hurt him to realise that because he was so close to her, but that is what it was all about in my opinion.'

That Sellers was deeply influenced and impressed by his mother was perhaps underlined in a revealing fragment of interview given between marriages: 'My problem,' he told a journalist with unknowing candour, 'is that as a child I think I was influenced by too many Mrs Miniver pictures. You know the sort of thing: ideal wife, loyal, devoted, mother enough to make you take your pills each day . . .'

Could it have been that 'Mrs Miniver', complete with that interesting hint of disparagement, was really a subconscious substitute for his own sometimes embarrassingly possessive parent? It is almost certain the answer is yes.

But if Peg were the kitchen architect of her son's ambition, was her motive pure, noble maternalism? Was it really the Ray 'family tradition' she felt so strong a need to continue through her son, or something less altruistic? Was there, perhaps, a darker shade of reason?

If the latter, and again the answer almost certainly must be in the affirmative, it was a most forgivable human design. He was, after all, quite clearly her last chance and her only chance to enjoy vicariously the kind of fame and success in the theatre that she herself had smelled but not tasted. She strongly believed it was her own deep frustration that fuelled the aspirations of her son and so he became, with his success, the cherished embodiment of all her dearest wishes, all her desperate needs.

Peg's one constant fear during the formative years, when he was idolised and protected with something more than maternal affection and sometimes less than pure unselfishness, was that too much of her husband's un-aggressive, contented, and gentle nature would surface in her son, an anaemic transfusion to dilute the rich blood of her own gift of ambition.

So, although he was not to know it for a long time, his future was set fast before the ink was dry on his birth certificate, which names him Richard Henry, but not, strangely, Peter.

In 1967, when she was seventy-two and only a few weeks away from her own death from a heart attack at the Royal Northern Hospital in Holloway, North London, she was to tell me: 'I know that some people, some relatives even, have accused me of spoiling him. But I don't think I went further than most mothers who have the kind of premonition I had about my son's future. I knew, you see, that his destiny was exceptional . . . so I took exceptional care.'

The vivacious soubrette of the Roaring Twenties, the girl in the scarlet Ford, was now a trim, grandmotherly lady with a calm outwardness that had grown markedly since the electrifying ambition she had carried for her child had been fused by his fame. To meet her in her fading years was rather like looking into a superb shop-window display with all the lights switched off. They came on, in short flashing moments, a brightness that lit up a long-dark corner of her youthful vitality, when the talk turned to Sellers and sometimes to her beloved grandchildren. But always those lights grew pale again until only her own shadows were left.

The achievement of his success had been as demanding on Peg as it had been on her son. But for him there was the bright, rallying, regenerating challenge of new channels to explore, new roles to play, new fights to fight; for her the work was done, his success had obliterated a very large part of her reason for going on.

She became an onlooker, cared for and protected, spoiled by her son as she had once spoiled him. But now, she believed with occasional crankiness, she had no active purpose in his crowded life. How true that was and how

150

much was the product of an old woman's fearful imagination and rejection fantasies is uncertain.

She was taken to Rome and New York, flown to the sun for the finest holidays that a grateful son could buy. On one occasion he even sent his secretary Hattie Stevenson from New York to London simply to keep her company on the flight – insisting that she turn straight round at London Airport because, explained the hardy Miss Stevenson in the calm of her resignation, 'he needed a friendly face' in the alien world of New York.

But could Peg Sellers' industrious and purposeful indulgence of her son have had a more extreme influence than she ever intended, knew or even dreamed of?

Shortly after the war, when he was more than occasionally short of the rent money, Spike Milligan was a guest at their flat in north west London. And it was here that he began to formulate a bizarre but compulsive theory that he finds more credible as the years pass.

He noticed with concealed disapproval that there was practically nothing that Sellers asked for that Peg did not eagerly provide. 'From the moment his eyes were open in the morning until they closed again at night, he'd be calling to Peg for something: a cup of tea, his slippers, the newspaper, dinner, a drink . . . and Peg would always loyally deliver.'

His father, thought Milligan, seemed surplus to his needs, 'relegated not to a place of lesser love but to secondary importance'. When Sellers went on tour he telephoned his mother almost every day. The conversations were long, chatty, close. 'He would talk to her for perhaps an hour at a time,' recalls Milligan, adding reproachfully, 'It is unhealthy for a grown man to be so needful of his mother.'

It was this extraordinary proximity, this unusually strong bond between mother and son, that Milligan believes succeeded in destroying Sellers' own personality:

'I think she had gained such an incredible influence over him that he virtually abdicated his own rights to any individual personality. He just couldn't register on his

151

own, without Peg. Finally, he had to invade other bodies to register at all. He had to inhabit, he was like a ghoul, he had to feast off somebody else! But he did it so well, it became an art. He was not a genius, Sellers, he was a freak.

'There was nothing worthwhile that he could do on his own,' he has also claimed without malice. 'He was a charming man, but I don't think anybody would have given him a job for that. So he requisitioned these bodies, any body, any sound, any voice . . . Cary Grant, he could even look like Cary Grant. It was a freak gift and he was the only man in the world who could do it and consequently he was a very rare product.'

There is an element of wild reason in Spike Milligan's theory: a satanic, tantalising kind of logic. But if his bizarre postulation is true it is certain that Peg went to her deathbed not knowing the consequences of her permissive power. Yet, strangely, despite his deep and troubled affection for Sellers, Milligan never attempted to free him from the seductive prison of this extramural womb; indeed, to his own astonishment, he found himself often in the role of jailer: securing and contributing to Sellers' pampered existence.

But time helps a man to rationalise even his most irrational acts and Spike Milligan explains now: 'The fact is, I suppose, Peter could look more vulnerable, more helpless, than anyone. He needed help, or convinced you he did. He was a man-child. And he always accepted that you would help, that you would not hesitate to do his bidding. It was his birthright.

'So he would say to me, "Spike, run downstairs and turn off the lights on my car. I forgot." And I would do it, you see. Because he needed it – like a fix.'

But without his mother's curious influence, would Peter Sellers really have become a stronger personality? Without the maternal pampering would he have grown up into a more explicit, absolute, distinct, and pronounced human being? And, if so, what then?

'If that happened, you know, his talents might have

been deviated into an entirely different form,' answers Milligan. 'Perhaps the old lady was right, because whatever route they travelled together the journey was wondrously worthwhile.

'His success was extraordinary in that it took almost a catastrophic pattern of circumstances to bring it about. I don't think the likes of it will be seen again for perhaps . . . well, I don't think ever again.'

Sellers was filming *The Bobo* in Rome when he heard of his mother's death in London. His immediate reaction astonished those around him, who expected a severe emotional collapse. Instead, according to one close associate, 'he withdrew deep inside himself', not even telling the loyal and trusted Bert Mortimer for several hours. That the valet remained totally unconscious of the situation is perhaps indicative of how tight Sellers held the reins on his feelings.

When Hattie Stevenson telephoned from London and learned that Bert was unaware of Peg's death, she presumed, not unreasonably, that Sellers was similarly uninformed. Overwhelmed by the burden of the news she had to bring him, she began to cry when he came to the telephone.

'Yes, I know, Hattie,' was all he said.

Peg had suffered a coronary a week earlier and, despite director Robert Parrish's pleas that he should fly back to London immediately, Sellers insisted on staying in Rome.

'She's going to be fine,' he said. 'I know everything about heart attacks, don't forget, Bob. I'm the expert.'

'Sure you know about *your* heart attack, but you don't know about *her* heart attack. She's an old lady, Pete. I think you should go back,' said Parrish, surprised at the actor's apparent emotional entombment towards his mother's crisis.

Sellers was adamant. He said, 'I've talked to the doctors at the hospital and I'm quite certain she is going to be fine.' It was little use arguing. The relationship between the two men, once close, had deteriorated anyway by this time to one of only partly concealed hostility, and the situation had not been helped by the actor's demand – 'It came with the same swift unfriendly surprise as Pearl Harbor,' commented Parrish later – for director's credit on the picture.

(Sellers had originally planned to direct *The Bobo* himself, but bowed out at the final moment, believing the dual effort of starring and directing would be too arduous: he had, however, continued to work closely alongside Parrish throughout the production.)

'But I look at you right now and tell you that you could not help but have total compassion for this man during that week his mother lay ill in London,' said Parrish. 'He was determined to finish the film, but clearly the strain was enormous. Deep down I believe it was weighing heavily on him, not going to see her.'

His sympathy and concern for Sellers during this cruel crisis, despite their overheated professional relationship, is not untypical of the manner in which people reacted to Peter Sellers; it is an interesting phenomenon in a business usually too narcissistic to notice the losers.

'One's feelings toward him in a situation like that were quite different from what one's feelings would be toward any other antagonist. He had this locked-in, vulnerable, little-boy-lost quality and your heart went racing out to him. I mean *racing*.'

It is a strange but far from a lonely echo of Spike Milligan's words. 'Yet you were not fooled,' Parrish says, without rancour and perhaps even a touch of wry martini humour. 'You still knew that the next day you could easily receive a letter from him that began, "Dear Bob: Please never speak to me again", or "I don't like your kids", or "Why do you drive that kind of car? I hate you for it."

'He was a man you could not anticipate with intelligence because there was no intelligent patter, no apparent reason, no visible cause.'

There were no paths for Sellers, I remembered one ex-colleague of his once telling me, and no paths away 'except a long slippery slope'.

The moment Parrish heard the news of Peg's death he

telephoned the actor at his villa. It was a Monday morning. 'You were right, Bob,' Sellers told him. 'I should have gone.'

'How do you feel?' Parrish asked.

'I don't feel too well,' Sellers said, his sorrow now giving his voice an age and a sound that the director had never heard there before. 'I'm going to get on a plane as soon as I can and go to London.'

It is interesting to reflect that while he could physically diguise his anguish from someone as close and involved as Bert Mortimer, he could not keep the dejection and withering sadness out of his voice.

He behaved, says one associate, with 'enormous dignity', but the shock waves below the surface were registering hard on the seismograph of grief. He did not break down, in fact, until after the funeral service, when he met Spike Milligan. 'I'm sorry, Spike,' he told his old friend, 'but seeing you, I didn't expect you'd be here, and seeing you . . . brought back so many memories. I would have been fine but for the memories.'

Sellers' resolute refusal to return to London when his mother was so ill is a mystery that perhaps not even he was able to explain satisfactorily. It may have been, quite simply, that he could not bring himself to acknowledge that she was in any real danger; and certainly he had been in a far more critical condition in Hollywood. Perhaps he allowed his concern for the already late production schedule to mar his judgment: he was under severe professional stress at that time, steadily warring with director Parrish and the producers, and greatly concerned with Britt's performance in the film.

But there is one theory that carried much support then: in not flying to his mother's sickbed he was making a final, perhaps unconscious bid to stand alone.

The Boulting brothers, who worked more closely and frequently with Sellers than any other film makers, believe that basically he hated Peg. (That he never called her Mum, always Peg, was a fact that at least one of his Hollywood analysts spent a great deal of time probing.)

'He was always quoting and citing Peg as the ideal woman', says Roy Boulting. 'He was trying to convince himself. I am absolutely certain from the things he told me that he was burdened by this guilt . . . that this woman he should have loved, professed to love, his mother, he genuinely hated.'

Says John Boulting: 'He hated her for burdening him with an ambition that he found intolerable. Peg was an avaricious creature, constantly pushing him, goading him, a relentless creature. As a child he had watched his parents 'die' on stage over and over again. He was determined not to let it happen to him . . . perhaps it was a kind of revenge he sought on their behalf. And that revenge was the whole motivation throughout his career.'

Yet the Boultings have a kind of sympathy for Peg.

'It is very hard for an actress who has had to hustle for work all her life to stop hustling. She had this compulsion to sell Bill, herself, and most of all Peter. It never left her, the hustling instinct. Long after Peter was a star, a rich man, she was still out there hustling for him, selling him to someone or other. Whenever she went into action . . . you could see Peter *squirming*. It made him very unhappy.'

A writer who knew Sellers well was with him in Rome as Peg lay dying in London. 'For an entire week he was steeling himself for her death. But I shall never believe for a single moment that it was a cruel, cold-hearted act of indifference.'

Agreed another, 'It had to be that way, as he saw it, and it took a lot of guts. He loved her too much to let her see just how much he still needed her. You won't understand . . . unless you happen to be acquainted with that particular relationship. And if you are, you'll know it was the only logical conclusion.'

If the Oedipal overtones are obvious, they are nonetheless theoretically valid. 'Peg understood the score perfectly,' believes one subscriber to this view. 'Every day Peter Sellers wasn't at his mother's bedside was a day of triumph – for them both.' If you accept this reasoning, then you must accept too that his puzzling absence was really the final agonising conquest of man over mater-familias.

Time Out For a Commercial

AT THE END of shooting on *The Bobo*, Peter Sellers said he wanted to give 'the boys on the unit something nice'. His secretary Judy Goodman, although an occasional beneficiary of his generosity, was surprised; by this time he was not about to win any popularity contests with the unit. ('If Sellers had ever asked me to work for him again,' said one member of the British camera team, 'I would have joined a very long queue for the simple privilege of telling him to get stuffed.') He decided that lighters would be an appropriate gift, and some forty Dupont gas lighters were purchased, each one expensively engraved with the appropriate initials. But when Miss Goodman showed him a sample the day before they were to be handed out, 'he went mad'. The engraving, he said, was 'disgusting'.

'Have it changed,' he told her.

'But you can't alter *engraved* initials,' she pointed out.

Sellers would not budge. Finally the jeweller made forty small gold plaques to put on the offending initials and these were duly re-engraved with lettering carefully approved by Sellers.

It was a revealing incident.

Most comics are notoriously stingy and incapable of cultivating the more manorial tastes that normally go with success in other branches of show business. A comic's largesse is a stage illusion; the last of the bigtime savers will be a very frightened clown. One day somebody will make a study of this strange penny-pinching phenomenon among the world's funnymen, and when they do they will find that Sellers is worth a thesis to himself. Not because he represented the norm, but because he was the exception.

'He would have given his right arm away,' says his

former agent Selinger, who for many years had the difficult task of curbing this tendency to dismember himself. Yet he had always maintained the comic's natural suspicion that life is just a bowl of cherrystones, and it was this only partly suppressed instinctive fear that drove him in the middle of a film (for which he was paid £310,000 plus ten per cent of the gross) to make a fast-buck television commercial. The top fee for providing a voice for a one-minute spot was unlikely to exceed £1,250 even for Peter Sellers. A millionaire, he did not find this at all incongruous.

'You've got to remember that five hundred quid is a lot of money, a lot of loot. It's what I call real money,' he explained. 'I don't think about $750,000 – that's too unreal for me, you can't count that kind of money, you can't hold it. It's just big business, a bank transaction, an exchange of signatures between corporations. But if I've got five hundred quid in my pocket . . . I'm a rich man, dad.'

The money, then, was an unabashed incentive; but it was not merely the mercenary considerations that drove Peter Sellers into the golden arms of advertising. For it was only here that he could again work, as he did in his early, happy radio days, solely with his voice. 'There is,' he said, 'still an enormous excitement about that.' In England, he supplied voices for an Omo washing powder advertisement, vocalised for the chimpanzees in the Brooke Bond Dividend tea commercials, and supplied the suave, upper-class dog's voice in a Kennomeat dog food cartoon.

But all his fine thespian genius was defeated by a canary. Trill, a company manufacturing birdseed, wanted a voice that sounded human *and* birdlike *and* funny without upsetting bird-lovers, who are, it seems, an excessively sensitive breed. Finally stumped, he suggested that Spike Milligan might 'do the trick'. At one stage the willing and imaginative Milligan rigged up a perchlike device, and holding his nose while swinging upside down, tried talking through a megaphone. It was a daring failure. 'The voice just couldn't be found,' said Sellers with amusement and regret and frustration in his voice.

Such happy excursions for birdseed and peanuts did not always endear Sellers to the more cynical citizens of the film industry; he was sometimes suspected of avarice. Others saw these supreme efforts for so little return as the involuntary reaction of 'the uncertain small-time comic inside the confident big-time actor'.

There was no discernibly regular pattern on which to judge his motives. When a London advertising agency had to launch a new Gillette razor blade they invited a man they knew to be very close to Sellers to persuade him to lend his name to the campaign. Actual endorsement of the blade itself would be cunningly avoided; they simply wanted him to 'say what he believes has that indefinable something called "style" '. It was privately estimated that Sellers would ask for 'anything between £5,000 and £10,000', and presumably a similar sum would be available.

Sellers liked the idea and agreed to do it – for nothing. A few days later he produced his list of stylish things:

My wife
A red Lamborghini Miura
El Cordobes
Private Eye Magazine
Habit Rouge de Guerlain
Leicaflex and Summicron-R f/2 50 mm
Elmarit-R f/2·8 35 mm Elmarit-R 2·8 90 mm
The music of Antonio Carlos Jobim
A Baglietto 18 m motor-yacht
The Daily Mirror
Hi-Fi
Vodka
Shakespeare
Sid Perelman
Roast beef and Yorkshire pudding
Italian shoes
Some Chinese food
Fred

The agency executives were understandly delighted; the list became possibly the most notable, certainly the best-remembered, in the impressive campaign, and Sellers was again pressed to accept some remuneration. After a while he said he would like 'some Swedish china' from Thomas Goode, the distinguished china and glass specialists in Mayfair. It was happily agreed; the total cost of his contribution was finally not more than £600, still a long way below his real market value.

Not long after this episode, the man who had been instrumental in fixing the Gillette deal found himself temporarily hard-pressed for money. He asked Sellers for 'a loan, a small sum by his standards'. Sellers replied that he had every sympathy – but was unable to help. 'I was genuinely astonished. I mean, only a few weeks earlier he had shown such a complete disregard for money, and here he was behaving like a double-eyed Scrooge,' he lamented. Not long after this refusal, Sellers sent him a gift worth more than £800.

It was this extraordinary inconsistency in his make-up that could both anger and amuse those around him. His gifts to friends and colleagues could often be embarrassingly generous (but not always too apt: 'he had an uncanny knack of stampeding your life with unexpected herds of white elephants', said one wary recipient), yet he had resisted the temptation to become a well-known charity benefactor or celebrated patron of the poor. Perhaps as an unconscious concession to the parsimonious traditions of his craft his public gifts were inclined toward the modest, even frugal.

Perhaps the most legendary example of his private generosity (and perhaps too his grave sense of the inept) was what Spike Milligan calls The Case of the Mighty Melotrone Organ. Although Sellers was not notably musical (the only thing he ever mastered on the organ was 'Lover'), the electronic gadgetry proved overwhelmingly seductive to him. According to Milligan, a man with a graphic and imaginative talent for explaining the *modus operandi* of such things, 'If you wanted the sound of marching feet in size ten boots accompanied by Chopin and a portrait of Salvador Dali shaving under water while whistling the "Blue Bells of Scotland" this was the machine you had to have.'

When Sellers' enthusiasm for the versatile organ had run its natural course, he decided to give it to pianist Alan Clare whose passing (but suspect) approval he had remembered. Unfortunately, the Melotrone is not a small instrument and Mr Clare did not live in a large apartment. The combination of these extreme and inconvenient factors produced something of a storage crisis for Clare's wife, Bloom. A place for it was finally made in the bedroom. It was a mistake. After a while the Clares found it had created a strong, depressing atmosphere of cathedral-like calm which was to become the butt of much merriment among their more sacrilegious friends. 'It was,' Clare has reflected, 'one of the more esoteric sights of London.'

Clare was on the point of selling it when Sellers asked whether he might have it back. A few days later a pantechnicon arrived and the organ was removed.

Some months afterward, Princess Margaret and Lord Snowdon (who did not have such pressing space problems) were persuaded by Sellers to acquire one. The shock, when confronted with it on a visit to Kensington Palace, was almost too much for Milligan, who had developed a weird fascination for it during its oppressive occupancy of the Clares' bedroom. With difficulty he managed not to laugh. 'It seemed so bloody incongruous stuck in the middle of the royal front room. Then I realised that Pete had got the Snowdons on the gadget kick. Tony's having to take these tape recordings three times a day in tablet form now,' he said.

But at least one connected closely with the Snowdon circles suspects that the mighty Melotrone was not too warmly welcomed by Tony. 'Nothing in fact could have been been more calculated to exacerbate feelings between Tony and Margaret,' reckoned Robin Douglas-Home, the late writer, nightclub pianist, nephew of the Tory ex-

162

prime minister – and final heir to Sellers' own Melotrone. 'She adored it; he positively loathed it, and was supremely bored whenever she went near it,' he said.

Sellers' tendency to indulge himself and his friends was more wildly extravagant towards the end of his life, but it was not new. 'He had been this way all his life,' says Dennis Selinger. 'It was just a need he had whatever the cost, whatever the consequences.' In 1949, when he was beginning to make a name for himself on 'Ray's a Laugh', the radio series, he walked into Selinger's office carrying an impressive number of very expensive cameras and photographic equipment.

'How about that, then, Den?' he said.

Selinger eyed the gear and mentally began estimating its worth. He gave up several hundred pounds over what he knew his client had in his bank account. (He was also looking after his financial affairs in those days.)

'It's very nice, Pete. What are you using for money, luv – shirt buttons?'

'I gave them a cheque,' Sellers told him carelessly.

Selinger was horrified. 'You know perfectly well you haven't got enough money in the bank to meet that cheque. Do you realise what you've done, giving a firm like that a cheque with your name on it, a cheque that's sure to bounce? Don't you bloody well realise you're becoming well-known now, a name on a hit radio show? You can't go around doing things like that. If that cheque bounces, and it will, the papers will get hold of the story and you're going to be in real trouble. You know you could blow that show right out of the window with a stroke like that, I suppose?'

He made his point. Sellers looked miserable. 'But I've bought it now, Den,' he told him. 'I didn't think.'

'Well, you've got to take it back. Ask for your cheque back, tell them you've made a mistake.'

'I can't do that. What excuse can I give? I shall look such an idiot, Den.'

'Look, leave the stuff here, I'll sort it out,' Selinger finally told him. That afternoon he telephoned the store in

Bond Street and explained that Mr Sellers was unfortunately going to be out of the country for a year 'on a world tour' and would have to return the equipment, since it was impossible to take it with him and it would be out-of-date when he returned. The manager agreed, the cheque was returned and burned.

'That was typical of him,' Selinger said. 'It wasn't done with any intention of harming anybody. It's simply that money didn't really mean anything to him. That episode worried him at the time, but it didn't make the slightest bit of difference, because he went on doing exactly the same sort of thing. He was a child, really. Totally irresponsible where money was concerned.'

On one occasion when money was scarce and a persistent creditor threatened to have the bailiffs in, Sellers told him that his method for paying overdue bills was to put all the names into a hat, shake it well, and pick one out. 'If you make any more trouble,' he concluded this pithy lecture on the dynamics of his private economy, 'I won't even put your name into the hat.'

It was foreseeable that a man who could be so magnanimous with his favours, so casual about his expenses, was going to be unduly sensitive to the smallest return of affection. When Judy Goodman bought him a record album she thought he might like – it was the music from the French film *A Man and a Woman* – she was quite unprepared for his reaction. 'He almost broke down with emotion,' she remembered. (He later reciprocated by buying her a splendid stereo record player.) 'The truth is, I suspect, hardly anyone bought Peter anything. He got so few gifts, yet he was still like a small boy who loved surprises. He could genuinely rave and rhapsodise over the smallest gift, like a record album somebody happened to think he might fancy,' she said.

This not unlikely view helps to explain an incident during the days of John Boulting's close friendship. At Christmas he would send Sellers a small token gift, often wine, sometimes Scotch or cigars. But when success came to the actor on such an affluent scale Boulting dropped the custom. The following spring, when he was discussing an idea with Bill Wills that he believed might interest Sellers, he could see that something was troubling the business manager. Finally Wills told him that his client was very upset that he had 'forgotten him at Christmas'.

It angered Boulting.

'I give presents to children and I give presents to a few people who are not doing too well,' he told Wills. 'To give gifts to somebody as well-heeled as Peter is nonsense, in my opinion. It may sound priggish, Bill, but I suppose I am priggish in that sense.'

Wills told him that whatever the reason it hurt Sellers. He suggested that he recommence the tradition the following Christmas. Boulting never did.

It is interesting to compare this incident with examples of his many kindnesses. Although their relationship eventually became another victim of *Casino Royale* for a while, Douglas Hayward, the tailor, remembers the first halcyon days of their friendship with affection and gratitude. 'He could be so great,' he said. 'When I first went into business on my own he was one of my first three customers. He ordered about eight suits without really knowing what I could do. He trusted me and I owe him a lot for that.'

When Sellers' first marriage was coming apart at the vows, Hayward was a frequent visitor to the Oliver Messel suite at the Dorchester Hotel. 'You could *feel* his loneliness,' Hayward recalled. 'I'd sit and talk to him for hours, just talking, about anything. He never wanted you to leave.'

One night, after Hayward had been with him for a long time, Sellers said, 'What do you want most, Doug?'

'Nothing really, Pete,' he said.

'A car? What about a good car?'

'I've got a car, Pete.'

'You must want something. Everybody wants something.'

'No, not really, Pete. I'm pretty happy with what I've got.'

'Finally he gave up, but it disturbed him,' remembered Hayward. 'He said if ever I wanted anything let him know, because he wanted to buy me something special. That's the way he was, no bullshit, he really meant it.'

When Douglas Hayward left that night he felt very sad for the famous actor he had left alone seven floors above London, amid the rented splendours of the Oliver Messel suite, with his jazz albums quietly and continually scoring the silence around him and doing nothing to stop the loneliness inside the man.

Who Was Peter Sellers?

Bids to find the true source of Sellers' personal identity, an enigma whose answer lay deep in the undergrowth of his psyche, have been many, imaginative, and global, psychological, journalistic, friendly, and hostile. It was suggested that he purposely abandoned his real identity in the crowd of his own making; others said he was simply afraid he might be a figment of his own incredible imagination.

But a more cynical view with an impressive body of support is that he was essentially in perpetual flight *from* himself; a man who knew himself only too well and was neither enamoured nor comfortable with that secret.

John Boulting is among those who believe that Sellers was really hiding from, and not searching for, himself.

He had been close to Sellers, both as a man and an actor, for almost a decade. His attitude is one of critical understanding, a kind of grudging compassion. To understand Sellers you must first recognise that he was 'busy running away from the reality around him', reasons Boulting; and 'he was obsessed with concealing his own reality from the world, from himself even, and from everybody with whom he was in contact'.

Again, 'I suspect that there were really two realities for Sellers, and one of them was always predominantly the character he was playing at the time. I have a horrible feeling that very likely he was incapable of living except in terms of a creation, a role.'

It is an explanation that acknowledges a demoniacal force within the star. Indeed, the incredible extent to which he himself felt taken over by a role can be judged from a conversation he had with a journalist at the time he was making *Doctor Strangelove*.

167

'When a role is finished,' he said, 'I experience a sudden loss of identity. It's a funny thing, but when I'm doing a role I kind of feel it's the role doing the role, if you know what I mean. When someone says "You were great as so-and-so" I feel they should be telling so-and-so and not me.' The impact of such total transference of identity on an actor's emotional equilibrium can only be guessed at.

Although a fine actor should always be in control of a performance, one English actor-knight much impressed by Sellers said, 'He seemed to abandon control; his roles enwrapped the man. He pushed a performance to the edge of incarnation.'

For Sellers it seemed necessary. One veteran film man, who knew him since the days when he was eagerly providing those assorted 'job lot' voices for sound-tracks back in the fifties, claims he was 'always at his happiest, most secure anyway, inside some guise'. This informant didn't think it was merely 'an actor's satisfaction' but 'a secret place' and a necessary 'bolt hole'.

He recounted an extraordinary occasion when Sellers was playing the dome-headed President of the United States in *Doctor Strangelove,* and Peg visited him at the studio. As usual he didn't come out of the character between takes, nor over lunch, maintaining the accent and mannerisms of the role. Peg 'seemed genuinely rattled when she left that afternoon'.

On the way home, he was to learn later, she answered the driver, who asked whether she had had a good trip: 'Not very, I missed talking to my son.'

Supposing the old lady had somehow missed Sellers, the driver explained that he was very busy playing so many parts and had most probably got involved in a meeting with the director or the producers.

'Oh no,' she said, 'we had lunch together all right – except it was more like having lunch with a stranger, and I didn't care much for that.' She couldn't she added plaintively, recognise 'my own flesh and blood'.

It is an incident that provokes a crucial but perhaps unanswerable question: in becoming squadron leaders and aristocratic lords, even schoolboy private eyes, was he not only, as Spike Milligan so persuasively argues, invading other bodies but subconsciously evading Peg's enticing and well-meaning martriarchal tyranny?

Or, just as she was living vicariously through her son, was her son living vicariously through bodies that eluded her influential love and perhaps his own passive existence?

The need to impersonate Lord Beaconsfield was pressing at the time, of course, but did it bite deeper than mere expediency?

'I suppose I had a basic need to be bigger and grander than I was,' he once reflected. 'I think I've always felt more confident playing somebody else.' Always his own attempts at explanation were feeble, unsatisfactory, and truthfully vague. What is certain is that these impersonations, on and off the stage, were the beginning of a duality that was to grow stronger and more complete with time.

Now John Boulting says: 'He was such a consummate artist that, as close as I was to him, I found it very hard to know when I was dealing with the actor and when I was dealing with the man.'

When he was playing Doctor Pratt in *The Wrong Box,* a business associate who had known him for many years went to the studio. Again Sellers failed to emerge as himself. 'He *was* Doctor Pratt. I suddenly thought, "My God, if he can be Pratt that truthfully, how truthfully is he Peter Sellers?" I was very disturbed.'

Yet, despite his constant reassuring acclaim as an actor of genius – even if it was to some a frightening, unattractive genius – he retained an uncomfortable wariness of his own talent, and seemed somehow fearful for its permanence. He learned the craft and the technique of screen acting, became a supreme studio craftsman; but he still did not understand where the rest came from, where or why the genius began.

'Sellers,' says one old acquaintance who had been close to the stress, 'was condemned to a life of professional insecurity, because you cannot harness genius the way you can harness the atom. It doesn't come with a lifetime's guarantee. The seam can give out tomorrow. It is a perpetual threat.'

If it is true that Sellers knew himself 'only too well' as a man, there can be little doubt that he possessed a troubled ignorance of himself as an actor beyond his acquired professionalism. The depth of his certainty was partly revealed not long after Peg died and he and Milligan came together for an evening; the occasion left Milligan 'uneasy and very unhappy'. Sellers, clearly depressed, had told him: 'Spike, this is all I can do well. This is all I can do.'

'It was strange,' recalled Milligan later, 'because it suddenly hit me that he wouldn't say "acting" or "impressions". He could only say "this", and it was a "this". It was a unique thing. No man in the world could do what Sellers did. What Sellers did was his own particular brand of freakery.' He avoids, one can't help noticing, the bigger word 'genius'.

After Sellers had completed *The Bobo* and an edgy rapprochement had been made with director Robert Parrish, he was again to reveal his basic bewilderment at his own art: 'The truth is, Bob, I don't know what happens.'

'Well,' Parrish answered with a speed that may have clouded his sincerity, 'I've done a couple of pictures with you now, Peter . . . and I believe you.'

Parrish has been in the business a long time. Behind his Boy Scout smile is an Indian Scout mind. As a child actor he worked with Charlie Chaplin on *City Lights,* in 1933, and knew him until his death. This durable relationship today enables Parrish to make an interesting comparison between the two actors, who have each been called a cinegenius in that neon cablese of Sunset Boulevard and *Time* magazine.

'The point is,' he says, 'there was a real Charlie Chaplin. He was not necessarily the most delightful man in the world but, my God you could sit down and say Chaplin was this and Chaplin was that.

'But Peter Sellers was something quite different, believe me. He walked this strange tight-rope of not being a real person at all.'

Parrish puts his sentences together with the smooth finish of a man who is thoroughly conversant with his subject. 'When Charlie Chaplin looked in the mirror he saw a comic genius who was mercenary to the nth degree, and it's quite clear that there was a hard little nut of something staring back at him.

'Peter could stare at a mirror all day and at the end he'd find somebody else's face, another personality to portray, to use. That was both his achievement and his failure as a human being. The very fact that he played all of these parts so well is because there was no real person there at all.'

It is a view held and retold in different ways by many of those who became close to Peter Sellers. Some suspect Sellers held the same opinion. 'Pete', says former co-star Peter O'Toole, 'had an extraordinary sense of not being there. He genuinely felt that when he went into a room no one could see him.'

Certainly Sellers himself had told friends: 'I seem to have absolutely no confidence in myself. I can't hold anyone's attention for more than a minute, not as Peter Sellers. I start talking and suddenly I see their faces freezing and their eyes going terribly dead and I know I've lost them, because really I have nothing very clever or very original to say.'

Always concerned with his lack of formal education, even, one suspects, shamefully conscious of his premature departure from school at thirteen, he was inclined for a long time to trot out impressive pieces of dialogue or potted philosophy that he had memorised from old films or plays or radio discussions. One evening at a dinner party in London he quoted verbatim a piece from *Gulliver's Travels*. It was the passage where Swift describes the Emperor of Lilliput: 'The Most Mighty Emperor, Delight and Terror of the Universe, Monarch of all Monarchs, Taller than the Sons of Men, at whose nod the Princes of the Earth shaked their knees, pleasant as the spring,

171

comfortable as summer, fruitful as autumn, dreadful as winter.'

It seemed to his audience an odd recital, some thought merely an actor's conceit. Then he said, 'Isn't that interesting. You know that Emperor, poor chap, was no more than six inches tall.'

One guest suspected he was slyly deriding a particularly pompous actor at the table; another thought he was making a general philosophical point about the profession. Yet it is more likely that he was simply using a remembered quotation to get him through a difficult time when he was expected to say something.

One man who knew how deep Sellers' uncertainty about himself went is Father John Hester, a Church of England priest whose former parish in Soho is closely associated with the Actors' Church Union. In 1962 he was helping to produce a series of long-playing record albums of readings from the New English Bible and was searching for actors willing to help.

Sellers was a member of the Union ('not through any great care or forethought, I suspect,' says Father Hester now, 'but simply because he happened to think one afternoon that it was a good thing to join') and was duly invited to contribute to the recording. A few days later, Father Hester received a handwritten invitation from Sellers to visit him and discuss it.

He was pleasantly surprised because, he explained later, 'most actors didn't bother to answer at all, or said they were too busy or that the money wasn't enough. I think we were offering a flat fee of £50 – anyway, certainly not a lot of money.'

He kept an appointment a few days later at the actor's office at the top of a narrow flight of stairs, through a door bearing the simple inscription: Welcome Within. The welcome, in the absence of humanity, would have been chilling. It was a small room with a gas-fire and the kind of office furniture that becomes secondhand very quickly. Outside the window, like a black iron varicose vein, a fire-escape clung to the brickwork. On one wall was a photograph of Sellers which somebody had captioned The President. Above this office, containing a secretary and a telephonist-clerk, was another, just slightly better furnished. This is where Father Hester first met Peter Sellers.

After a few minutes, tea and biscuits came and they got down to the serious business of discussing the album. Sellers, remembers Father Hester, 'asked a lot of intelligent questions: what were our motives, where would the records sell, what other actors had we signed, who were the potential customers?'

The priest enjoyed the interrogation and liked Sellers. 'He was quite clearly fascinated in the project, although as I remember it he didn't bring up the question of his fee at all.'

Sellers eventually said he would like some time to consider the matter; he would ring the priest in a few days, he promised. 'I went away,' Father Hester has since admitted, 'half suspecting I would never hear from him again.' He was wrong. Three days later he received a note from Sellers: politely but flatly turning down the offer.

Yet, 'it was a categoric no, which oddly endeared me to him because most actors, you know, aren't very good at such positive decisions, especially when turning down work is involved'.

Before another week had gone by Father Hester was to hear a third time from Sellers. In a brief note he was invited back. 'It explained nothing, and I must say I was terribly intrigued.' A second appointment was arranged and kept. More tea, more biscuits, some preliminary small-talk. The priest waited, watching the actor's face and knowing whatever it was all about it was something that troubled and perhaps embarrassed him.

Finally, Sellers explained that his participation in the album was 'still quite out of the question – although I would very much like to do it'. The priest said he didn't understand.

Just to *read* something, even a passage from the Bible, Sellers explained, 'is beyond me'. Speaking, recalls Father Hester, with a crisp economy of words, rather like an

173

actor who wants an early curtain in a long-running play he know too well, Sellers told him how he had always 'hidden behind a voice, a make-up, a characterisation.

'To read something in my own voice, as Peter Sellers . . . I can't do it,' he said. 'I don't know myself well enough.'

He had thought, he added, that the priest 'deserved an explanation'. Such a revealing confession, coming from a man he barely knew, impressed the priest. 'He was afraid and yet had the courage to admit he was afraid,' he commented later. 'I think that really did take enormous guts.' It was the beginning of a close and lasting relationship between them.

That Sellers' lacking sense of identity (whether or not it was subconsciously self-induced to avoid an unpleasant confrontation with the truth, as John Boulting believes) was a continual concern is shown by a similar confession he was to make to a newspaperman several years later:

'I have no personality of my own. I reached my present position by working hard and not following Socrates' advice, Know thyself. I couldn't follow it if I wanted to. To me, I'm a complete stranger.'

When in 1966 he decided to appear on the screen for the first time as himself, in the role of Evelyn Tremble, the gambling-club croupier hired to impersonate James Bond in *Casino Royale,* it was a milestone in the art and life of Peter Sellers. Yet not a single critic recognised or acknowledged it. The role was, on the whole, singled out neither for praise nor for condemnation. In the general and occasionally hysterical abuse heaped on the film, Sellers almost disappeared.

'I have to have a strong character to play,' he had once remarked with prophetic accuracy, 'otherwise I become virtually unnoticeable.'

Some sensed Britt Ekland's strong subtle influence in his decision to appear à la Sellers. 'She got tired of being married to a public enigma,' reckons one close to them both.

'Perhaps she needed the reassurance, maybe she simply

needed to reassure others that her husband could satisfactorily exist on his own terms. She didn't give a damn about whether she was helping to stretch him as an actor, but only whether it would establish him as a human being.'

Sellers was less than happy with the adventure and displeased with the performance. 'I was up there pretty naked,' he told me later. 'You saw an aspect of me you've never seen before on the screen. Me. I didn't enjoy it. It isn't my idea of what acting is about.'

It is interesting to note that this was the performance that director Joe McGrath believed 'suffered because Sellers had not put enough work into it . . . had not done his homework'.

Knowing that Sellers was a man quietly obsessed with a belief that he had failed to achieve recognition or even substance outside the roles he played, Peter O'Toole rapidly felt deep affection for him when they first met on *What's New, Pussycat?* in Paris, despite the fact they had tossed a coin for top billing and O'Toole had lost.

One night, in a bid to reassure Sellers that he had indeed forced his own personality on the world, he told him about his experience in London the night the news came that he was so near to death in Hollywood.

In the lobby of Claridges Hotel there is a ticker-tape machine, and as O'Toole with his then wife, actress Sian Phillips, and producer Jules Buck, were leaving that evening, the porter handed them a piece of the tape. It was the news that Sellers had suffered a heart attack.

'We were all pretty badly shaken,' recalls O'Toole. 'We went straight to the cocktail party, and don't forget we'd just got the news red-hot off the tape machine, and already everybody was talking about Sellers.'

They left the party and went to the Trattoria Terrazza, an Italian restaurant in Soho: 'Nobody was talking about anything else. The news was beating us all the way through town, right down the line. It reminded me of Raimu's death, the great French actor-clown. He died during the war in Marseilles, I think it was, and apparently within fifteen minutes of his death every bistro along the

175

whole coast was mourning him.'

But the real point about that evening in London, said O'Toole, was that nobody was talking about the Goon that died or the talent that was lost or the actor who would be missed; 'they were all talking about the *man*'.

When he had finished telling this story to Peter Sellers, O'Toole, the passionate Irishman, said, 'Look, luv, you must understand, they weren't talking about the layers, they were talking about the centre. *You*. Not the myth, not the legend, but the man. Because you do bloody well exist, you know.'

Sellers listened quietly, his face a passive shield in front of his emotions. At the end, recalls O'Toole, 'he said something noncommittal like "really" or "I didn't know that".'

'I don't know,' Peter O'Toole reflects now, 'whether it did any good or not, my telling him that story. I got the feeling he didn't believe me.'

Most star actors are cunning experts in the art of interview, experienced in the guile of self-projection; the dark lanes of their lives are illuminated by shining neon that blots out the darkness with a glow so utterly blinding it shows you nothing. You may talk to such men for hours and longer and learn only that they are articulate, entertaining, and purposely elusive.

The elusiveness of Peter Sellers was of another kind. He had found a safer hiding place in the roles he played. That the face behind the mask was another kind of mask made the man more complex certainly, yet no less human. The species that are most vulnerable, least secure, always make the greatest camouflage. 'A tramp,' said Spike Milligan, 'has more security than Peter Sellers.'

The Mined Wonderland

To ENTER THE world of Peter Sellers was to enter a mined wonderland; although the deep, sensitive detonators were laid during his childhood. Suspicious, vulnerable, pressured by his own fame, he was often doubtful of even himself and his own motives. His self-imposed social siege was almost total. 'He had so few friends, young friends, new friends,' said Britt Ekland during their marriage. 'And the friends he had talked mostly of the past, of things I knew nothing about. It was very difficult. He told me to go out and make friends, but a woman can't easily do that; you can't slip out and order half a dozen friends and hope your husband is going to approve.'

There are less than six people in the world who were really close to him, and half of those must sometimes suspect the real measure of their friendship. 'He was quick,' says Harvey Orkin, 'quick to love and quick to hate.' In full flight he could make a bullet look as if it was backing up. It was the trait that dismayed those around him the most.

Herbert Kretzmer, who first met Sellers in 1958 for a profile piece for the old *Daily Sketch* ('It was overwritten,' he has admitted since. 'One always overwrote about Sellers the way one always overwrites about bullfighting.'), was well acquainted with his great gusts of enthusiasm and has been, too, a victim of the lulls that followed. 'How many people did he champion down the years?' he questions. 'Writers, actors, directors, all kinds of people. And they would go home screaming with pleasure to their wives and mistresses, "I'm doing it, I'm doing it for Peter". But by the next day when they were planning to move from Wembley to Holland Park, from Brooklyn to the East Fifties, he had discovered somebody else and

177

quite forgotten he had even had lunch with them yesterday.'

Yet Kretzmer finally had an affection for the man that transcended criticism. 'The great thing about Peter was that he was a lovable man. You loved him despite everything, you loved him in many ways because of his almost tragic shortcomings.

'To be a friend of Peter Sellers you had to be a very sophisticated man, because you had to understand why he did the things he did. Perhaps it didn't make him any more endearing, but the man was singularly free of malice in the ordinary sense; it was often simply that he so easily forgot too many of yesterday's promises and yesterday's passions.'

John Boulting believes that 'he was a friend to nobody. I think he was a human being who had need of friendship but whose great tragedy was that he was incapable of the real sacrifices that flow from deep friendships.'

Princess Margaret has told friends, 'He is the most difficult man I know.'

It was this particular friendship that puzzles and sometimes nettles citizens who were close to Sellers. In the early days, recalls John Boulting, 'we had great fun at the expense of the monarchy', but Sellers 'succumbed' when the crested invitations came.

The truth is, reasons Boulting now, Sellers did not dismiss the idea of royalty on a political or philosophical level, but 'because he feared that it revealed in some way his own sense of inferiority. So their final recognition became so much more important to him.'

Princess Margaret is known to be slightly stagestruck, and once invited Sellers to co-star with her in a homemade film. With Lord Snowdon as cameraman, Sellers played an old-time vaudeville quick-change artist who announces he will do his famous impersonation of Princess Margaret, then according to one well-informed report: 'He goes behind the screen. Clothes are flung over the top. Then out from the other side of the screen steps Princess Margaret. She simpers and squirms like a music-

178

hall ingénue. She curtsies. She blows a kiss. She retires behind the screen and Sellers appears boasting of his great impersonation.'

He was confidently well in with the Snowdons. Even so 'his boisterous humour could turn into morose introspection if somebody didn't smile', said Robin Douglas-Home. 'You suddenly found him in some corner asking, "What have I done wrong?" He had a greater capacity for self-examination than any man I know. He was continually undermining his own success.'

Just how close Sellers was to the Royal couple was a matter of speculation. 'Tony and Margaret had practically no friends,' claimed one acquaintance. 'They were too obsessed with the revolving fashion scene to sustain and develop real chums. Sellers was simply a durably fashionable fixture.'

Cruelly, perhaps, some suspect that the Snowdons regarded him as something of a court jester. And, 'Peter had certainly been known to humour them with a vulgarity he seldom displayed professionally,' says an informant. 'He knew of course that traditionally the Royal Family has a great sense of humour, and Margaret particularly upholds the reputation.'

Yet Sellers' position in the Snowdon set-up was not submissive nor kowtowing. 'He argued very well with her, because she is a very argumentative lady,' says an intimate observer of that scene. And once, when Queen Elizabeth asked him at a royal première line-up what he was doing, he replied tartly, 'Standing here.'

Indeed, just how seriously Peter Sellers valued his privileged position in the Snowdon circle was questionable. Occasionally, it had seemed to some he had 'gone out of his way to embarrass them' and 'risk their serious displeasure' knowing that Princess Margaret's humour, particularly, is not 'easily predictable'.

Inevitably, perhaps, Sellers' relationship with Princess Margaret became the subject of speculation among their close friends. 'PM can be a terrible flirt', Robin Douglas-Home explained. 'There was no doubt that she enjoyed teasing Sellers.' But it was nothing exceptional, he insisted. 'It was the sort of social flirting that never gets out of the drawing-room.'

Sellers did not have the sophistication to understand the rules of those sort of games in those sort of circles.

'He convinced himself that there was going to be a big thing between them', said Douglas-Home. 'It was suddenly forbidden-fruit time.'

The cheek, the romantic grandeur of the actor's design, amazed his friends.

'PM was fond of Sellers. He could make her laugh when there wasn't always much to laugh at in her life. I'm sure it went no deeper than that', recalls another Sellers intimate who had watched events at close quarters.

Sellers refused to accept that.

During their 'sittings' at the clairvoyant's Hampstead home, Sellers returned again and again to the possibility of a romance with somebody *exalted:* 'Somebody *very* high up the social tree', he repeatedly prompted Woodruff.

Woodruff had heard the gossip. He knew the score. He also knew that one word out of place could mean the end of their relationship.

Even so, the clairvoyant could not see what Peter Sellers wanted him to see. Woodruff was very sincere about his 'gift'; at the same time, he understood the wisdom of guiding people's anxieties about the future toward practical conclusions. He was thinking very hard.

'I close my eyes', Sellers prompted him still further. 'I see the colour purple.'

'There is an affinity', Woodruff said guardedly. 'A woman of high birth. But she is not free as other women are free.'

'She's married', Sellers said glumly.

'She is beholden beyond the sacraments of marriage.'

'It's not on then, Maurice?'

'I see a lot of hurt if you continue in that direction. She cannot help you. She cannot help herself', Woodruff told him.

180

A few days later, Woodruff received a very old sepia postcard picture of an empty dining room of a hotel in Lahore. On the back was scrawled: *With equal pace, impartial Fate knocks at the palace as the cottage gate.* It was signed P.

'It was never on the cards', Woodruff told me. 'I think Peter in his heart of hearts realised that. That's when he started to get so bloody bolshy, answering the Princess back and all that. He had a very strange sense of grievance sometimes.' (Woodruff had invited me to write his biography; he died of a heart attack in Singapore before the idea got beyond several exploratory interviews from which this story comes. I eventually used him as the model for the character Waldo Bragg in my first novel *Titles,* called *Royal Title* in England.)

According to Woodruff, Sellers was 'over the moon' when Tony Snowdon agreed to photograph Britt Ekland at Kensington Palace a few days before their marriage. 'I can't wait to see a certain lady's face when a certain lady claps her eyes on the next Mrs Peter Sellers', he said to Woodruff.

'It was very sweet, really. Very sweet and a bit sad. He was like a kid with a new toy he wanted to show off. "To hell with you, dear", he wanted to say to Margaret, "look what I've got instead!" '

Woodruff's story bears out Britt's later version of events. At the first meeting with the Princess, Britt was photographed dressed in little more than one of Snowdon's own shirts. While Princess Margaret looked on, Sellers encouraged his bride-to-be to unbutton the shirt even lower.

Those who believe that there was 'something' between Sellers and the Princess (and that 'something' veers from the view that it was 'a deep emotional attachment' to the more forthright explanation: 'sex') suggest that the gifts Sellers sent Tony Snowdon – they included a Riva speedboat as well as expensive camera and stereo equipment – were evidence of his troubled conscience. 'We used to call them Peter's guilt offerings', a former Sellers aide told me. 'He had very expensive tastes in pangs of remorse.' (When I tried to verify this story with another Sellers aide, she said: 'Yes, but remember Peter could imagine pangs of remorse as easily as he could imagine slights, strange looks, slurs.')

Perhaps genuinely unaware of the rumours, perhaps choosing to ignore what she heard, Britt Ekland admits in one cruel sentence in her memoirs that she would 'squirm with embarrassment at the demeaning lengths' to which Sellers went to please the Royals. The explanation *she* heard 'on the grapevine': Sellers was after a knighthood.

Princess Margaret's subsequent affair with Roddy Llewellyn affected Sellers in a curious way.

'I don't know whether Peter and the Princess had had a thing going or not – don't forget that Peter was a wilful megalomaniac with no sense of limits and all the exigencies of vanity – but he certainly carried on as if he had had. He behaved as if the public recognition of the Margaret-Roddy business was something that should have been accorded to him. There were certain things you quickly learned never to mention around Peter – and Mr Roddy Llewellyn was top of his shit-list.' (He kept a permanent shit-list, carefully memorised by his entourage; mostly it contained the names of journalists, producers, directors and so on to whom he would not talk or who were somehow out of favour. The list altered every week, often for no discernible reason.)

By the end of the sixties when it was becoming increasingly obvious that Princess Margaret's marriage was doomed (Snowdon had begun a close relationship with Lady Jackie Rufus-Isaacs) Sellers was telling friends that he was in love with her and that they were having an affair. Several nights a week, he said, she visited his Clarges Street apartment in Mayfair for cosy dinners *à deux*. To convince her detective that she was attending large dinner parties, Sellers (having discreetly dismissed the staff for the evening) would open the door disguised as a very old manservant in white wig and *pince-nez* eye glasses. In the background, on tape, were the sounds of a lively gathering of people, laughing, chatting. Having seen her safely to the door of the apartment, the detective waited downstairs, unaware that Her Royal Highness was entirely alone with the actor, enjoying 'picnics' sent across from the Tiberio restaurant, and occasionally from Mr Chow's in Knightsbridge.

At that time he was making *The Magic Christian* (and smoking quantities of pot), a film whose message, he said, was corruption by money and power. 'We wanted to show that the Establishment is absolutely destructible. Rules are made to be broken,' he told Helen Lawrenson in an *Esquire* profile. 'It's a film for heads.' Certainly he had his own 'heady' moments.

Impersonating Tony Snowdon, he telephoned Princess Margaret and embarked on a fairly raunchy confession of his burgeoning friendship with Lady Jackie Rufus-Isaacs. Unfortunately, he had completely miscalculated Her Royal Highness's sense of humour, as well as her *sang-froid*: her attitude to that whole delicate situation turned out to be considerably less 'civilised' than Sellers had imagined.

Realising that the joke had gone badly awry, he ended the conversation hurriedly, without self-disclosure.

He fretted about it for weeks. Finally, one evening at Laurence Harvey's apartment in Grosvenor House on Park Lane, he unburdened his dilemma. His co-star in *The Magic Christian,* Harvey had a splendid air of *savoir-faire* that Sellers admired a lot. Harvey told Sellers to forget the whole business.

'In my experience, dear heart,' said the late Mr Harvey, 'actresses and princesses have the most dreadful memories for trivia.'

Encouraged by the worldly Mr Harvey's assurance and abetted by a joint of Acapulco Gold, Sellers confided cryptically: 'The thing is, you see, she has the same size breasts as Sophia Loren. The same cup-size exactly.'

Harvey, who preferred his women on more boyish lines, said blandly: 'Large breasts and small husbands must be an irresistible *mélange* for some chaps.'

'They're my undoing,' said Sellers glumly.

Had he, perhaps, imagined his affair with Princess Margaret?

'Pete was a romantic fantasist', says his former agent Dennis Selinger. 'I'd heard all the stories. My guess is that Princess Margaret was very fond of him and Pete built it up from there. Perhaps they did console each other when their marriages were going wrong. They were friends, it would have been understandable. But an actual physical affair . . . no, never, in my opinion.'

An English actor told me, 'Pete could tell a few tall tales like all of us. At one time, listening to one of his stories about the Royals, I thought: "He's a fucking bigger egomaniac than I am." I didn't believe a word of what he was saying. Now I'm not so sure. You have to bear in mind what has happened to Princess Margaret's life since then. I mean, she's no angel, is she?'

The Boulting brothers, who probably knew and understood Sellers as well as anyone in the business, are divided on the question. One is certain that there had been an affair; the other agrees with Dennis Selinger that it was probably all a figment of Sellers' imagination.

Spike Milligan celebrated the friendship in a poem that is said to have delighted Her Royal Highness:

> *Wherever you are*
> *Wherever you be*
> *Please take your hand*
> *Off the Princess's knee.*

'There's only one thing I can say to Spike about Princess Margaret and myself: *we are just good friends,*' Sellers was quoted as saying later. It was a provocative quote, probably the most provocative thing he ever said for the record. 'He knew the implications of that hoary line. He knew *exactly* what he was saying,' reckoned one associate.

Sellers' spiky involvement with Princess Margaret and her set was well-established by the time Britt came on the scene. A year earlier, in 1963, he had taken part in *Fool*

Britannia along with Tony Newley, Joan Collins, Daniel Massey, and songwriter Leslie Bricusse), a comedy album satirically mocking the notorious Profumo scandal that had threatened the position of Prime Minister Harold Macmillan and almost toppled the Tory government. The Palace, it was known, was especially concerned at the strong anti-Establishment feeling the crisis had caused in the country.

The album, recorded in New York, was called 'nasty, smutty, and offensive' by the London *Daily Herald* critic Anthony Carthew. Especially he had 'reservations about a Buckingham Palace scene (in which Sellers impersonates the Queen) which is mostly rather nasty innuendo, only slightly redeemed by lines like, "We are at home now, dear, you don't *have* to keep on smiling and waving". And, "Anne, how many times have I told you not to ride your pony on the tea table?" The rest is either unprintable . . . or feeble.'

The enterprise, thought one member of the Snowdon group, 'was very foolish from Sellers' point of view, amounting almost to a personal affront'. Sellers was unrepentant. 'Only a prude,' he insisted, 'could possibly be offended by it.' Nevertheless, the major record companies declined to handle the album in Britain. A spokesman for Decca said: 'It was in bad taste.'

This was followed two years later by an incident that many thought thoroughly tested the entire Royal Family's sense of humour, if not their more fundamental sense of democracy. On the Queen's thirty-ninth birthday she was taken by Princess Margaret to see Spike Milligan in his London hit play *Son of Oblomov*. In the party were Prince Philip, Prince Charles, Princess Anne, Lord Snowdon, and Britt and Peter Sellers.

Suddenly, disregarding the play, Milligan asked, 'Is there a Peter Sellers in the house?'

Sellers, in the middle of the Royal party, shouted back, 'Yes,' and started an amazing cross-talk act with his former Goon colleague.

Milligan: 'Why can't a lady with a wooden leg change a

pound note?'

Sellers: 'I don't know. Why *can't* a lady with a wooden leg change a pound note?

Milligan: 'Because she's only got half a nicker.'

Sellers: 'I don't wish to know that.'

Milligan: 'Why does Prince Philip wear red, white, and blue braces?'

Sellers: 'I don't know. Why *does* Prince Philip wear red, white, and blue braces?'

Milligan: 'To keep his trousers up.'

The audience was in uproar; the press eagerly reported the irreverent exchange, noting that the Royal guests 'shrieked with laughter'. But later a well-connected host said, 'To see the Queen dutifully reacting in public is not to know her. I can only guess at her real embarrassment. After all, it was a private visit and not a Royal Performance, where a certain liberty is expected and even encouraged.'

Perhaps even more speculative was Sellers' own reaction on this occasion: to be thus singled out in the stalls of a theatre, even by Milligan, might normally have discomforted him intensely. That he should have reacted with so much encouraging enthusiasm puzzled a lot of people.

'Admittedly he was put in a spot by Milligan,' said one established member of the Snowdon scene, 'but I suspect that he welcomed that chance to publicly show his equality and independence in that illustrious company, to prove he wasn't some sort of mascot the way I think he suspected his great-great-grandfather Mendoza was the mascot of the Prince of Wales.'

His 'extravagant independence' might also merely have been an unconscious prologue to the end of an acquired relationship that deep down he found less rewarding and more demanding than he cared to admit even to himself. For he seldom was the one to take the obvious initiative in ending a relationship.

'He tended to push people until they made all the important decisions, even against himself,' says former secretary Hattie Stevenson, who finally 'sensed the need to quit'. Thus, Anne Sellers left him, just as tailor Doug Hayward left him, Janette Scott and Britt Ekland and innumerable others who had 'sensed the need' to say goodbye.

'I don't like people leaving me,' he once reflected. 'But in a strange way I feel secure only in change.'

On the several occasions that he brought himself to fire Hattie Stevenson the results were less than satisfactory. On one occasion during the filming of *The World of Henry Orient* in New York he woke her in the early hours of the morning to enquire after the plans for his new home in Elstead. They had somehow been mislaid and he fired her on the spot, adding that she should return to England immediately – 'and tourist'.

During the course of that day, however, he maintained a particularly heavy barrage of requests, orders, instructions, and demands. 'By the middle of the afternoon,' recalls Miss Stevenson, 'it was perfectly clear he had no intention of letting me go. So I simply stayed. But he never told me I was unfired or re-engaged. He just made it impossible for me to leave. That was very typical of him; he hated to make that kind of decision. Finally, the decision had to be my own and he accepted it.'

Both she and Doug Hayward left Sellers within a short time of each other during the chaotic days of *Casino Royale*. It is likely that he needed to divest himself of their services at that time in some sort of streamlining of his emotional commitments. Still convinced of his initiative in ending the relationship, Hayward said, 'I had to stop seeing him. He had this incredible talent for draining people, he sucked you dry as a human being. You became a shell. He could get more out of people than anyone else I know. There was nobody else in the world who could make me do the things I did for Pete. He had these enormous, flattering, demanding, driving crushes on people, on talent. It may have gone on for a month, six weeks, three months – then it was over, finished, finished, finished.'

Hayward crossed the finishing line one night when he

187

failed to turn up for a tentative appointment at the Dorchester. The next morning Hattie Stevenson was told to pass on Sellers' irritation on his non-appearance with a warning hint that such a lapse should not occur again. But knowing Hayward's Cockney pride it must have been a calculated incentive for him to terminate the relationship; certainly that was the result.

Tired, overworked, the tailor reacted with fury, ordered his staff to drop everything but the Sellers assignment, and that evening took the finished work to the Dorchester and handed it over.

'That's it, Pete,' Hayward told him. 'Goodbye.' He didn't see him again for nearly three years.

'It was a rotten way to end a friendship,' he was to say later. 'But he gave me no alternative. You can't cope with that kind of sensitivity.'

'He was *so* sensitive,' says Harvey Orkin. 'He was like a dog that could hear whistles that nobody else could hear: insults, innuendoes, snubs – he could detect them dripping away in a Niagara of praise.'

'He was a very difficult friend to have, especially to keep,' admits Father John Hester, the Soho priest. 'He reacted with extraordinary quixotic violence.' Once early in their relationship, when Sellers was exploring religion, he failed to keep an appointment that had been made for some weeks. 'It was a thoughtless and inconsiderate act. I was pretty mad and let him know in no uncertain terms,' recalls the priest. Sellers seemed oblivious to his rage, explaining that he had had to attend a back specialist.

'What can a back specialist give you that I can't?' demanded Father Hester, now exasperated to a point of evangelical immodesty.

'This,' he confesses, 'put the fat in the fire. We shouted at each other for a while. It was all a bit juvenile, I suppose, but after that we got, as the Americans say, a good relationship going.

'You see, he had managed to put his finger on a bit of pomposity in me, a touch of self-importance and ego that is quite unpardonable.'

Perhaps the most notable survivor of that quixotic temper is David Lodge, the English character actor. They first met in the Royal Air Force during the last tedious days of the war. The place was Gloucester where boredom can easily set in once you have visited the cathedral.

Lodge was poking life into the ancient stove when he heard 'a bloody great argument' at the far end of the hut; Sellers was involved in a dispute with an airman considerably larger than himself and 'heading for a right bashing'. Lodge removed the red-hot poker from the fire and walked down the hut.

'Leave off,' he said to the large airman, 'or come outside with me.'

'I've got no argument with you,' the large airman replied.

Lodge gave Sellers the poker. 'Here, take this, mate, and if he comes near you again, belt him across the head with it.' It was the end of hostilities and the beginning of one of the most remarkable friendships in Sellers' life.

'Pete just looked at me with those lovely sad eyes of his,' Lodge has recalled that occasion, 'and something just happened. I was a couple of years older than him, no more, but I became his big brother, father confessor, favourite uncle, the lot. Pete was the kind of bloke who always needed somebody there. There always had to be somebody in his life he could telephone at three o'clock in the morning and know there would be a friendly voice.'

Most of the friendly voices in Sellers' life went back a long way, most often to the early postwar years, and only very few joined that small band of 'real mates' in recent times. Peter O'Toole was one of the few to forge a warm and insightful relationship with him during the growingly guarded years of his gathering fame. It was an interesting bond. For the two men were in almost every way opposites. O'Toole is a tall, lean, handsome leading man with a laugh that was bred in some of the best bars in Dublin. He is volatile and incautious and proud and mindful of his wild heritage. He is still very much the vagabond actor beneath the veneer of moneyed respectability and more

189

recent sobriety, a man in perpetual pursuit of his own temptation level, yet sensitive enough to its dangers. Talented, controversial and ambitious for things beyond material satisfaction, he regards the achievements of Peter Sellers with an admiration that comes close to awe. 'I knew Pete,' he says, 'and I think he knew about me. We were totally comfortable together – not cosy, it was far from cosy, it was sometimes downright edgy – but it was the sharp edginess of stimulation and exploration.'

They had tried hard to work together more often. In 1964, shortly before his postcoronary disenchantment with Billy Wilder, it was announced he would play Dr Watson to O'Toole's Sherlock Holmes for Wilder. He had, Sellers disclosed, 'accepted the role without seeing a script. Wilder is the only director I would do that with. He is a phenomenon. He seems to have a large number of admirers who even copy his way of life. Perhaps he attracts them because he is a completely honest man.' The enthusiasm, as we have seen, was soon to wane; the deal fell through.

'That,' said O'Toole, 'was really very sad, because something quite exceptional could have come out of that set-up.'

Perhaps the most extraordinary thing about this relationship is that it was one in which, by and large, Sellers brandished the major influence. 'I found myself completely eaten up by Pete's personality,' says O'Toole. 'I took far more from him than he took from me – yes, I was hugely influenced by him when we were together. I found myself listening more than I did with most people. I even found myself imitating him.'

It was a remarkable confession, especially from an actor whose own personality is determinedly vivid and sometimes violent. Inevitably it produces at least one explanation in a now familiar vein: 'You understand that when they first acted together Sellers played O'Toole's analyst [Dr Kleiner in *What's New, Pussycat?*], an obviously dominant position which spilled over into his private attitude toward O'Toole,' estimates a writer who knew them well. 'It is weird when you remember that O'Toole isn't too easily impressed with *anybody*. He more than holds his own with the big-league hell-raisers and personality-boys like Richard Burton and John Huston, yet he practically *shrivelled* beside Sellers. It isn't that O'Toole was still unconsciously playing the analyst-patient game but Sellers *was* . . .and to devastating effect.'

Understandably O'Toole finds this rationalisation, despite its author's sober repute, 'a bit bloody way-out'. Yet the fact remains there are few people, especially of that kind, whom Sellers could impress with such sustained confidence; that he should achieve it with a man like Peter O'Toole was perhaps otherwise inexplicable.

Outside these few tried-and-trusted mates his social forays were frequently disastrous and wounding. 'He had a genuine contempt for the easy familiarity you find in show business,' observes a former acquaintance. 'He had a very small capacity for camaraderie.' When he was interrupted in a restaurant by a well-known producer he reacted pleasantly, but later he asked Harvey Orkin, 'Somebody like W.C. Fields would have told him to drop dead. Why can't I be like that?' (Although when a fan approached him and asked, 'Are you Peter Sellers?' he answered briskly, 'Not today,' and walked on.) 'He tolerated so many people he really hated,' says Orkin.

'I think he did strongly dislike a lot of people,' says Father John Hester with a smile that is both incredulous and indulgent. It was, he suspects, 'part of the classic confusion of his life – the sensitive artist expected to exist as a willing piece of public property, having to cope with some very tough businessmen'.

When he was still intensely interested in Christianity, Sellers invited Father Hester to Paris one weekend to pursue various points that bothered him. They were lunching at the Plaza Athene when an internationally renowned producer arrived rather loudly with his entourage. 'Peter,' recalls the priest, 'didn't react at all like a film star should. He didn't preen or push himself because here was an important and influential man in his business. He

191

simply became very uncomfortable because he was reminded of the kind of world he himself was part of.'

'Sellers,' thinks one actor he outpaced in the pursuit of stardom, 'lived in two incompatible worlds: emotionally he was with the losers, but physically he lived with the kings.'

Proof of this perhaps was the death of Marilyn Monroe, whom he never knew, although he had a close and personal understanding of her problems; it happened at a time when he was parted from his first wife, Anne, and the emotional rigours of his own fame were keenly felt. On Sunday 5th August, 1962, he was in Paris when he heard that Monroe had been found dead from an overdose of sleeping pills in her Hollywood home.

Until that moment, recalls Jerry Juroe, then European Press Director for United Artists, he had been in a 'particularly jaunty mood, very amusing'.

The news seemed to shatter him. 'It was as if it were the death of the closest person to him in the whole world,' says Juroe. Juroe was her publicity director during the filming of *The Prince and the Showgirl* and was not himself untouched by her death, but he became particularly concerned for Sellers. 'He became very withdrawn and after a little while said he had to leave.' Worried, he felt he should go after him but a friend who had arrived at Juroe's apartment with Sellers urged, 'Leave him alone, Jerry. Let him work it out for himself.'

It was, says Juroe now, 'a moment of real grief'.

This was the man who could also be almost totally insensible to the more simple suffering of those close to him. Before *Casino Royale* started, Sellers invited Joe McGrath to Elstead one Sunday to work on the script. The director arrived shortly after breakfast and Sellers suggested that they first take a bicycle ride 'to get some air in our lungs'.

McGrath was given a bicycle and they started out at a brisk pace. 'He was going with fantastic ease, shooting these questions about the script at me. I'm a pretty fit guy, I play football every Sunday, but he was wearing me down,' recalled McGrath. It was not until the end of the ride that he realised the actor was riding a super featherweight machine with every possible aid to vehicular propulsion short of steam.

Feeling the iron lump of his own bike (circa 1910, Metropolitan Police model, if McGrath's judgment at that moment is to be trusted) against his tired and aching legs, he felt the need for some pithy comment.

'That's a very *light* bike you've got there, Pete,' he observed, hoping there was sufficient needle in his tone to compensate for the diplomacy of his words.

Only delighted at his apparent approval, Sellers mindlessly 'did a twenty-minute bit' on the bike's features: Italian gears from Milano, Japanese bamboo rims made by hand by craftsman in Kyoto, miracle-weight alloy frame from France . . . 'He didn't,' said McGrath, 'mention my bike at all.'

'I don't blame Peter,' says Judy Goodman who knows most of the stories. 'He was a helpless victim of a system that must make a man less than he is. The system lays down that everything has to be right for the star; the world is adapted and rearranged to please him. If he trips over a cable the nearest electrician is fired. The bigger the star the more power he has, the more lunatic it becomes and the more he loses touch with the needs and feelings and reality of the ordinary people around him.'

Most celebrities only live out their celebrity in the company of other celebrities: a constant reminder of their own acceptance and fame and achievements. It was perhaps the final division that Sellers fought. Certainly he understood it. He grieved too much for Monroe.

Red Cloud

FROM AN EARLY age religion fascinated Peter Sellers, worried him, puzzled him, and pursued him through the years. The howling mob of his conscience was most probably no more than the Twelve Apostles. It was understandable: his mother was Jewish and his father a Protestant and, perhaps revealing a fundamental schism of that seemingly docile relationship, Sellers was neither baptised nor barmitzvahed. 'Why didn't they commit me as a child?' he would ask in moments of religious anguish. 'Why have they left me to grope like this? I don't know whether I'm a Jew or a Gentile. I'm nothing.'

Not all his friends could get too worked up at this theological dilemma, however. 'That's just Peter talking,' said Harvey Orkin. 'He'd be going on the same way if he were a Catholic, a Presbyterian, or a Russian Orthodox.' He inherited dilemmas, said another associate, the way the Rothschilds inherit money.

Yet this particular quandary sank deeper than that. One Christmas when Spike Milligan bought him a synagogue candlestick he broke down completely. 'He burst into tears,' recalls Milligan. 'He was utterly overcome. I think now he somehow thought I was casting a slur on the Jews, and he already certainly had his own guilt complex about that.'

It is interesting, as Milligan points out, that the impressions he did of Jews were often 'less than adulatory. He never did a refined Jew; we even got letters from listeners saying that "The Goon Show" was anti-Semitic.' (A commercial he made for Barclays Bank in which he played a conman called Monty Casino, was attacked on the same grounds. It was about to be withdrawn when Sellers died. The commercial was immediately cancelled, the Bank said, as a mark of respect.)

Could it be, as some thought, that here was a subconscious revelation of the ambivalent feelings he felt for Peg and the meddling implantation of her own ambition?

Later, after her death or close to it, Sellers did turn down two notable Jewish roles: Fagin in the film musical *Oliver;* and the lead in *The Fixer,* a role he was initially keen to do.

'I couldn't,' he told me, 'finally see any way of playing either role outside the usual interpretation; and Alec [Guinness] had done the definitive Fagin already.' (This performance was much attacked as anti-Semitic and largely blamed for the disappointing reception of David Lean's *Oliver Twist* in America.)

The complex subject of his divine confusion was not unexplored by his friends nor by his enemies, and many agree there was more solace to be found for him on psychiatrists' couches than in any church, synagogue, mosque, or joss-house he may spiritually have ransacked for answers.

'I don't especially believe in the analyst route to contentment or stability, but if ever a man needed to put his cold backside on a cool couch it was Pete,' says one associate who had more than once been a victim of the actor's whim. 'He should have just laid down and talked, "I hate my mother, I hate my father, I hate being a Jew, I hate not being a Jew" . . . honestly, he was a mess.'

One man who was to become an expert on the spiritual peregrinations of Peter Sellers, however, was Father John Hester, the Church of England priest he had first met during the discussions of the New English Bible record album. When his father died not long after those meetings, Sellers invited the priest to conduct the funeral service. And for quite a long while Sellers was to find a sophisticated kind of spiritual comfort in the young, bearded, and worldly priest.

Bill Sellers' death had emphasised the feeling of a religious void in his son's life, a disturbing and challenging emptiness that possessed him shortly – and significantly –

before he was to start filming *Heavens Above* in 1963. In this controversial comedy, he was to play the Reverend John Smallwood, a crusading priest whose fine Christian principles embarrass the Church Establishment and cause havoc and a financial slump in his own parish.

Emotionally he was going through a bad patch. And, unable to fix on a satisfying, credible character for the Reverend Smallwood, he felt, he told one friend, 'surrounded from the inside'. Motivated by private needs and driven harder still by an obsession 'to find' the Reverend John Smallwood, he began seriously questioning Father Hester about his faith, probing aspects of religion and religious doctrine with an intelligence and depth that demanded sharp respect, even on occasions careful reflection.

Says Father Hester, 'A large part of Peter's basic fascination for Christianity was motivated by his role in *Heavens Above*. He had become deeply involved with that part, it obsessed his thinking. He saw the man as a kind of . . . ideal.'

The true extent to which Sellers was involved can be judged by an interview he had with Malcolm Muggeridge on 'Meeting Point' in 1963. He became, he said, so beset by the role of Smallwood (the portrayal was finally based 'quite a great deal' on Brother Cornelius, his old teacher at St Aloysius College, he later told him) that he was almost thinking of becoming ordained.

'During one section of the film I was completely taken over with the idea of doing good for people,' he said. Muggeridge, honestly religious although generally regarded as a cynical egghead, was enthusiastic about the idea. 'I think,' he declared, 'he would make a terrific clergyman.'

During this time he visited the Sea of Galilee; and as he walked on the shore where Jesus once walked, he was later to tell David Lodge, he felt a strong desire to demonstrate his Christian determination and sincerity. After some thought he announced he was going to give up smoking.

'It sounds funny now, but he made it sound so bloody serious then that you somehow accepted it as a very reasonable and generous sacrifice,' recalls Lodge.

His interest in the Bible became intense: 'He read it,' says Lodge, 'almost every day.' He visited boys' clubs in the East End of London, met parson David Shepherd (former England cricket captain and later the Bishop of Woolwich), who had become heavily involved in social work in the slums.

The impact on Sellers was considerable. 'It made him feel that his own life was meaningless,' remembers one friend.

'In other words,' says Lodge, 'he got religion. I don't mean he was Bible-punching, but he definitely found some very real comfort in it. It didn't last of course, but that doesn't matter, it doesn't mean it didn't make some very real impression on him.'

When Lodge noticed Sellers had started smoking again, he knew the passionate romance with religion was nearing its end.

'When Peter got enthusiastic about something, there were no limits to his enthusiasm. Then suddenly, were it people or possessions, *finish*.'

He was no longer under the spell of the Church when he was seemingly dying in California. Yet, 'I suddenly felt I had to go to him,' Father Hester says. 'I felt an enormous need to be with him, almost as if he were demanding it. It wasn't a vision, but did come to me in a flash.'

(At approximately the same time David Lodge experienced a more exact occult sensation. Deeply depressed by the news, he was shopping in Richmond, Surrey, when he heard the voice of Peters Sellers saying very clearly, 'Don't worry, boy. I'm going to be all right now, Davey.' Lodge returned home, slightly shaken but no longer under a cloud. He told his wife, 'Peter is going to be fine; I'm not worried now.' It seemed a surprising thing to say, Mrs Lodge thought, in view of the continuing headlines that gave small hope of recovery.)

In Soho the priest left his small, comfortably untidy

197

office overlooking the churchyard where office girls eat their sandwiches in summer, and vagrants wait for the dark to hide them. It was a scene that Sellers once said he found 'encouragingly peaceful'. Father Hester walked briskly to Sellers' office. There he met Bill Wills, the actor's financial caretaker. 'What about it, Bill, should I go?'

Richard Dawson Azerley Wills was the man who controlled and manipulated the vast Sellers market, negotiating his complex contracts, investment programmes, insurances, and always paternally watching over his day-to-day expenditures. He was not, naturally, a man of impulse. Ten years before, he had been asked by Sellers to sort out his financial affairs. 'They had been,' he recalled affectionately, 'in a hell of a mess.' They were no longer in a mess: but with Sellers in such a critical state and with the sudden shadow of death-duties thrown menacingly across his schemes to preserve and multiply his client's fortune, he was even more wary than usual.

Wills assured the priest that Sellers would be much comforted by his presence, as both minister and friend. But, he added sadly, if the news was 'as black as it now sounds', he could offer no financial help for the trip. Father Hester didn't want it. 'I simply wanted his approval. I always planned to pay my own way and I did. It was enormously expensive, but it was a good investment from a priesthood point of view.' (Later Sellers offered to repay all his expenses, but the priest refused. 'If I'd accepted it it would have undermined and defeated the whole object of my going. But he did offer and that was enough.')

The following day he was in Los Angeles. He drove straight from the airport to the Cedars of Lebanon, where Sellers was now coming through the last crucial hours of his ordeal. The priest offered to anoint him: the simple Christian service was conducted in the room where he had, at least clinically, died eight times.

Almost at once the priest from Soho was faced with a problem: how to ward off Sellers' renewed eagerness to embrace the Church? Father Hester wanted to give him time to consider his fresh outbreak of religious fervour from somewhere a little less prejudicial than a hospital bed in which he had clinically died. He avoided discussing the question of commitment in any depth.

'I didn't feel any desperate need to hook him, to land him . . . there was no hurry with Peter,' Father Hester believed. 'He was already an honest man to himself, and that was as much as most of us can ever hope for on this earth.'

This decision, from at least a clerical point of view, may have been a supreme mistake. But by this time Father Hester was acutely aware of Sellers' often sincere but short-lived passions.

For, only a few years before, Sellers had been deeply involved with clairvoyancy. His preoccupation had been so well known that at least one producer attempted to use it for his own ends. Having failed to persuade him by conventional methods to star in his comedy *Too Many Cooks,* Mario Zampi embarked on a frankly devious scheme. An ingenious idea, if not the most honourable experiment in psychical research, it was based on the simple premise that Sellers was reputed 'not to make a move without consulting Maurice Woodruff'.

Sellers had had cause to be impressed by the little Cockney clairvoyant. On his first visit, sometime in 1955, he had been told he would work for a producer with Z in his name and play several roles, winning much critical acclaim. The following year Sellers, still considerably better known for his radio and television work, was signed by Mario Zampi to star in *The Naked Truth.* The picture was made in 1957; Sellers played five roles and collected due praise.

Now Woodruff wasn't seeing a Z in Sellers' future at all. But, 'I have to have Sellers,' Zampi told writer Michael Pertwee. He offered to almost double the £5,000 he had paid Sellers for *The Naked Truth.* 'Mario,' says Pertwee, 'was pretty desperate.'

Zampi then put his plan into operation: he became a sudden and devoted client of Maurice Woodruff. During each visit he poured out his own predictions of the fame in store for the actor fortunate enough to star in his next picture. Woodruff recalls he seemed 'bloody uninterested' in his own future and had some difficulty slipping in a prediction edgeways. It was, perhaps, a pity.

After three fast and voluble visits Zampi felt convinced he had insinuated the idea and waited for Sellers to get the message, via the unsuspecting Woodruff, and change his mind. Certain of his powers of persuasion, he told several friends that 'Sellers is certain to change his mind' and on another occasion, 'Sellers won't be able to resist.'

Several weeks later Sellers was still resisting, and even Zampi recognised that his bid to brainwash Woodruff had failed; Terry-Thomas was cast in the role, and the producer went to his grave never recovering his faith in clairvoyancy nor in his own gloriously glib tongue.

It was inevitable, perhaps, that Sellers' questing, impatient mind, which had taken him beyond clairvoyancy into the Church, would one day lead into the trickier world of spiritualism. During his days in Ilfracombe he had known a boy called Terry Roberts whose mother, Estelle Roberts, was among the most distinguished and accomplished mediums in Britain. It was to this diffident, dignified, and quite extraordinary old woman that he went, in the early sixties, to investigate psychical phenomena.

Born in 1889, in Kensington, Estelle May Roberts, *née* Wills, left school at fourteen, and from her earliest recollection 'heard voices' – and was frequently beaten with a leather belt by her stern Victorian father, who felt such imagination demanded realistic disciplinary measures. The voices survived the strap. When Sellers heard about her paranormal gifts he, together with his first wife, Anne, arranged to attend a séance at her home in Esher, Surrey.

At this first sitting Mrs Roberts' spirit-guide, an Indian known as Red Cloud, brought forward a man Sellers immediately 'recognised with a shock'. It was, he was convinced, Larry Stevens, a talented young writer on the early Goon shows who had died suddenly and on the threshold of a deserved fame.

'He sent messages that Estelle Roberts couldn't possibly have known about,' says Sellers. 'He used words and whole phrases that we only used together. It was . . . convincing.'

It was, he felt, the beginning of what he had long been searching for: a solace that was more than mortal, an answer that seemed to resolve his religious desolation. This ethereal enchantment was to be temporarily interrupted and even questioned during the making of *Heavens Above* and his involvement with Father Hester, but it would be rekindled after the death of Peg. At his mother's cremation service – conducted not by a rabbi but by Father Hester – he decided not to have denominational music. (For some mourners the playing of her favourite tunes, including 'I'll See You Again', caused uneasy moments.)

'Peter,' said Estelle Roberts, 'was psychic. He would have made a very fine medium, indeed.'

This information did not surprise him. 'I've had a strange thing that has followed me all my life, some special person in the other world who takes an interest in me and guards over me. It's very weird, it's like a sort of curse in some ways. I mean, people who go out of their way to bring bad things to me have great misfortune in their lives. I can quote you many instances. You can argue that what I'm going to say would have happened anyway: but one man just died who had been very much against me,' he once told me.

'I don't believe that I'm any special person but I do know that things do go very badly for people who are particularly evil towards me. It's most odd.'

It seems he did not overstate his case. Wolf Mankowitz was recalling the names of the people involved in an ambitious but finally abortive film company he was setting up with Sellers in 1960 (included in their production programme was the life of the actor's great-great-grandfather, pugilist Daniel Mendoza, whose fighting

201

stance was to be the company's colophon) when he stopped in his tracks.

'My God,' he said, 'so many people died during Sellers' lifetime. I'm amazed I'm still alive, you know that?' He was perfectly serious; he does not drink to excess.

Sellers' sense of divine protection could possibly be seen at work in the fortuitous circumstances of his presence in Hollywood at all in April 1964: so close to the Cedars of Lebanon with its then unique Intensive Care Unit, almost certainly the one place in the world where his life stood a ghost of a chance of being saved. (A British medical conference was told in 1966 that 'if Peter Sellers had been taken to ninety per cent of British hospitals, he would have certainly died'.) There he was in exactly the right place at the right time, making his first film in Hollywood, one of his few films outside Britain.

Sellers' investigation into the world of spiritualism, like most important things in his life, was not entirely unconnected with his career. For some time prior to his first visit to Mrs Estelle Roberts he had felt very strongly the presence of potent influence on his work; an influence that he knew was far greater and infinitely more strange than that of the impressive but irrepressibly mortal Maurice Woodruff.

For a time he toyed with the thought that it was the guiding presence of Grimaldi or perhaps the ancestral fighter Mendoza, both of whom could make viable mentors.

Joey Grimaldi, a famous pantomime clown of the nineteenth century, is in fact a frequently claimed ghostly influence on performers at the Drury Lane Theatre, where he gave some of his most memorable performances. And Daniel Mendoza, he knew, had done some theatrical touring – at £60 an appearance – after his days in the ring were over. Indeed, Mendoza was not a stranger to the art of impersonation: on one occasion, while celebrating a victory, he had dressed himself as a sailor, and was arrested as a deserter. Another time he sold himself to the organisers of a Jewish festival in the East End of London as a popular entertainer, a lie that was swiftly unmasked.

It was not until a later and more sophisticated sitting with Estelle Roberts – to whom he had never disclosed his longtime uncanny feeling that he was being professionally protected and guided by some supernatural force – that he learned the true identity of his mentor.

'Dan Leno,' Estelle Roberts told him, 'has come into the room, Peter. He wants you to know he is taking a very special interest in your work.'

Dan Leno, born George Salvin in the slums of St Pancras in 1857, was the most revered comic of his age. Highly praised for his timing and inventive humour by contemporaries, he won the personal approval of King Edward VII, who commanded his presence at Sandringham, a remarkable accolade in that class-conscious era. But at the height of his fame both his health and his mind snapped. He died, after a brief come-back, in 1904, aged forty-three. His cortège through the city of London was mourned by weeping crowds five feet deep and four miles along.

This was the man Sellers became convinced had guided his career so carefully for so long. A man who died just twenty-one years before he was born. He remembered taking this information from Estelle Roberts with 'a sort of satisfied relief, really, but, no, not surprise because it . . . made sense somehow'.

How or why 'it made sense' he admitted he was unable to explain. But in January 1968 the BBC produced a remarkable and revealing television show on Leno's life based on his autobiography *Hys Book*. The following morning the critics were almost unanimously astonished at the resemblance between the Edwardian's bizarre free-wheeling material and style and 'The Goon Show' of the fifties.

'What struck one most forcefully about the content,' wrote Michael Billington in the London *Times,* 'was the way it anticipated the material of our own most far-out modern comedians.' He duly noted the surrealist, anatomical jokes like, 'She winked at me with her ear and not her eye' and added admiringly, 'A description of some-one's voice as "thick with passion and bulging at both ends" would have fitted happily into any Goon Show.'

Dan Leno, it should be recorded, is not entirely an unknown psychic influence in the world of show business. On at least one occasion the old-time English comic Stanley Lupino, father of Hollywood actress Ida Lupino, claimed to have seen and talked with the ghost of Leno in his dressing room at Drury Lane.

It is, of course, entirely possible that the sincere and highly regarded Estelle Roberts was able, through some unconscious paranormal telepathy, to pick up Sellers' secretly held view that he was being helped from 'the other side'. Her revelation that Dan Leno was the spirit guiding his career – although 'he was as clear as you are now, dear' – would be a natural piece of casting in view of Mr Leno's established penchant for personal appearances in this rarefied theatre.

But even allowing that Mrs Roberts had quite asto-nishing telepathic powers, so that when she seems to be communicating with the dead she is merely picking the minds of the living, it does not satisfactorily explain everything.

Alternatively, then, one must seriously consider Sellers' own powerful, perhaps unique, creative energies. For this factor, allied to his formidable memory-capacity as a trained actor, could create illusions of enormous and inexplicable reality: indeed, a phenomenon easy to attri-bute to some outstanding paranormal force.

Nevertheless, Peter Sellers himself remained quite con-vinced that Dan Leno was his guiding spirit. 'He follows me around everywhere,' he said, and his voice carried the simple conviction of that simple statement. 'For years I felt his help, especially with my timing, before I knew who it was. He has been great for me. I knew it had to be someone in the business because his knowledge was so perfect. He has given me some wonderful advice.'

One evening as we talked in his flat in Mayfair, I asked how Dan Leno communicated with him. 'Do you hear his voice the way you hear my voice now?'

'Yes, absolutely as clear as that. I mean a clear, clear voice, as if someone is speaking, but in here' – he pointed a stiff finger down into the middle of his skull – 'and not through here' – he tapped his ear with an index finger. 'It's a strange, strange difference; it's as though somebody is speaking inside your head, which is why many people dismiss it, dismiss spiritualism as being dotty, of course.'

'Is the voice spontaneous, unpredictable, or must you call on it, summon its presence?' I asked.

'Sometimes I ask for help, sometimes it just happens. It can happen anytime, anytime at all.' He talked with that brand of calm, quiet conviction that intelligent zealots use, the ones who don't care a damn whether they convert you to their cause or convince you of their right; they *know* and their own acceptance, a private and reassuring thing, is all they need. He never let Dan Leno become an Edwardian skeleton in a silk suit; he was not a haunted man, neither burdened by nor afraid of the good spirits he believed sought to guide him.

(Although an alien spirit did severely panic him out of a home he was renting on Long Island once; he was convinced it moved a pair of blue socks from a chair to the bed one evening while he was taking a shower. The following morning he took up residence in the Regency Hotel, Manhattan, where his socks, along with his nerves, remained undisturbed.)

He discussed the subject with the respect that fell short of unction, with authority that was not dogmatic; he spoke with care because it was important, but the care did not become caution, for caution is the defence of the weak, the first barricade of the uncommitted. It is a very personal subject, spiritualism, prickly with prejudice and controversy, yet as he talked one began to feel a closeness to the man, perhaps even a flicker of understanding.

A few days before, he said, he had been staying at his country home with his son, Michael, who was then thirteen and already over six feet tall. During the afternoon Michael announced he was going riding with a friend

205

named Stanley. It was a bad moment for Sellers. 'Somebody, I don't know who it was, said as clear as a bell in my head, "Oh don't let him go, he'll have a bad accident". I felt paralysed.' But unable to explain his reluctance to agree to the ride, Sellers felt trapped. 'I didn't want to let him go, but I didn't want to seem like a spoil-sport either. I felt awful. Finally I said a thing I don't normally say to my children: "If you go out riding will you promise me to be especially careful?" '

A hundred yards from the stables a dog ran across the road and startled the horses. The two boys were thrown. 'Michael, very fortunately, was guided down and fell correctly . . . but his friend was kicked and quite badly hurt. I felt terrible.'

As he struggled with the words of his simple story, full of parental pain, one wondered whether the varnish and the veneer had been stripped away to expose the grain of Peter Sellers – the original humility of the man before the gloss of sophistication had soaked into his pores and completed the groomed camouflage of the twentieth-century celebrity: impenetrable from the outside and the in.

Estelle Roberts, perhaps, knew something of the man inside. She lived alone in semi-retirement in a large new flat furnished in the comfortable taste of the thirties. There were signed photographs of dead politicians and deposed kings with fixed, unknowing smiles wasting away in unvisited rooms or lost amid the Dresden china and bric-à-brac of an old woman's crowded life. She was a slim elegant woman, with the kind of style you buy only with the currency of the years. At a distance she might have been an aristocrat; as you moved closer you noticed the hands, and guessed correctly that they once scrubbed floors. Her clothes were the clothes of the smart dowager duchess, but they didn't quite disguise the tough sinewy body made by hard times and missed meals, and not by diets and croquet. There was a permanent pleasure about her face, even in repose, and she laughed well, without noise. She was very fond of Peter Sellers and regarded him with the affection of a childless aunt without being unaware of his faults. Her attraction for Peter Sellers, aside from her potent mediumistic appeal, was not hard to appreciate.

'Peter,' she said, 'was working out his own salvation in his own way. Whatever one does in this world one is criticised for, but nobody can take away the fact that he made millions of people happy. Nobody has the right to criticise another person, and often you find that such criticism is merely the expression of self-guilt, self-doubt. They defile themselves, the critics, not Peter.'

She talked without prompting, moving gracefully among her themes, again and again returning to Sellers:

'He came when his mother passed over . . . she's very much alive . . . she told him he was carrying her ring in his pocket and he was . . . Peter has a great talent and he is very much helped from the other side . . . he was very pleased when I told him Dan Leno was standing behind him, as clear as you are now . . . it is the simple law of attraction, you see . . . he didn't die in Hollywood because the unbilical cord didn't break . . . the living are tied by an unbilical cord, you know, just as a child is tied to its mother we are tied to life . . . this would account for the dreamless sleep . . . he is too highly strung and loses his temper very easily . . . but he is getting help from the other side . . .'

The sittings were carried out simply, without ceremony or symbols of any sort; she passed on messages, advice, reassurances, words of love. She was an undemonstrative woman, only occasionally allowing herself to screw her face into threads of concentration or cocking her head, listening, smiling, nodding through her private communication with Red Cloud.

'You see,' she said afterwards, 'it is all so natural. That was what Peter liked. It is the most natural thing in the world.'

But having satisfied his own private needs, and provided a balm for his bereavement, is it possible that the world of occult, of spiritualism, and psychical happenings, could have opened up the frontiers of his talent?

Shortly before he was due to begin work on *The Bobo*, in which he was to play Juan Bautista, a much-gored, mediocre, singing matador, he was still groping for the character. He was concerned that he could not find the voice, that vital foundation of all his roles. Not many days before production was due to start he got a 'compulsive feeling' that he would 'find Juan Bautista' in a particular bar not far from the bull-ring in Barcelona. He immediately took off alone.

It was not, on the face of it, a particularly paranormal attraction. It was the usual kind of bar favoured by players and punters and hangers-on in hard sports the world over. Bullfighters who died young and died brave look down from their rosetted frames, so solemn, so sad, as the survivors grow noisy and old, just as they do in the saloons on Eighth Avenue that cater to prize-fighters with broken faces now healed, and broken hearts that never will. It is only a very short journey to a spacious apartment in England where dead kings and forgotten politicians smile in silver picture frames. In both places, in different ways and for different reasons, people are clinging to the past with ageing fingertips. And in both places Peter Sellers had searched and looted for what he wanted.

Night after night, in the bar in Barcelona, he waited for Juan Bautista. He ate there, drank there, played there, waiting. It was an extraordinary vigil, something far beyond an actor's research.

'I knew,' he told me, 'that sooner or later my man would walk through that door and I would recognise him instantly. And of course he came. I watched and listened. The way he walked, picked up his glass, laughed and spoke with that funny lisp . . . Bar*the*lona . . . the way his mouth worked, everything.'

It was at this point, on this occasion, that Peter Sellers moved, perhaps deliberately or perhaps unconsciously, into the unmapped area of the paranormal. 'It's rather like being a medium,' he said, 'and laying yourself wide open and saying, "I want a character to inhabit my body"

208

or "I want a spirit to take charge of me so that I can produce what I hope to produce".

'I've been aware of a whole new thing happening to me when I've been like that. I think that in there somewhere is the beginning of the advanced form of mediumship, although I think at that point you must start thinking in terms of spirit-guides, because if you didn't know your way around in that area you could get taken over by all kinds of wrong things.'

Despite Estelle Roberts' high opinion of his psychic potential, Sellers was cautious. 'Whether the powers I have become more acute as I grow older I obviously can't tell. But I think not. Because I don't, to myself, appear to be that kind of person.'

Did he, I asked him, have any premonition about his future?

'Yes,' he said evenly. 'I shall live till I'm seventy-five and will die in my sleep shortly after that. I know that. I suppose I knew all the time I would never die during that Hollywood business. But you have to watch things. Even so, I think I shall most probably die about then, seventy-five, that age.'

A Fragile Flower

Peter Sellers is behaving like a brat. He has threatened
to walk off his new movie *I Love You, Alice B Toklas*
unless the entire crew is changed. He contends there's a
spy on the set – and indeed all his latest little sorties
behind the camera have been reported with unaccus-
tomed rancour by a certain Hollywood columnist.
Sellers' temper is hardly a secret deserving of espion-
age. It may now be time for Peter Sellers, one of our
great comedy actors, to return to acting in earnest. *The
Bobo,* his most recent picture, shows a Sellers who's
lost something in transition.

Joyce Haber in the *Los Angeles Times*
8th January, 1968

THE COLUMNISTS, particularly the female breed, were
gunning for him. Particularly peeved at being banned
from the set during Sellers' presence, they mounted a
steady campaign of abuse; one gossip writer let it be
known that she would 'pay very well' for any anti-Sellers
stories she received. He was, said one studio veteran,
Hollywood's biggest 'scapegoat, whipping-boy, and fall-
guy since Fatty Arbuckle'. Some of the stories had roots in
reality: he *did,* for example, object to a purple sweater
worn by a script-girl. It was his 'unlucky colour' and,
fearfully superstitious, he asked the girl to change it. It was
reported he 'flew into a rage' and 'screamed at the poor
girl', who 'fled in tears'. Some of the columnists didn't
even get the colour right: 'My own spies tell me,' confided
one, 'Sellers exploded . . . because someone was wearing
green.'

'I'm a sitting duck, I can't possibly win,' he said.

'People who write these things just don't know the real Sellers,' complained Leigh Taylor-Young, his co-star on *Toklas*, in which he played a lawyer-turned-flowerchild hippie. 'He's not perfect, but they've been very unfair to him.'

Toward the spring of 1968, when the picture went into the editing stage and still the anti-Sellers stories showed no sign of relaxing, publicists at the Warner-Seven Arts studio were told to feed some of the actor's 'more endearing ripostes or inimitable epigrams' to the baying ladies who write the columns. There were, alas, few to feed. 'He just isn't concerned with covering his brawls with badinage,' said one press agent. 'He's an obsessive actor and that's that.'

The bid to build a 'nice guy' image was doomed from the start. Even when Sellers generously took page advertisements in the trade papers (as well as telephoning at least one influential London critic) to laud Mel Brooks' film *The Producers*, it was rumoured that it was part of the studio's campaign to rehabilitate him in Hollywood's affections. Yet neither Brooks nor the studio knew about the advertisements until the day they appeared. 'I was just knocked out with the picture, that's all,' Sellers said simply. 'I thought it would be nice to give it a plug.'

Certainly it did nothing to enhance Sellers' popularity. Shortly after it appeared Donald Zec wrote in the London *Daily Mirror:* 'To the wagging-tongued fraternity here, who like their celebrities to fall into line, all servile and gift-wrapped, Sellers is probably the most unpopular chap in Hollywood.'

The professionals were not surprised. The picture of perfection in acting, in art, in anything, is only pretty when it's finished. The pursuit of it, they know, is an ugly, sweating, painful business. The gossip columnists displayed only their own intolerance or ignorance or both. Certainly they failed to report or convey the creative stress that provoked his real and imagined tantrums. And it is to the film-makers and fellow artists themselves that

211

you must turn to understand the agony of Peter Sellers. Not all of them liked Sellers as a man, but there were few who did not in the final analysis respect his supreme artistry and sympathise with his peculiar torment as an actor of genius.

Joe McGrath had this to say after the debacle of *Casino Royale:* 'When the camera turns, whatever the political intrigues, the front office wrangles, the back-stage fights, it all comes down to the actor. A close-up. And that's what drives people like Sellers to such lengths . . . knowing that finally in wide-screen and Panavision, fifty yards across by twenty yards tall, it's going to be his face they're looking at and nobody else's.'

Billy Wilder now says, 'Sellers was a highly original and effective star who achieved a tremendous rapport with vast audiences. That is a rare thing. And audiences, you know, don't give a damn whether an actor is difficult or tough or downright impossible. All they care about is what they see up there on the screen in their local cinema.' After the completion of *The Bobo,* when the strains and tensions of that production were behind them, Sellers told director Robert Parrish: 'Well, Bob, we've finished it. They said we'd never complete it and we have.' (Sellers had by now completely fallen out with the producer Elliot Kastner, who had firmly resisted his claim for a director's credit on the picture. Angrily Sellers cabled him, 'Have received your message and am not surprised. It is typical of you. I have given all there is that any artist can possibly give to you. *The Bobo* is the last time we will work together.' It is framed in Kastner's London office.)

'I think,' said Parrish, 'it's the best thing you've ever done. Your contribution to it on all levels has been tremendous, I mean *tremendous*.'

He added, 'I've been very angry with you at times on this picture, Pete, and I guess there have been times when you've been just as mad at me . . .'

'*When* were you angry with me?' Sellers interrupted. His shocked tone surprised Parrish.

'On this picture,' Parrish answered evenly. 'We both

212

decided to be ruthless very early on – everybody and everything had to go if it stood in the way of making this picture work. Right?'

Sellers agreed.

'I've been most angry with you when you've invented a marvellous piece of business and then scrapped it against my advice. You didn't trust my judgement. That hurt. That was angry-making.'

Parrish was particularly incensed at the actor's point-blank refusal to keep in a piece of business he especially admired:

During rehearsal Sellers had emerged from a bath of blue dye and, woefully examining himself, said, according to the script, 'I'm blue everywhere,' then, noticing his little finger, ad-libbed, 'even my pinky is blue.'

Sellers had refused to use the joke in the scene.

'That,' said Parrish, 'is the sort of thing which made me mad at you. After all, we were making a comedy, and funny lines are what make people laugh.'

It was wrong, Sellers insisted. Then, 'It was too cute, it wasn't Juan Bautista talking. It was me.'

Unlike most comics, especially those reared in vaudeville, he would not corrupt the integrity of a performance for any easy laugh. It was often this pitiless attitude toward himself and others that caused so many items like the one quoted earlier from the *Los Angeles Times*. His explanation to Robert Parrish was one of the few occasions when he found the words to justify or even explain his behaviour as an actor.

'The trouble with Peter,' says one affectionate critic, 'is that he lacked eloquence and he lacked discretion. He either flew into a tirade or clammed up. Either way he lost. He was a blundering genius.'

His tirade against Hollywood, however misinterpreted, cost him the nominated Oscar for *Doctor Strangelove*. 'If he'd died and kept his mouth shut,' one influential academician told me later, 'it was in the bag. The man tripped up the actor.'

'Sellers was so damn self-destructive,' says Robert

Parrish. 'If he had been a painter he would have had to cut the canvas; but he was a film actor and there were too many canvases. So he cut the nearest thing to him at that time . . . sometimes the director, sometimes the producer, and even sometimes himself.'

Yet, 'he was the only actor with whom I have worked that I would call without any doubt a genius', says John Boulting. In a business where the coinage of praise is peanuts, Boulting is not a big spender. 'I had an affection for Sellers because I thought he was a very sad, vulnerable and basically a very unhappy person. He needed to be comforted because deep down he was a child, with all the innocence and all the cunning that belongs to childhood,' he says.

Richard Burton once told Sellers, 'You are one of the finest actors in the world today.' Even allowing for his natural Welsh exuberance (probably tempered anyway by his respect for the English language), Burton's words were a remarkable testimony to Sellers' real achievement. For seldom before has a man, essentially a comic actor, been recognised as a serious theatrical force. W.C. Fields, Stan Laurel, Buster Keaton, even the urbane Cary Grant, have never been given the credit they've deserved as actors. Comedians are the perpetual outsiders. That humour has its own absolute measure – if a laugh misses it fails – is of little, consequence in the erudite world of dramatic art, where so many failures survive as artistic triumphs, buoyant on a sea of pretentious mediocrity.

'A clown,' Buster Keaton said to me in Paris not long before he died, 'is a fragile flower. Treat him kindly.' Richard Burton's words of praise were as tender and as nourishing as any green-fingered nurseryman's. 'I don't believe,' remembers Harvey Orkin, 'Pete had ever been quite so stunned by a remark in his life. But Burton was right. Sellers revealed more truth in a cameo performance than a dozen tragedians in a lifetime.'

To get to that truth was a tortuous business; it left him no less bruised than those around him. But tolerance, as the gossip writers have shown, is the most perishable produce in the bright display windows of humanity. Writer Wolf Mankowitz felt his own rotting as he watched *Casino Royale* warp and buckle beneath the creative stress of the actor's performance.

'I don't know why my professional relationship with Sellers was subjected to this extraordinary malformation,' he was to say later. 'Except I doubt whether he had ever had any working relationship that finally was not.'

It is worth recording here that Mankowitz, who once survived and was prepared to forget the collapse of their business partnership, was not willing to forget nor forgive what, in his opinion, was an actor's self-indulgent destruction of a fine screenplay. Now he says bluntly, 'I wouldn't have considered myself confident to write for him anymore, in any circumstances. If a producer had come along to me and offered £40,000 for me to write a screen-play for Sellers I would first have asked whether I had to work with the man. If the answer had been yes I would have given back the money immediately. It simply wouldn't have been worth the effort, the heartbreak.'

To bring a man like Mankowitz to this state of sacrifical determination must have involved a traumatic experience of epic proportions.

This is what *he* says happened on *Casino Royale*. 'Sellers had rejected the property once. Then I wrote a character and evolved a situation [the three-ringed circus treatment] which he found very funny, and he agreed to do the picture. But then, with Joe McGrath, he started to rewrite it . . . nobody knew what the hell was happening. If Sellers hadn't adopted that meddling attitude, which in the end didn't produce such a marvellous sequence anyway, the whole film wouldn't have gone into the mêlée that it did. For me that is the unforgivable crime of Sellers.'

But even Mankowitz recognises the stature of his adversary. 'He was a hard man to analyse,' he finally concedes, 'because he was a genius. He was an acting-genius there was no question about that. But he was not a genius writer, director – he wasn't even the greatest producer that ever happened. It was,' says Mr Mankowitz, shrugging heavy shoulders, 'a bloody shame.'

Yet Peter Sellers did have a superb grasp of the cinema business, of the economics, the chemistry of casting, the complex technicalities of picture-making, far beyond the understanding or interest of most actors. There are even some who believe this was part of the real tragedy of a singular talent caught up in a collective art. For whatever his contributions, and they were often staggering in their variety and inventive brilliance, he still *needed* writers and directors and cameramen and producers.

'He was hung up on that,' says one former associate. 'He never succeeded in doing a Chaplin and he never could have, because the business became too diffused, too risky. You cannot distil a three-million-dollar motion picture to one mentality, to one psyche. No studio, no man was going to finance that kind of gamble. Chaplin did it but in another age, in a less sophisticated and less expensive time. It was what Peter would dearly have loved to have created and knew he never could.'

But did Peter Sellers really 'loose something in transition'? Did 'the man' once more and finally 'trip up the actor'?

Roy Boulting says: 'As a man he was abject, probably his own worst enemy, although there was plenty of competition. But as an artist I loved him. He was so close to being a natural genius that his genius almost excused his behaviour. He would have continued to flourish, his talent would have ensured that . . . and his keen sense of survival.'

Again, to imagine that Peter Sellers was indifferent or unwary of such feelings would have been ingenuous; to think that he was not hurt by them, often very deeply, would have been insensitive. Each film he finished left him tense, emotionally bankrupt. There was a moment as we talked on his yacht *Bobo* in the Mediterranean when he revealed something of the besieged loneliness of his fame. 'It's not a status symbol for me,' he said of his yacht. 'It's really a . . . simplicity symbol. A sort of free pardon

216

from all the pressures. The sea is the only true solitude left in this world. I suppose that space is really the last loneliness, but we can't reach it yet.'

There was longing in his voice. The sound you heard when he talked of yesterday. In 1967, after the running disappointment of three films *After the Fox, Casino Royale, The Bobo,* he seriously contemplated returning to his old and first agent Dennis Selinger, now a super-agent guiding the affairs of such stars as David Niven, Roger Moore and Telly Savalas.

There was an exploratory dinner: it only saddened Sellers. The following morning he wrote a brief, self-betraying note to his old friend, expressing regret over their estrangement. He was unprepared, he wrote, for the surprise he got when he 'sat back and heard us both talking'. Clearly, he felt, Selinger had become 'dotty with power', and 'I am a hard cynical article'. Dismissing the idea of a renewed partnership he said: 'let's not make it nasty and uneasy' for each other. 'I remain as ever your friend.'

Selinger was amused by the almost melancholy seriousness of the note. 'We both knew it would never work out,' he said later. 'Not even old Pete could put the clock back. But it obviously really shook him when he realised we had both changed. That must have been a very hard little note for him to write.'

A Species of Revenge

On Monday, 29th April, 1968, back from Hollywood, Peter Sellers returned to Maurice Woodruff for a reading. It was almost two years since he had consulted the clairvoyant. Woodruff, the man who had predicted he would marry Britt four years before, now told him that the marriage was soon to end.

Clairvoyancy played no part in Woodruff's prediction this time. It was there for all to see. Their fights had become more and more public, their separations more frequent. Both were having more or less open affairs. Locked out of their Mayfair apartment, excluded from their country house, Britt was loaned a friend's cottage in Fulham.

The marriage ended in December 1968. Britt got a £30,000 settlement, no alimony, and custody of their daughter, Victoria.

In her ghost-written autobiography published a few weeks before Sellers' death, Britt remarks that at this time 'our friends PM and Tony had also run into heavy marital squalls . . . I hesitated to contact PM to tell her that we too were having problems, although I guessed she knew.'

Indeed, Sellers was already hinting to close friends that his friendship with Princess Margaret was something more than platonic. They were, he said, 'two people consoling each other at a very difficult time in our lives. She's good news.'

'The trouble was that Pete could never believe that he was a social force in his own right', one former girlfriend told me. 'The Princess Margaret story was just one of the stories he told himself, to reassure himself when things were going wrong.'

On 5th June Sellers announced in Rome that he and

Britt had decided to part and planned to get a divorce. Britt returned to her parents in Stockholm, lamenting: 'I don't like the way he allows his life to be governed by soothsayers.' Yet even at the final breaking point she told friends: 'The strange thing is I know in my heart that if I had the choice I would do it again. He is a genius. Impossible, moody, temperamental, jealous, all those things, but life with him was extraordinary, stimulating, memorable.'

Britt sued for divorce, citing mental cruelty.

In London, Sellers examined the debris of his second marriage and once again he felt the loving spectre of Peg touching his life. 'I suppose what I lack, what I really want, is some sort of mother figure in my life,' he conceded. 'A man needs that, particularly if he adored his mother, as I adored Peg. Yet one wants a great bird as well. It's a problem. But, I don't know, most men seem to solve it without too much trouble – but then other people always seem to find the happiness you've been looking for . . .'

By this time, after a brief interlude with the actress Mia Farrow, his affair with Miranda Quarry, a 22-year-old flower of the British aristocracy, was well along the garden path. Her stepfather was Lord Mancroft, a former Tory cabinet minister, a bastion of the Establishment. 'I'm not sure if anything'll come of it,' Sellers said, spotting at once the idiosyncrasy and style of her class. 'She's the sort of girl who either marries old money and has masses of frightfully debby daughters, or opens a boutique in Beauchamp Place.'

Despite the manner in which he had courted royalty, the upper-crust was not his favourite *milieu*, a fact he was not always able to hide. 'You could only imagine him mixing with that set to absorb material, to eavesdrop on characters and accents,' said one of his old mates, uneasy at the direction Sellers' social life had taken. But, if nothing else, the Establishment epitomises stability and stability was something he needed badly at that time.

I had finished and delivered the manuscript of the

original version of *The Mask Behind the Mask* to my New York publishers. We were still talking, although his enthusiasm had cooled considerably since 1965 when we had first discussed the idea of a biography. Once he had tried to stop it completely. On September 12 1966 he wrote:

I have given a very great deal of thought to our proposed project on my life story, including dying and everything, and I have a strong feeling that this is not the time to do it, even though I think your idea for the general layout is the best yet. I won't bore you with the whys and wherefores; enough that you know, in the words of Fred Kite, that: 'I have withdrawn, meditated, consulted, convened and my decision has been democratically arrived at.'

I think later on, much later on, would be better for me – perhaps in about eight or nine years. Of course it may be that nobody will be interested by then, but the reverse also applies, and I know I am just coming into my most productive period right now.

I wish that you will understand my feelings, Peter, and not be disappointed.

All good wishes,

As ever,

I immediately flew to Rome where he was preparing *After the Fox*. I told him that I had gone too far to stop; I was too committed, too keen to see how it would end. With or without his cooperation, I said, I intended to finish the book. He didn't fight me. Now he simply accepted that a book was in the works. Like many things in his life, it became a subject he preferred to ignore. I knew he was unhappy about some things I had done:

'He's talking to all the wrong people,' he had complained to Bert Mortimer.

'He's talking to people who know you,' Mortimer replied.

'He's talking to people who *think* they know me.'

'He talking to just about everybody, Pete,' the loyal but

220

truthful Mortimer told him.

Now Sellers' career, as well as his private life, was shaky. Behind her gentle Pre-Raphaelite beauty that was very fashionable in the late sixties, Miranda Quarry was a self-possessed, tough-minded lady. 'She's a hard bird to handle,' he admitted ruefully, but with a kind of pride, after one of their frequent rows. He had made a succession of poor pictures; pictures mauled by the critics and left alone by the public. *After the Fox, Casino Royale, The Bobo, Women Times Seven, The Party, I Love You Alice B. Toklas* . . . it had become more than a bad patch. Few superstars have fallen so far so fast. Yet still he had not been able to moderate his behaviour or his demands. He was unable to own up to his portion of blame for the slump in his career, for the wretchedness of his private life.

'People don't understand,' he said. 'People don't understand what I have to do to protect myself from mediocrity, from shit, from all those third-raters.'

But producers were not interested in the tactics behind his tantrums. They only knew that his volatile temperament – alternating humility with sheer tyranny – was always liable to wreak impossible mischief on the studio, on the production, on people. 'Sellers,' said Bob Parrish, 'had gone into the mutual assured destruction business.'

Sellers knew all about the kind of business he was in.

'The movie business isn't exactly known for its observance of Queensberry Rules,' he said. 'A contract isn't exactly a Magna Carta.'

'You can't argue with Sellers,' Charlie Feldman had said to me once. 'His idea of winning is to emerge from a fight less mangled than the other guy . . . the biggest smithereen, if that's how it has to be.'

He had been in one crisis after another since *I'm All Right, Jack*. Now he was exhausted. 'I'm about as done in as I've ever been in my whole life,' he said to me one evening. 'It's been a heavy load.' There was something poignant and terrible about him then. It had finally borne in on him that he was being abandoned. He had ceased to deliver the goods. Producers believed that he was washed up as a major box-office star; he was no longer a bankable name.

The arbitrary shifts in his emotional behaviour became more reckless, more public. Some people thought that he had finally lost his marbles. At London Airport, he grabbed a customs officer by the throat following a small contretemps over some camera equipment ('for years afterward, anybody known to be remotely associated with him got a terrible going over at Heathrow,' recalls one publicist); he slugged his doctor cold at a dinner party for suggesting that his heart was as sound as a bell despite the 1964 heart attack; he overturned a food-laden table in a restaurant because they didn't have the vegetable his guest had asked for; he took a swing at a nightclub doorman who, failing to recognise him, asked if he were a member.

Unable to make those compromises, those adjustments to the ego, forced on slipping movie stars, his depressions deepened alarmingly. When I gave him a special leather-bound first edition of *The Mask Behind the Mask* in Daphne's restaurant in London, he burst into tears. 'I hope it's a good book,' he sobbed, 'because it's been a bloody miserable life.'

His decline had coincided with a crisis in the movie industry. The year before, five of the seven major Hollywood companies had lost over 100 million dollars between them. 'Peter Sellers,' reported *Newsweek* magazine in February 1970, 'who has been paid as much as $750,000 for appearing in a film, was recently offered to a producer for $50,000 and a small percentage of any profit from the movie.'

Frustrated, feeling the pinch ('I had just paid my income tax and that came to almost every penny I had,' he told me later) he became more and more reclusive, more and more prickly.

The Magic Christian did nothing to resurrect his career; *Hoffman* flopped badly; a picture called *A Day at the Beach* was shot and presumably buried in Denmark.

He knew now that he was engaged in nothing less than a struggle for survival. With a supreme effort, he managed to put on a brave philiosophical face, another mask. 'You know, luv,' he said, 'the trials we poor bloody actors are heir to . . . They come with the territory.'

Privately he was convinced that there was a Hollywood conspiracy against him. 'They need a scapegoat, so I'm being sacrificed,' he said. 'I'm the bag-holder.'

He began to mould a theory that part of his brain had been destroyed during the 90 seconds his heart had stopped beating in Hollywood. His weakened mind was a subject he turned to again and again. 'I know I'm going soft in the head,' he said. 'All my troubles upstairs started after that business in California.' Brain surgeons he consulted in London and New York tried to disabuse him of the idea. He wouldn't be shifted.

He had become a somewhat eccentric hypochondriac.

He was especially hooked on patent medicines.

'He always had a cold or a sore throat – coming,' recalls one former girlfriend. 'One evening he jumped up and left me in a restaurant in the middle of dinner because he said his throat tickled and he was about to come down with laryngitis.'

Visitors to foreign locations, anxious to put him in a good mood, were often advised to bring him small gifts of his favourite nostrums; guests came with gift-wrapped packages of Benylin, Lem-Sip, Beecham's powders, Night Nurse, Day Nurse, Liquid Anbesol (he often suspected he had a mouth ulcer on its way) and vitamin tablets.

'Most of the time he was dosed up to the eyeballs with some syrup or salve,' complained a studio nurse on one of his last pictures. 'If the instructions said "take three times a day", he'd take it three times an hour.'

Reports circulated in Hollywood that he was on the needle. It wasn't true, although he was often glassy-eyed. He did smoke marijuana occasionally; he took cocaine occasionally; on the whole he preferred vodka and champagne. But he seldom got drunk. 'Half the time he was just heaped to the gills on Benylin or bombed on Lem-

Sip,' an aide said wryly.

During this bad time, the Boulting brothers, who had given Sellers his first big break in *I'm All Right, Jack,* had been bidding against Columbia Pictures for the film rights to the successful West End play *There's A Girl in My Soup.* At a point in the bidding, Columbia's Mike Frankovich suggested that the Boultings and Columbia should make the picture together. It made sense. Columbia wanted the property for Goldie Hawn who had just had a big success in *Cactus Flower* for Frankovich. It was agreed that John Boulting would produce the picture, with his brother Roy directing.

'Now what about the guy?' Frankovich said. 'Do you have any ideas?'

It was the role of a lecherous middle-aged television personality.

'Peter Sellers,' John Boulting told him. 'He really is the only actor for this part. All along we wanted the play for him.'

'You can have anybody you want,' Frankovich said, 'except Sellers.'

'Sellers is perfect,' John Boulting insisted.

'A perfect son of a bitch,' Frankovich said. 'My board would never hold still for a minute for Sellers – never again.'

Columbia had lost a very great deal of money on *Casino Royale.*

'Every film is a prototype, Mike. Every time you invest in a film you're going to the races, you know that,' Roy pointed out. 'This is entirely a new race.'

'Get me,' said Frankovich, 'an entirely new jockey.'

Experienced film-makers, with gifts of brinkmanship and persuasion, the Boultings continued to lean on Frankovich. They knew it would not be easy; they knew that Frankovich had very strong and valid reasons for not wanting Sellers. During the making of *Casino Royale,* the Boultings had had a sizeable stake in Shepperton: studios enriched by Sellers' goings-on. 'Finally, you know, the workers themselves came to us and complained that

224

Sellers' behaviour was threatening the whole industry. They were building sets that could never be used because he was suddenly unavailable. They said, "It's all right for us now, guv, we're getting lots of work and plenty of overtime . . . but what about tomorrow, what is he doing to the fucking industry?" That was typical of the scale of his irresponsibility. He did not care,' John Boulting admitted later.

Nevertheless, the two Englishmen were convinced that they could handle the erratic star. It became a personal crusade, but it was a shrewd commercial crusade. 'We wanted Columbia to think again about the sense – we weren't arguing about the justice of it – of burying perhaps the greatest comic genius since Chaplin,' said Roy Boulting.

The situation was brittle. They were both aware of the dangerous ground they were treading. Frankovich was anxious to safeguard the studio's investment in Goldie Hawn. She had won a Best Supporting Actress Oscar for *Cactus Flower;* critics were comparing her favourably to Marilyn Monroe. She was the hottest thing around. Columbia saw *There's A Girl in My Soup* as a star-vehicle for Miss Hawn. The Boultings also saw it as an opportunity to rehabilitate Sellers.

'Sellers could unbalance the picture,' Frankovich said cautiously.

'We won't let him,' the Boultings said.

Finally convinced that they had the tactical guile to handle Sellers, Frankovich agreed to put the idea to his board of directors in New York. 'These guys can have practically any actor they ask for, but they still want Sellers,' he said. 'I think we should go with Sellers. They think they can control him. They're confident they can control him – and I have confidence in them.

The board approved the casting, but with no real enthusiasm. Frankovich was told, 'It's on your head, Mike. Nobody here believes that there's a man alive who can control that asshole.'

'I'm surprised he's still running around loose,' one

executive added gloomily.

Sellers was signed for $350,000 plus ten per cent of the net profits. It was by far the best deal he had had since *Casino Royale*.

The picture got off to an ominous start. Before the end of the first day's shooting, Sellers wanted the continuity girl fired.

'She's been looking at me with an expression,' he told director Roy Boulting.

'What sort of expression, Peter?'

'She hates me. That sort of expression. Would you please get rid of her. Tonight,' Sellers said.

Roy Boulting, who found 'the burden of dealing with Sellers on that level extreme,' summoned his brother. The producer listened to Sellers' complaint.

'But Peter, my dear chap, she adores you,' he answered, remembering how once, holidaying together in the South of France, Sellers had also 'seen a look' on his face and decamped in the middle of the night. 'I happen to know that she only took this picture because you were going to be in it. She's a tremendous admirer of yours.'

'Yes?'

'Absolutely. Tremendous. She's simply very shy. You're her hero.' Boulting laid it on thick. Sellers never talked about removing her again.

It had been eight years since the Boultings had last worked with Sellers. Roy was depressed by 'the marked change for the worse' in the star. 'He had been spoiled rotten by Hollywood. He had discovered that his talent gave him special privileges. Only now he wanted nothing less than licence.'

It was a constant battle, but the Boultings kept control. The picture was finished pretty much on schedule and close to its $2.5 million budget.

From the final wrap, Sellers was supremely confident about *There's A Girl in My Soup*. His suspicions of being Hollywood's scapegoat were forgotten. 'I have a real good feeling about this one,' he told friends. 'I think I've turned the corner. It feels like old times. I have to admit I went through a pretty rough patch, some real stinkers. I'm going to be a lot more careful about what I do from now on – and who I do it with.'

He was also satisfied that his two-year relationship with Miranda Quarry – a feuding and forgiving, clashing and kissing affair – was finally worth putting on a more legal basis. He had proved to himself, he said, that he had outgrown his fear of serious involvements: it was time for a new emotional commitment.

'Peter is a dear sweet man,' Miranda told reporters at their wedding at Caxton Hall registry office, London, in August 1970. Her 'bridesmaids' were her favourite Pekingese dogs, Tabitha and Thomasina.

It was left to Spike Milligan to put the pertinent question: 'Whatever happened,' he asked, 'to Fred?'

Sellers and high society were images of mésalliance.

'I don't know why either of them went through with it,' one of the actor's oldest friends said afterward. 'For respectability's sake? Out of embarrassment? Out of boredom? Perhaps they had really kidded themselves that there was something there. Miranda enjoyed his fame. And Pete . . . well, Miranda was twenty-two-years-old, beautiful, bluebook. He was flattered, dazzled, a bloody fool as usual.'

Sellers was forty-four. 'I think that now I have matured, learned a few lessons. Now all I want is to be happy,' he said.

A sneak preview of *There's A Girl in My Soup* in San Diego had been a big success. Mike Frankovich telephoned Sellers and told him, 'It really connects, Peter. Congratulations.'

That evening, the actor took a party of friends to dinner at the Tiberio restaurant in Mayfair. There was an air of quiet celebration about Sellers, but nobody knew why. He ordered champagne and caviar. Somebody asked, 'What's the toast going to be, Pete?'

'Jack's return home,' he said, lifting his glass.

He was convinced that he was on his way back to the top. Scripts and offers started to arrive again as word got around that *There's A Girl in My Soup* was a winner, vintage Sellers. But when the movie opened in London at the end of 1970, the critics were less than enthusiastic. The star's performance was 'surprisingly amateurish,' summed up David Shipman in his book *The Great Movie Stars*. It was a performance, Shipman wrote, 'that did go some way towards reflecting the dilemma of the latter-day Sellers : he couldn't decide whether to play it for laughs or romance, as character actor or leading man.'

Although the picture opened to excellent business, the notices undermined Sellers' confidence. He decided he had to strike while the iron was hot again. Ignoring his avowed intention to be more selective in the roles he played, he quickly signed for three more movies. 'Peter needed money,' said one of his overruled advisers. 'His recovery programme went out the window. He was grabbing movies the way other people buy sweepstake tickets, hoping that one of them would pay off.'

None of them did. One, *The Blockhouse* – described by its producer Lord Anthony Rufus-Isaacs as one of the finest things Sellers ever did, 'his Macbeth, if you like' – has never been commercially released.

Sellers moved to Ireland. He bought a mansion house in the village of Maynooth, near Dublin. It was a home that provided not merely a tax haven but also genuine isolation. 'It's a place where I can wind down between movies, and prepare myself for the next role, the next round.'

Ireland was also where he went to lick his wounds . . . and sharpen what Maurice Woodruff had once called 'his strange sense of grievance.'

His depressions returned, deeper and more lasting than ever. One morning he came down to breakfast with his thinning hair shaved to the bone. He announced that he intended to become a monk. Later he often claimed that he had spent some months in a monastery ('the happiest time of my life') but where, or when this blessed time was, remained a mystery. He spent days locked in his room, seeing no one, working on his shit-lists, those changing columns of names of people he hated. 'I suppose,' said a director whose name was no stranger to the list, 'it was occupational therapy of a sort.'

His always uneasy relationship with the press had given way to open hostility; his shit-lists invariably contained many critics' and reporters' names. Reporters were dismissed as 'lavatory-wall scribblers' or, sometimes, 'those loo inscribers'. (He contemplated introducing an Oriental journalist in *Fu Manchu* called Loo In Dong; the joke was finally considered to be too esoteric and dropped). He sent one reporter, a compulsive nose-picker, a wicked caricature (drawn by makeup man Tom Smith) of him at work with his finger deeply embedded in his nostril. Sellers had the cartoon duplicated and all the Fu Manchu unit were invited to submit suitable captions. 'Peter,' I was told, 'was really quite upset when he never got a thank-you note!'

Sellers' low opinion of journalists was undoubtedly hardened by his discovery that one columnist had cuckolded him. He said nothing but put the erring wife under surveillance. The private detective's reports were conclusive but he never used them. 'He just read them and read them – like a cricket buff reading old scores in backdated *Wisden* almanacks,' an aide told me. 'Her infidelity didn't seem to make him sad or angry. I think he blamed his own sense of sexual inadequacy at that time. He never minded talking about it, when he couldn't get it up. But one day . . . one day, he would have found a good use for those reports. That was Peter, nothing was ever lost and nothing was ever forgotten. It was very strange the things he could live with – and the things that could destroy.'

At the end of a dismal comedy called *Where Does it Hurt?* he took to his bed for weeks. He had lost so much weight from not eating, he quickly developed bed sores.

Miranda was feeling the strain. She became ill and moved back to London. Sellers had returned to Rome to dub *Where Does it Hurt?* when she was admitted to the London Clinic. Doctors diagnosed meningitis. Sellers stayed in Rome. Tax problems, he said, prevented him being at her side.

Privately he was telling friends, 'I'm pissed off with the pleasures of society and Miranda's pissed off with me. That's what you get for being such a bloody snob. I think that all Miranda ever really wanted was a bit of rough, a stroll across the tracks.'

His assault on society over, his marriage almost over, Sellers' career was again in sharp decline. He tried, and failed, to put together a movie of Bernard Kops's play *By the Waters of Whitechapel*. 'It's about a mother-dominated Jewish boy who is now well on in years and still hasn't left home,' he told the late Sydney Edwards, a reporter on the London *Evening Standard*. 'I'm Jewish and know that scene very well.'

Every Friday he lit a candle to his mother's memory.

There was about him again an aura of being lost, a sense of total defeat. He distrusted most friendships, and all women. His shit-lists grew longer with society names; for a short time they contained more society names than American names and names of newspapermen.

'There are some satisfactions you can only find in work,' he said. 'It's good to be a father sometimes. It's good to be in love sometimes. But the return you get on a really good performance, of making something real and understandable . . . nothing touches that, nothing gets near it.'

He sold up in Ireland ('All that green, I hate green, green's very unlucky') and returned to England and another picture for the Boultings. *Soft Beds, Hard Battles* was a comedy set in occupied Paris in which he played six roles, including an ancient French general, a Gestapo chief, a Japanese officer, and the sort of British major who is always at the first day of Lords, the last day of Wimbledon, and in the middle of most military cockups.

'It was a bad movie,' the Boultings recognise now.

'Sellers was superb but the thing as a whole just didn't hang together. The fault was in the script. We had a script that on paper seemed to be funny, seemed likely to extend Sellers' enormous talent for mimicry, but in the end just didn't work out.'

It was during the making of *Soft Beds* that Sellers embarked on his famous and frenetic affair with Liza Minnelli. Within forty-eight hours of meeting at a dinner party, he was announcing their engagement. He was still married to Miranda.

'I've fallen in love with a genius,' Liza said.

'This girl walked into my life and I'm walking on air,' he said.

Liza moved into his Eaton Mews home and quickly realised that she was walking on eggshells.

When she heard that Fredrick Davies had predicted on the BBC's *Today* show that she would never marry the actor, Liza immediately telephoned the clairvoyant for an appointment.

Davies read the Tarot cards and confirmed his radio prediction.

'That,' Liza told him, 'is what I thought.'

Three days later she announced that the affair was over. It had lasted exactly one month.

When Sellers heard that Liza had been guided by a clairvoyant, he said: 'Why didn't she go to *my* fucking clairvoyant?'

Columbia had now finished counting the profits on *There's A Girl in My Soup*. Ignoring the accusations of unprofessionalism again being levelled at him, ignoring the renewed box-office doubt surrounding his name, the studio was anxious to find another Sellers vehicle. They came up with a seventeenth-century pirate adventure-comedy called *Ghost in the Noonday Sun*. The role, a rascally ship's cook, was ripe with opportunities and the script, co-authored by Spike Milligan, abounded in the sort of gags that recalled the early Goons.

It was his fortieth film. Location filming began in Cyprus in September 1973. The Miranda divorce was moving to its final stages. In any other circumstances the picture could have provided an idyllic break in pleasant surroundings with agreeable people. Milligan would soon be joining him with a part in the film and David Lodge, another old chum, was also among the cast.

Trouble started on day one.

Sellers took an instant dislike to the American actor Tony Franciosa. Franciosa was playing a Douglas Fairbanks Jnr sort of role; when costumed and made-up, he bore a striking resemblance to the former film star. The likeness seemed to disturb Sellers considerably. He began inventing dialogue that the American, a dour introverted man who took his acting seriously, suspected was a veiled slur on his swashbuckling ability.

Franciosa asked him to stop changing the dialogue and get on with the script as written.

Sellers retaliated by stopping everything and getting on a plane to London to attend Princess Anne's wedding.

The production came to a standstill.

The hiatus did nothing to improve relations between the two actors.

Shortly after Sellers came back from the royal wedding, Franciosa had to be physically restrained from attacking him. 'I'm not,' he roared suddenly one morning as he sat in the make-up chair, 'going to take another day of insults from that English cocksucker.'

'It was very unpleasant,' remembers one of the crew who helped to calm the American. 'But I got the impression that Sellers was enjoying every minute of it. Some actors can only get off through gamesmanship, they need polarity and predicaments. I had never worked with Sellers before but from the moment he walked on the set he looked like a man stepping back into a terrain that was remorseless and very familiar to him.'

A few days later, the two actors came face to face in the picture's big duelling scene. Sellers received a slight nick beneath his right eye.

It was an accident but Sellers became convinced that Franciosa was trying to kill him.

Again he disappeared without notice from the island.

Returning several days later, he explained that he had gone to London to consult his ophthalmic surgeon.

'I've had worse cuts shaving,' said Franciosa.

'There obviously wasn't much wrong with Pete's eye,'

said one actor on the picture. 'He came back with just about the leggiest dolliest bird I've ever clapped eyes on.'

The lady was model Christina – Titti to her friends – Wachtmeister, daughter of Count Wilhelm Wachtmeister, Sweden's ambassador to the United States.

Titti, unfortunately, did not possess her father's diplomatic skills. When a man at the next table in a waterfront restaurant in Kyrenia began to pay her compliments she responded with obvious satisfaction.

Sellers left the table, drove back to the villa they had rented in the hills, and packed all her clothes. When he returned to the restaurant, Titti had joined her admirer's table. Sellers, with a great Clouseau-like flourish, threw the suitcase onto the table. Wine bottles, glasses, coffee cups crashed to the floor. *'You,'* he said, pointing to the wrong girl in the cafe's candlelit gloom, 'I want you out of Cyprus on the next plane.'

'But I *live* here,' said the astonished girl.

'A lot of Peter's outbursts had their funny side', said a former girlfriend. 'He nearly always went over the top. Afterwards you could laugh about it. But at the time . . . he had this gift for making you wish you were in whatever country or town or room he wasn't.'

Shortly after this incident in Kyrenia, in a lingering mood of misogynic morosity, Sellers gave a remarkable interview to a local 'stringer' for the London *Daily Express* in which he said some extremely unkind things about Miranda and their marriage.

Later in the day, he had second thoughts about the interview. He told Mike Russell, the picture's publicist, to call Jocelyn Stevens, an executive at the *Express,* and ask him to use his influence to kill the story. The well-connected Stevens, former owner of the society gossip magazine *Queen,* married to Princess Margaret's lady-in-waiting, said at once: 'Tell Peter it's done.'

When Sellers got the message he crossed Stevens' name off the shit-list. ('The idea that Peter was an extreme innocent who stumbled into situations is the judgement of a very naive person,' says Roy Boulting. 'He was very calculating. He used everybody.') He went back to work in a sunnier mood.

The sunny mood was short-lived. The production was now a long way behind schedule and the situation in Cyprus grew daily more serious. Sellers lost faith in the producers; Gareth Wigan was flown out to try to get the production back on an even keel. Sellers lost faith in director Peter Medak; Spike Milligan took over the direction.

'Milligan might very well be some kind of genius but it isn't film genius,' said an assistant director. 'He didn't know Camera Right from Camera Left. Nothing was matching. The continuity girl had a nervous breakdown.'

Unaware of the logistics and planning that go into a major production, Milligan couldn't understand why, at a moment's notice, on a whim, the entire crew of the pirate ship could not be dressed and wigged identically. Sellers, in a sort of sympathy tantrum, tore off his own wig and hurled it into the sea.

In New York, one Columbia executive considered the growing crisis in the Mediterranean and said bleakly: 'Sellers is a born again bastard.'

With Sellers aiding and abetting Milligan, the production sailed closer and closer to the anarchic surrealism of the Goons. (In one scene Sellers, as the ship's cook, serves up a ghastly looking swill. 'What's that?' asks Milligan. 'Bean stew.' 'I don't care what it's been, what is it now?' In another scene, Milligan tells Sellers, now the ship's captain, that the crew have a complaint. 'So have I,' ad-libs Sellers. 'We'll all see the doctor when we reach land.')

Franciosa was not amused by 'this grab-bag of adolescent jokes.' Neither was his performance helped by Spike Milligan's unique style of directing. His complaints fell on deaf ears. Columbia, like Charlie Feldman on *Casino Royale* seven years before, had put their money and their hopes on Sellers' comic genius and inspired improvisation . . . not realising that improvisation was his last refuge when he sensed a picture was going awry. Columbia knew

234

it was loo late to back out now. They considered the possibility of retitling the picture *Goons at Sea.*

The day they were to shoot the final scene at sea, a terrible storm blew up and lasted for ten days. The production was recalled to England. It was planned to shoot the scene on a tranquil stretch of water off the English south coast the following spring.

The scene was never filmed. The picture was shelved. It still lies buried in some Wardour Street vault.

In just four years he had made nine films: three were never released; five had flopped (although *The Optimist,* based on Anthony Simmons' excellent novella *The Optimists of Nine Elms,* was critically admired); only *There's A Girl in My Soup* had done well.

'I was only just hanging on,' he conceded later.

'Sellers had gotten away with murder for years because his talent was unique, he was too good to dump. But he had blown it this time,' said a producer. 'This time the word was out.'

The word was that Peter Sellers was washed up for good.

The Last Siege

In 1974, in the middle of what many of his friends considered to be a nervous breakdown, Peter Sellers heard Dan Leno talking to him. The Edwardian comic, the man whom Sellers believed had guided his early career, told him to 'return to Clouseau.'

It was, Sellers told me later, very clear. He had not heard from Leno, who died in 1904, for some while and was deeply impressed. 'Leno said he would look after me through the picture, watch my timing and all that sort of thing. He said he'd see me back on the right road. As clear as a bell,' Sellers said, pointing a finger at his temple. 'In here.'

Director Blake Edwards, who had been looking for a success after his own somewhat lean period *(Darling Lili, Wild Rovers, Tamarind Seed)* was thinking along similar lines to Dan Leno.

Sellers and Edwards had fallen out after *A Shot in the Dark* in 1964 and Sellers swore he would never make another Clouseau movie. There had been a rapprochement – and a sort of compromise – in 1968 when the director and the actor got together again for *The Party* in which Sellers played an Indian extra in Hollywood, a character that was clearly an amalgam of Clouseau and the doctor in *The Millionairess*.

The Return of the Pink Panther in 1975 put Sellers back on top; the sequels made him a millionaire. 'The *Panthers* saved his ass,' said one film man with no affection for the star. 'They renewed his bastard's licence.'

More exactly, Clouseau gave him clout. He was a bankable name again, an object of reverence in studio boardrooms. Almost immediately he set about using his restored muscle to get *Being There* off the ground. He had first read Jerzy Kosinski's novel in 1972. He saw the blank and isolated gardener, Chance, whose only experience in life is from watching television, a man of such simplicity that it borders on idiocy, as the greatest acting challenge of his life. 'The role is so reductive that only a truly professional actor could fill it with meaning without becoming boring,' he told Kosinski. Keen to play the part himself, the author had endowed his hero with an Olympian beauty to match his own Polish good looks.

Sellers saw Chance as middle-aged, pallid, overweight – 'all those years watching television, doing nothing . . .'

His compulsive identification with Chance was extraordinary. 'If I were to tell you that (Chance) was the ultimate Peter Sellers, then I would be telling you what my whole life was about,' he said to Kosinski. 'If I don't portray him he will ultimately portray me.'

Kosinski was convinced.

It was less easy to convince the moguls that *Being There* was a suitable idea for a Peter Sellers movie. It took Sellers, and director Hal Ashby, four years to get it into production.

Sellers did not hang around. In that time he made *Murder by Death,* two more *Panthers,* and *The Prisoner of Zenda.* It was sometimes hard to remember while reading about the films he was making and the women he was dating that Peter Sellers was a thrice-married, grey haired, middle-aged man with a pacemaker sewn into his body.

Marriage, he insisted after his divorce from Miranda Quarry in 1974, was something he had put behind him, like the latest car, thoroughly explored and tested and of no further interest to him. But in 1976, he met actress Lynne Frederick and promptly fell in love again. Miss Frederick, a 21-year-old brunette, had scored some success on British television. They met at a party given by Sellers' old friend and former agent Dennis Selinger. Peter talked, Lynne listened. She was fascinated, but not smitten. At four o'clock the following morning, Sellers phoned Selinger. He wanted Miss Frederick's number.

'That time of the morning, the urgent tone of Pete's

voice – talk about *deja vu*,' said Selinger afterward.

So began the last romance. They were married in Paris in February, 1976. He gave her the wedding ring that had belonged to Peg. The bride's mother, Iris Frederick, a casting director for a London television company, was distressed by the affair. 'What mother can be expected to approve of the marriage of her daughter to such a man?' She said the marriage was doomed.

What gave Miss Frederick the confidence to become the fourth Mrs Sellers was the conviction that her husband's needs were for a woman who would dedicate herself to him entirely, and the knowledge of her willingness to fill that role. 'I happen to like mothering people a bit. I love cooking and spending evenings at home. I'm content to put Peter's career first.'

In his eyes, Lynne became what he had always said he needed – a beautiful young Peg-like figure through whom he could release the pressures of his filial love. Their marriage, from the outside and in the beginning, looked like a mother's conniving sufferance of a spoiled child.

In August 1978, Sellers flew to Vienna to begin filming *The Prisoner of Zenda*. Lynne accompanied him as wife – and leading lady. After his unhappy experience with Britt Ekland on *The Bobo* it was, many thought, a most dangerous fusion of roles. People waited for the explosion.

The couple set up home in the Hotel Bristol. Sellers was overweight and stand-offish but generally well-behaved. He was particularly conscious of a thin red scar that circled his neck, the result of recent plastic surgery to tighten sagging jowls.

'He *seemed* to have settled down. His eccentricities weren't too obvious. The film went over-schedule but that wasn't totally Peter's fault. He turned up every day except for a couple of days when he really did have a cold and filming had to stop,' remembers one assistant.

He didn't want publicity, he turned down all requests for interviews. He declined Robert Mitchum's invitation to dinner. He said no to Richard Burton's invitation to the

238

Vienna opening of *Wild Geese.*

Lynne, in front of the cameras for the first time since their marriage, was eager for some attention. 'She was like 23-years-old. She wouldn't have said no to a little night-life occasionally,' I was told. 'But suddenly Peter was behaving like an old man, a recluse.'

'Lynne was slightly scared of him,' agrees one Sellers aide. 'She was very wary of him.'

The explosion that many expected never came. The marriage continued to tick over quietly, like a time-bomb.

In December 1978, at the end of *Zenda,* Sellers collapsed on an aeroplane going to Switzerland. It was a very serious angina attack. He spent a month in a Geneva clinic. It was the best-kept secret of his career.

Doctors told him that he must take a year off.

'What would I do?'

Rest.

'Do you know would that would do to my mind?'

You must slow down.

'You mean die more slowly?'

It is one way of living longer, they told him.

'I'm not an invalid,' he said. 'I won't live like one.'

His reaction was not just defiant, but alarming. There was, according to his thinking, a very good reason to risk everything. In a few weeks time he was due to start shooting *Being There.* 'If you think I'm going to pass that up because some quack wants me to spend a year in a rocking chair,' he said, 'you're crazier than I am.'

In Vienna he had been worrying about Chance. He was scared that he had coarsened his talent with too many *Zendas,* with too many rough-grained scripts. For years now he had indulged in excess, unnecessary exaggeration, although he knew that his genius lay in baring the sinews of a character through observation and subtle under-play. Now Hollywood was making reparation by finally allowing him to make *Being There.*

And he was scared.

Chance was still eluding him. He had little bits of the character. He had put on weight ('All those years watching television, doing nothing') and had had some minor plastic surgery on his eyelids because he felt they were too crêpey-looking for Chance. But he had no voice and everything started with the voice; he didn't know how the man walked, and he knew how a man lived from the way he walked. He stared for hours at himself in a mirror – waiting, as he had always waited, for the character he was to play to stare back at him, to inhabit his body as if he were a medium. That was how it had always worked for him, the way he had found Juan Bautista in Barcelona, how he had found so many other characters in so many other places.

'What Peter was seeing in the mirror was his own essential blankness. That's what baffled him. For the first time in his life *he* was the character,' said an English publicist who knew him well. 'Chance was the quintessential Sellers. He had become a perfect cypher.'

The day before shooting began in Asheville, North Carolina, he told his wife: 'I don't know how I'm going to play Chance. I thought I knew everything about him, how he spoke, how he walked, acted, thought, but I realise now that I have to do it tomorrow, and I really don't know.'

He did not sleep the night before shooting began in the winter of 1979. At about three o'clock in the morning talking to himself in the bathroom mirror, the voice came to him. It was a thin voice, an American voice with a trace of accent that might have begun life in the North of England. It was, he recognised much later, the voice of comedian Stan Laurel. It may or may not be significant that Laurel's earliest ambition according to biographer John McCabe in *Mr. Laurel and Mr. Hardy* was to be 'another Dan Leno.'

After the voice, Chance began to fall into place. 'Click, click, click,' said Sellers, explaining the ease with which that chillingly serene creation began to inhabit his body. Everything about him began to change. It was not just his walk and the way he held himself, it was not simply his voice, but his expression, his eyes, his gestures were all different . . . 'a leading man plays himself, I must create a whole new human being every time,' he had once said. It had never been more truly demonstrated than now.

He became passionless, totally unresponsive. The cold depressed him. The role he carried with him wherever he went emphasised his gloomiest and most pessimistic behaviour-patterns.

The strain on Lynne was intense. Sellers had closed up completely. He hardly ever talked to anyone. He seldom smiled. He rarely made eye-contact with people at the best of times; now, behind his tinted glasses, he had a look of habitual glazedness. 'You knew he often didn't hear a word you'd said to him. He had gone on another planet for a while. I think what happened in North Carolina was a shock to Lynne's whole system. I don't think she every quite recovered from North Carolina,' I was told.

The role of Chance did not go away the day they stopped shooting the movie. It stayed in Sellers' system for months afterward. As it fell away, layer by layer – the blankness in his eyes went first, then the walk and the gestures, and finally the voice – he behaved very strangely.

In London, he announced that his marriage was over. The first his wife, who was in California, heard of it was when a friend telephoned to commiserate.

Sellers regretted the outburst when he read the headlines the following morning. He tried to telephone Lynne and apologise. She refused to take the call. He sent his assistant Michael Jeffery to California to reason with her. 'Make her see my side,' was his somewhat cryptic parting instruction to the emissary. Jeffery, his dresser on *Zenda,* had replaced the ousted Bert Mortimer in Sellers' entourage.

After some delicate negotiations, Lynne was mollified; a kind of harmony was restored. 'But that's when the shift in their relationship happened,' reckons one of Lynne's closest friends. 'Before that moment, he had been the dominant one. Lynne had been fairly acquiescent. By the start of *Fu Manchu* the balance had tilted totally in

241

Lynne's favour. Sellers was very much courting her.' Part of the *modus vivendi* was that Lynne maintained a home in California, a place Sellers had come to dislike intensely – 'full of shit and oranges' – while he basically lived in Switzerland, a country he loved best after England. Lynne was not fond of Switzerland.

But some things stayed the same.

Two directors (Richard Quine; John Avildson) had been hired and fired on *Fu Manchu* even before the script was finished. Working with screenwriter Jim Moloney on his yacht in the south of France in the spring of 1979, Sellers fancied he 'caught a look' in Moloney's eye. He demanded that the writer be removed from the yacht at once. 'It must have been a hell of a look,' recalls one production executive, 'because he never forgave it.' Months later, during some horse-trading over a luxurious mobile home he wanted to use for a dressing-room, Sellers happily agreed to forgo the out-of-favour Hollywood writer's presence in Paris; the money was spent instead on the mobile home.

'He really didn't want to do the film at all. He just didn't have anything else to do. Artistically he knew it was a step backwards after *Being There*. That upset him,' said an associate. 'He was obviously sitting down there in Cannes thinking up ways to irritate the producers, to screw as much out of them as he could. He hated producers. He came down very hard on producers.' (Typically unpredictable, when *Fu Manchu* producer Leland Nolan happened to mention that it was his ambition to own a gold Rolex watch, Sellers gave him one the next morning.)

The Fiendish Plot of Dr Fu Manchu began shooting in Paris in September 1979 with the Englishman Piers Haggard directing.

Sellers failed to turn up the first day; he pleaded a domestic crisis. It was not the most promising start. He arrived the second day looking emaciated. He had lost about 28 pounds, and very fast. It showed in his face. 'His face was much too thin, his head looked much too big for his body,' remembers English publicist Ann Tasker who had worked with the actor on *The Prisoner of Zenda*. The change in his appearance since Vienna was startling. 'As *Fu Manchu* went on, he just looked worse and worse. His skin started to go a strange colour. It looked as if he had eczema. Several people on the set were already saying that they thought this would be his last film. I thought they were being a little histrionic, but in retrospect he did have a strange air of . . . of wanting to be rid of it all.'

Lynne accompanied him to Paris. After a summer of rumour about a new rift in their marriage, her presence surprised the press; it also surprised many of the people close to the actor. Her presence contradicted some of the things he had been saying during the summer.

The producers were pleased Lynne was around; Sellers was easier to handle. (She was eventually put on salary with an ornamental title to encourage her proximity.) Her wife-mother role had escalated to a kind of domestic gynarchy. 'She had a no-nonsense approach to Sellers,' recalls one observer. 'It was very much a question of belt up and stop moaning, you've only got a sore throat: don't make such a drama of it.' She confiscated all his patent medicines after he collapsed in a restaurant one night from what doctors warned was probably an overdose of Lem-Sip.

He needed watching all the time. He was becoming more eccentric every day. He called up the Crillon hotel on his car phone and asked his maid to run a bath for him at once so that it could cool down and be ready for him when he arrived in about thirty minutes. She pointed out that it was possible, with mixer taps, to draw a bath at the exact temperature he required when he arrived. This made him very angry. 'I want,' he said, 'a very hot bath that has cooled down.'

Being There had opened in America to great acclaim. *Time* magazine began a series of interviews for a cover story. The interviews were done in three sessions. The first session was four hours long; there were two more sessions of over two hours. 'To me,' says a publicist who

243

sat in on the interviews, 'it was an agonising experience. He started off being very stilted, not really giving much. The girl from *Time* kept probing. He kept changing his tack. I wouldn't say he lied because "lie" is too strong, but I think he romanced about things. She didn't understand him at all. She kept saying she wanted to get at the real Peter Sellers. I mean, the real Peter Sellers was what she saw . . .'

He was, says another friend, tripping off more and more into fantasy land. 'He told everyone at the studio how Jacques his driver was taking him back to the hotel in Paris when they got stuck in heavy traffic. Three or four thugs started to attack the car. He got out and gave them a few karate chops and laid them out cold. We all knew this didn't happen. Peter was convinced it did. It was very puzzling.'

Every weekend, he flew in a private jet to his home in Gstaad, an Alpine residence complete with fallout shelter, telex machine, and plastic gnomes in the garden. It was here, alone one weekend at the beginning of December, that he began to feel unwell. He drove himself to Geneva and checked into a clinic. He was ordered to rest for a month. This time he followed doctor's orders. The picture was closed down until the New Year.

He returned to Paris on January 4 1980 and for the first time saw some *Fu Manchu* footage. He hated his performance as the ancient villain. He immediately wanted to get rid of Piers Haggard – it had never been a comfortable relationship – and take over the direction himself. It was a familiar manœuvre, not totally unexpected, but it was obvious that a serious crisis could erupt at any moment. He still looked very sick. In everyone's mind was the awareness that if the situation got out of control, if Sellers walked out at this stage, the picture might never be completed. There were people in Paris, who had worked on the unfinished *Casino Royale;* people remembered that unfinished *Ghost in the Noonday Sun.* Sellers' chagrin was everybody's crisis.

After a great deal of backstairs diplomacy, he was

allowed to reshoot and direct some earlier scenes which especially displeased him.

'He was very good, very professional, not at all self-indulgent,' admired one crew member. 'He didn't mess around. He got through a lot of stuff very quickly.'

He worked with the urgency of pain. He had continued to lose weight during the making of *Fu Manchu*. He had been unable to sleep. The unit nurse, a Frenchwoman, went to his suite every night to try to massage him into a relaxed state, to try to get him to sleep. His body was now dangerously emaciated. The bed sores had returned. It was the body, said the nurse, of a very sick man.

Directing and acting in the reshoots – his make-up took two hours to put on (black contact lenses, gum to shrivel and age his skin, four-inch fingernails) and was very uncomfortable to wear – was a ferocious drain upon his energies.

'It was extraordinary. Why bother? I mean, he'd made a personal fortune from the *Panthers*. Why put himself through all that agony – it was as if he was determined to self-destruct,' said one *Fu Manchu* executive.

I talked to a lady who knew him well for a great many years. She loved him very much but I don't think they were ever lovers. She saw him for the last time at the party he gave at the end of *Fu Manchu*. She said:

'I looked at him that night in Paris and it just made me want to cry, there was something so sad about him. It was his party but he was on the outside of it. I think he had lost the taste for living. I think he really was ready to die. He didn't know how to cope with life. He had got everything he wanted. He'd got money. He told me once that he had made something like eight million dollars on the last *Pink Panther* movie alone. I think possibly the only thing left that he might have wanted was a knighthood. He didn't even have *Being There* to look forward to any more. He had done it. There was nothing left to reach for. I think I really was ready to die.'

His behaviour from that moment is hard to interpret in any other way. Certainly it is hard to fathom. He flew to

Dublin to make a television commercial for Barclays Bank for a fee of just £80,000. In Dublin he collapsed again. The doctors told him to rest. His response was to fly to Cannes for the opening of *Being There*. In Cannes he became very unwell and blamed a heavy cold.

Being There had finally given him the *succes d'estime* he deserved and needed. Yet it did not win him the prize at Cannes (the French jurists hated it) nor did it bring him the Oscar.

'Never mind,' he shrugged, and there seemed to be genuine acceptance in that small movement of his thin shoulders. 'I still think it's my clincher. I'll settle for it as a monument any time.'

In July 1980 he flew to London to keep a reunion date with the Goons Harry Secombe and Spike Milligan. Shortly after lunch on Tuesday, July 22, he collapsed in his suite at the Dorchester with a massive heart attack. He was rushed to the Middlesex hospital.

Lynne flew back from America. Britt Ekland visited him with their daughter Victoria, then fifteen years old. Michael, his 26-year-old son from his first marriage to Anne Hayes, was at his bedside.

At 12.28 a.m. on Thursday July 24 Peter Sellers died without regaining consciousness. A hospital spokesman said, 'His death was due to entirely natural causes. His heart just faded away. Every effort was made to keep his heart going, but it just did not respond.' He was 54 years old. He left a widow, three children, three ex-wives, two opulent homes, a fortune, a mass of mechanical and electronic gadgets, millions of fans – and a national gallery of portraits that would remain his country's heritage.

At the end of the short private funeral service at Golders Green crematorium in North London, conducted by his old friend Canon John Hester, Sellers played his last joke: the mourners filed out of the chapel to the strains of Glenn Miller's *In the Mood*.

It was a nice try. But people will remember that the

weather on that day was the worst summer's day in living memory. At midday, black clouds, six miles deep, plunged the nation into darkness.

'Bluebottle,' said Harry Secombe, 'is deaded now.'

One Memory

I ONCE ASKED Peter Sellers if he had a favourite view in London.

'That penthouse up at Hampstead,' he said. 'That had a fantastic view.'

To the west were the Harrow hills and in the south the big exciting sweep of London; you could see the Thames like a dark green thread of ribbon wrapping up the town, around St Paul's Cathedral, on past the South Bank and down past the Houses of Parliament at Westminster . . .

But that wasn't it at all.

'Do you know,' he said, 'on a good day you could almost see Jimmy Grafton's pub. Where it all started. Spike, old Harry, Mike Bentine . . . it was a lovely view . . . such a lovely view . . .'

He could almost see yesterday. It was the only thing he could ever be sure of.

PETER SELLERS FILMOGRAPHY
Compiled by Danny Nissim

Title followed by (year and director) and other leading players

Penny Points to Paradise (51 Tony Young) Harry Secombe, Alfred Marks

Down Among The Z Men (52 Maclean Rogers) Spike Milligan, Harry Secombe, Michaël Bentine, Script: Jimmy Grafton

Orders are Orders (54 David Paltenghi) Margot Grahame, Maureen Swanson, Tony Hancock, Sidney James

John and Julie (55 William Fairchild) Wilfrid Hyde-White, Sidney James, Andrew Cruickshank

The Ladykillers (55 Alexander Mackendrick) Alec Guinness, Cecil Parker, Herbert Lom, Danny Green, Katie Johnson

The Smallest Show on Earth (57 Basil Dearden) Bill Travers, Virginia McKenna, Margaret Rutherford

The Naked Truth (58 Mario Zampi) Dennis Price, Peggy Mount

Up The Creek (58 Val Guest) David Tomlinson, Wilfrid Hyde-White

tom thumb (58 George Pal) Russ Tamblyn, Terry-Thomas

Carlton-Browne of the F.O. (58 Roy Boulting) Terry-Thomas, Ian Bannen, Miles Malleson.

The Mouse That Roared (59 Jack Arnold) Jean Seberg, David Kossoff, William Hartnell

I'm All Right Jack (59 John and Roy Boulting) Ian Carmichael, Terry-Thomas, Richard Attenborough, Dennis Price, Margaret Rutherford

Battle of the Sexes (60 Charles Crichton) Robert Morley, Constance Cummings

Two Way Stretch (60 Robert Day) Wilfrid Hyde-White, Lionel Jeffries, Liz Frazer, Maurice Denham

The Running Jumping Standing Still Film (60 Dick Lester) Spike Milligan (11 minute short) (Produced by Peter Sellers)

Never Let Go (61 John Guillermin) Richard Todd, Elizabeth Sellars

The Millionairess (61 Anthony Asquith) Sophia Loren, Alastair Sim, Vittorio De Sica, Dennis Price

Mister Topaze (61 Peter Sellers) Nadia Gray, Herbert Lom, Leo McKern, Billie Whitelaw, John Le Mesurier, Michael Sellers

Only Two Can Play (62 Sidney Gilliat) Mai Zetterling, Virginia Maskell, Richard Attenborough, Kenneth Griffith

Lolita (62 Stanley Kubrick) James Mason, Shelley Winters, Sue Lyon

Waltz of the Toreadors (62 John Guillermin) Dany Robin, Margaret Leighton

The Dock Brief (63 James Hill) Richard Attenborough, Beryl Reid

Heavens Above (63 John and Roy Boulting) Cecil Parker, Isabel Jeans, Eric Sykes

The Wrong Arm of the Law (63 Cliff Owen) Lionel Jeffries, Bernard Cribbins

The Pink Panther (63 Blake Edwards) David Niven, Robert Wagner, Claudia Cardinale

Dr Strangelove or How I Learned to Stop Worrying and Love the Bomb (64 Stanley Kubrick) George C. Scott, Sterling Hayden, Slim Pickens

The World of Henry Orient (64 George Roy Hill) Paula Prentiss, Angela Lansbury

A Shot In The Dark (64 Blake Edwards) Elke Sommer, George Sanders, Herbert Lom

What's New, Pussycat? (65 Clive Donner) Peter O'Toole, Romy Schneider, Woody Allen

The Wrong Box (66 Bryan Forbes) John Mills, Ralph Richardson, Michael Caine, Peter Cook, Dudley Moore

After The Fox (66 Vittorio De Sica) Victor Mature, Britt Ekland

Casino Royale (67 John Huston, Ken Hughes, Robert Parrish, Joe McGrath, Val Guest) Ursula Andress, David Niven, Orson Welles

The Bobo (67 Robert Parrish) Britt Ekland, Rossano Brazzi

Woman Times Seven (67 Vittorio De Sica) Shirley MacLaine, Rossano Brazzi

The Party (68 Blake Edwards) Claudine Longet, Marge Champion, J. Edward McKinley

I Love You, Alice B. Toklas (68 Hy Averback) Jo Van Fleet, Leigh Taylor-Young

The Magic Christian (69 Joseph McGrath) Ringo Starr, Richard Attenborough, Christopher Lee, Raquel Welch

Hoffman (70 Alvin Rakoff) Sinead Cusack, Jeremy Bulloch

There's A Girl In My Soup (70 Roy Boulting) Goldie Hawn

A Day At The Beach (70 Simon Hesera) Mark Burns, Fiona Lewis (not released)

Where Does It Hurt? (72 Rod Amateau) Jo Ann Pflug, Rick Lenz

Alice's Adventures In Wonderland (as the March Hare) (72 William Sterling) Fiona Fullerton, Michael Crawford, Dudley Moore

The Blockhouse (73 Clive Rees) Charles Aznavour

The Optimist/The Optimists of Nine Elms (73 Anthony Simmons) Donna Mallone, John Chuffey

Soft Beds And Hard Battles (73 Roy Boulting) (Sellers 7 parts) Curt Jurgens

Ghost In The Noonday Sun (74 Peter Medak) Spike Milligan, James Villiers, Peter Boyle (not released)

The Great McGonagall (as Queen Victoria) (74 Joseph McGrath) Spike Milligan, Julia Foster

The Return of the Pink Panther (74 Blake Edwards) Christopher Plummer, Catherine Schell, Herbert Lom

Murder By Death (76 Robert Moore) Eileen Brennan, Truman Capote, James Coco, Peter Falk, Alec Guinness

The Pink Panther Strikes Again (76 Blake Edwards) Herbert Lom, Colin Blakely, Leonard Rossitter, Lesley-Anne Down

Revenge of the Pink Panther (78 Blake Edwards) Herbert Lom, Dyan Cannon, Graham Stark

The Prisoner of Zenda (79 Richard Quine) Lynne Frederick, Lionel Jeffries, Elke Sommer

Being There (79 Hal Ashby) Shirley Maclaine, Jack Warden, Melvin Douglas, Richard Dysart

The Fiendish Plot of Dr Fu Manchu (80 Piers Haggard) Helen Mirren, David Tomlinson, Sid Caesar, Bert Kwouk

INDEX

253